ONLY THE BRAVE ARE FREE

ONLY THE BRAVE ARE FREE

A condensed review of the growth of self-government in America

"Courage to experiment in government has made us strong and kept us free."

By DONALD R. RICHBERG
Former Lecturer on Constitutional Law
University of Virginia

and

ALBERT BRITT
Former Professor of History, Scripps College, and
Former President of Knox College

THE CAXTON PRINTERS, Ltd.
CALDWELL, IDAHO · 1958

© 1958 BY
THE CAXTON PRINTERS, LTD.
CALDWELL, IDAHO

Library of Congress Card Number 58-5332

342.73
R 397 o
Govt.
Apr. 16, 1958.

Printed and bound in the United States of America
by American Book–Stratford Press, Inc., New York, N. Y.

Dedication
(A. B. and D. R.)

THE PURPOSE of this book is to offer in one small volume a reliable summary of the sources, the methods, and the results of more than three centuries of self-government in America. The authors seek to provide a guidebook for students, politicians, and voters who are concerned with the origins and significance of our political ways and their bearing on the determination of our future course.

What are the outstanding characteristics of our democratic system?

In what respects are we federated and in what others centralized and why?

How have we sought to balance individual freedom with political control through three centuries of rapid change and growth?

With what equipment do we face the future and how shall we use it?

Are we facing a revolution that involves a radical break with our past, or can we solve the problems that we face by continued application of the hard-earned lessons of our history?

These are some of the questions clearly implied in the study that the authors have undertaken.

To understand, to debate, or to vote upon such questions one should know how they have been arising, and how we have been answering them throughout our history, what social and economic questions we have been seeking to solve by what means, where we have found light, and where we have continued searching in darkness and confusion.

Two men of scientific training in history and in law have tried to pack the essence of a wearisome ten-volume study into a brief exciting narrative of the most fruitful experiment in self-government ever known. They have tried to explain what we Americans have done and why we did it. Their exposition is unpartisan. It had to be because the authors do not agree as to what we should do in the future, nor how we should do it. But they do hope, with all thoughtful men, that the final judgment of the American people may rest upon reason founded upon knowledge and experience.

So this book is an adventure in popular education. Ardent liberals and staid conservatives alike may draw upon it to support their arguments, or to find reason for doubt or modification. Our history is like that. The authors agree completely on two things: First, each has written his chapters as candidly and as accurately as he could, and "to the best of his knowledge and belief" all of his statements are "true in substance and in fact." Second, both believe that our national experiment in self-government will and should be continued and that its success will depend in the future, as it has in the past, on the number of voters who read and think for themselves, compared with the number who play by ear and avoid the labor of thinking.

Accordingly, this book is dedicated to that hope of a free world: The Men and Women Who Read and Think.

Contents

CHAPTER		PAGE
	Dedication (A. B. and D. R.)	v
I.	Learning in Spite of Themselves (A. B.)	1
II.	Revolution and Confederation (A. B.)	24
III.	The Great Compromises of the Constitutional Convention (D. R.)	46
IV.	Creating a Federal Government (D. R.)	61
V.	Jefferson and Marshall (D. R.)	70
VI.	A Time of Ferment (A. B.)	85
VII.	Jackson in the White House (A. B.)	116
VIII.	Cotton Threatens the Union (A. B.)	131
IX.	Taney to Lincoln and Civil War (D. R.)	144
X.	Reconstructing the United States (D. R.)	156
XI.	Peace and a New America (A. B.)	166

CHAPTER		PAGE
XII.	The New Nationalism and Social Responsibility (A. B.)	188
XIII.	New Wine in Old Legal Bottles (D. R.)	219
XIV.	World War and Halfhearted Internationalism (A. B.)	235
XV.	The New Treaty Power (D. R.)	254
XVI.	The Roosevelt Revolution (A. B.)	265
XVII.	The Old and the New Supreme Court (D. R.)	290
XVIII.	Hopes of a Welfare State (A. B.)	309
XIX.	Fears of a Welfare State (D. R.)	328
XX.	That Manifest Destiny (A. B. and D. R.)	346

ONLY THE BRAVE ARE FREE

CHAPTER I

Learning in Spite of Themselves
(A. B.)

THE HISTORY of the United States is something more than a chronicle of growth in numbers and in wealth, the conquest of the wilderness, and considerable accomplishments in scientific and technological ways. Those things we have done and the record stands. But impressive as the list may be, if that were all that we have done it would not be enough. While we have been exploiting the resources of a continent, perhaps to our own ultimate harm, and building great power, to our present bewildered embarrassment, we have at the same time been conducting an experimental laboratory and training school in politics, most of the time without conscious intent.

Politics is a word of ill repute in certain superior quarters, suggesting low arts and devious practices for selfish and ulterior ends. In such circles to call a man "a politician" is to damn him beyond redemption, and to "go into politics," except in the exalted mood of consecration and condescension of a missionary to the heathen, is to forswear one's birthright. But the word is not without its defenders. The *Standard Dictionary* states the case for it in impressive terms: "The branch of civics that treats of the principles of civil government and the conduct of state affairs; the administration of public affairs in the interest of the peace, prosperity, and safety of the state; statecraft; political science; in a wide sense embracing the science of government and civil polity." So the word stands. Politics it is.

For more than three centuries in this political laboratory that is now the United States of America we have been carrying on a series of experiments seeking ways in which we can best guarantee the peace, prosperity, and safety of the state. What is the "state"? There are various answers. Constitutional historians have one, usually in two volumes. They may be right but it takes a long time to understand and it doesn't sound quite real. A French king had another, short and easily understood, "L'état c'est moi." Unfortunately his was wrong, as one of his successors discovered a trifle late. The plain American, and that means most of us, has another, also a short one. This American, if he must testify, believes that at long last and when all the returns are in, "We are the state." And, there is a lot of history between the French *moi* and the American "We."

At the present time we are much concerned about what is happening or is about to happen to this government of ours, this state in which we have the last word. Historians are not always good prophets, especially when they beat their breasts and cry "Woe" in the market place. Prophecy is not their business; their proper concern is with the past and with the lessons that it teaches, but, if from such a source there can be drawn light on the way ahead, the historian can be thanked for an extra dividend. Since we are all politicians as well as bankers, lawyers, farmers, shopkeepers, and the rest, in such degree and form as the peace, prosperity, and safety of the state are important to us, what about the record and meaning of our political experiments for three centuries? What have we learned and how? From the earliest feeble beginnings of English settlements on the Atlantic seaboard, men have been forced by circumstance to do something to advance their own order and safety. In a word, government. Few of them were qualified for the task; some were unwilling to undertake it. The home government made little or no provision for the ordering of daily affairs at Jamestown or Salem or Plymouth. So needs must. England was far; the wilderness and the Indian were at their backs. Observe what the little handful did on the *Mayflower* even before they went ashore.

The Pilgrims who settled at Plymouth in that tragic winter of 1620–21 must not be confused with the Puritans who founded the Colony of Massachusetts Bay ten years later. They were a small company of obscure, simple people, small artisans, shopkeepers, servants, and farm laborers for the most part. William Brewster was the nearest to a man of substance among them, a landowner in Nottinghamshire, some time a student at Cambridge and then a secretary to Davison, one of Elizabeth's secretaries for foreign affairs. Such men as John Carver and William Bradford were above the average in shrewdness and capacity. All had been members of John Robinson's church at Scrooby and had followed him in his separation from the Church of England. Most of them had been exiles in Leyden before attempting the American adventure.

The plans of the Puritans were large and sweeping, nothing less than the control and purification of the Established Church. The Pilgrims desired only to be let alone. When they sailed from England they brought with them no charter or plan of government, only permission to sail and a vague promise from King James to let them alone as long as they did nothing to disturb the king's peace. A group of London merchants gave them scanty backing, enough to insure the westward voyage. Not much warrant here for such a risky enterprise, but it was all they could get.

It was a long, hard voyage, sixty-three days of head winds and October and November gales across the northern Atlantic. Naturally there was bickering and discontent on board; a hundred and two passengers crowded into a small ship of 180 tons, ninety feet long with a twenty-four-foot beam, are not likely to live in tolerant harmony. When they finally dropped anchor inside Cape Cod where Provincetown now stands, the more sober men took counsel together. There were murmurs of rebellion and some of the dissenters were plotting to strike out for themselves as soon as they were on shore. To meet this threat the elders, forty-one of them, drew up and signed the Mayflower Compact, in reality the earliest document in the American record to declare the intent and principle of self-government in the New World. These are the significant phrases: "We, whose names are underwritten, ... do, by these presents solemnly and mutually, in the presence of God, and of one another, covenant and combine ourselves together into a civil body politic, for our better ordering and preservation and furtherance of the ends aforesaid; and by virtue hereof to enact, constitute, and frame such just and equal laws, ordinances, acts, constitutions, and offices, from time to time, as shall be thought most meet and convenient for the general good of the colony, unto which we promise all due submission and obedience." They were a small and feeble group, lacking even the more obvious preparations for that first terrible winter, but in this compact they served notice that the political laboratory was open and the experiments were begun. The necessities of time and place had produced their first results.

There were three main factors at the beginning of the colonial period which combined to throw upon the feeble settlements much of the burden of establishing and maintaining law and order. The first was England's concentration on trade. The use of the term "plantations" in early charters and writings is revealing. These were not colonies but plantations, factories, to borrow a term from the East Indian trade, trading posts directed toward the increase of England's wealth.

They had no need of special provision for their own government. Another factor was the distance from England, four weeks each way at the best, and oftener six or seven, three months between the report of a need or emergency in America and a reply from England. In the meantime the people in the wilderness must fend for themselves. Later Burke called attention to this distance in time and space from center to circumference as a political handicap to England and a stimulus to self-government and an independent turn of mind in America.

Finally there was the steady emergence of new and urgent problems of a sort unknown and unforeseen by the people at home. These were all associated with life in a new land: how to make a living, defense against the constant menace of the Indian, adjustment to a new and often hostile climate. As numbers grew there were disputes over land titles and boundaries, threats from the French at the north and the Spanish at the south, and always the shadow of the unknown and dangerous wilderness at their backs. How could they translate these matters to English ears so that they would be clear to English minds? England asked chiefly for profits, the colonies sought mostly to live. Meanwhile the settlers dealt with the daily need by such means as they could contrive. The laboratory was at work.

In any consideration of these enforced beginnings attention must be given to the official policy which Whitehall pursued. Trade was active with Russia, with the Near East, and beginning with India. For the better control of this trade the device of the chartered company had been evolved. America was to be another source of gold and precious stones and of raw material for the manufacturers at home, hence charters for the plantations in America. These documents cannot be ignored. The earliest and most significant were those granted for Virginia. These Virginia charters are important not only for what they say but for what they fail to say. The first one granted by the king in 1606 made generous gift of the Atlantic Coast from 34° N. Lat. to 45° N., from Cape Fear to the Bay of Fundy. But there were conditions. This colony of Virginia was divided in half between two companies, the London Company from 34° to 41° and the Bristol Company from 38° to 45°. Furthermore, to prevent crowding, each plantation or habitation must have at least fifty miles of unsettled coast line north and south on each side of it. The trading purpose begins to be manifest later in the document where it charged that outsiders found "trafficking" anywhere along this coast are to be fined two and one-half per cent of the goods in their possession, if British, and five per cent if foreign. The only form of specific activity stipulated by the king is in his injunction "to dig, mine, and search for all manner of mines of gold, silver, and copper," frugally reserving to his majesty a fifth of the gold and silver and a fifteenth of the copper.

Provision for the government of the colony was simple, a council of thirteen in England, appointed by and answerable to the king. Grudging recognition was given of the possibility of local problems requiring immediate handling in the provision of a local council of thirteen in the colony also appointed by, and answerable to, the king.

As for the land no provision was made for ownership other than by the original company of Virginia, under the overlordship of the king. As for the individual settlers, they were servants of the company, living in company houses and working on company land for company profit. Such local power as lay with the council in Virginia was held wholly at the king's pleasure, which usually meant the pleasure of the council in London.

This charter stood for three years, years of famine, sickness, and Indian massacre. In 1609 the so-called Second Charter, really a series of additions to the first, was granted. This purported to give new powers to the council in Virginia, but its chief importance for us lies in its granting to settlers in Virginia and to their posterity the same liberties, franchises, and immunities as were enjoyed by English subjects in England. To tell the truth this was not much in 1609, but it was better than the status of company serfs. A third charter in 1612 provided for the establishment of a local court and assembly "for the better Order and Government of the said Plantation."

It was the second charter that first raised the question of title to the unknown wilderness stretching westward from the mountains. One of the duties imposed upon this forlorn handful of Englishmen in the New World was to find a way to the Western Ocean. It might be the Potomac or the James or the Chickahominy, but by 1609 that hope had begun to grow dim and now the king generously granted them "all that space and circuit of land, lying from the seacoast of the precinct aforesaid, up into the land, throughout from sea to sea, west, and northwest." This grant appears in the charter almost as an afterthought, but here was the foundation of the vast area of western lands where the American experiment was to have larger elbow room in which to present new forms and greater strength. We shall encounter these lands later.

By this time it had become clear that company ownership and operation of the land was a failure, and private holdings began to appear in individual grants and headrights. Tobacco was coming in and the demand for labor was heavy.

The headrights, usually of fifty acres, were grants to ablebodied men coming into the colony at their own expense or bringing in another under indenture of five years' labor. Landowners were appearing in Virginia and the shape of the tobacco economy was beginning to appear. The next steps were agricultural. John Rolfe brought in better and more sturdy tobacco seed from the West Indies and devised a means of curing and storing the leaf. Virginia settlers found little gold for all their hunting, but they had stumbled on something much richer than mines or nuggets.

On July 30, 1619, Governor Yeardley, by authority of the

Virginia company, convened the first assembly, the beginning of representative government in America. The document authorizing and calling this meeting has never been found, but the Ordinance for Virginia published in 1621 probably repeats the substance of the earlier document. Two councils were created in the colony, one the Council of State to advise and assist the governor and the other the General Assembly to be made up of burgesses, two from "every town, hundred, or other particular Plantation, to be respectively chosen by the inhabitants." Of course there was no thought in Virginia or in England then, or for many years to come, of anything resembling popular franchise. Landowners chose other landowners to speak for them. Charles I made Virginia a royal colony in 1624, but the House of Burgesses survived this change and became a fixture in Virginia life. The dream of a great trading company reaping rich profits from the western trade was done with, a stable economy had appeared with the spread of the tobacco culture, and landowners were soon to create an echo of aristocratic England in an environment that was anything but English.

Next in time and equal in importance to Virginia among the great colonies was that of Massachusetts Bay. Plymouth preceded it by ten years, but the Pilgrims were few in numbers and of small wealth. Their appeal to imagination and to pride is powerful and their contribution to our saga out of all proportion to their population and extent, but the share to be attributed to the Puritans on Massachusetts Bay is infinitely greater. The wording of the charter granted them by Charles I on March 4, 1629, is of small importance to us here. We must look to another document, the Cambridge Agreement, signed at Cambridge in England on August 26. By the terms of this agreement the signers undertook to organize and lead a colony to Massachusetts Bay on condition that "the whole government together with the patent for the said plantation be first by an order of court legally transferred and established to remain with us and others which shall inhabit upon the said plantation."

Why King Charles so casually tossed the reins of his royal power over to the leaders of a group of religious and political dissidents has never been made clear. Perhaps it seemed an easy way to get rid of troublemakers, with a fair chance of trading profit on the side. Whatever the reasons, the plain facts are that the laboratory of politics now began to work overtime. The leaders of the new colony had no misunderstanding as to their own purpose, nothing less than the creation of a Puritan theocracy in which power should rest in the hands of the religious and secular leaders in the colony, all of them devout believers and strongly entrenched in the Calvinist doctrine.

The colony grew fast, a thousand the first year, by 1640 close to fifteen thousand. Villages sprang up around Boston, wealth increased, chiefly the result of fishing, shipbuilding, and overseas trade to the West Indies and England. In the face of this rapid growth the heads of the church held fast to their rigid control of church membership. It was their pride that admission to the church was not to be had for the asking, but was gained only by passing rigorous tests of religious and political doctrine. Only the fully orthodox could meet them. As a result the members in good standing were always a minority, probably seldom more than thirty per cent. This would have been of slight importance if the colony had remained small, held in narrow bounds and easily controlled. But the outlying villages broke the orderly theocratic pattern and opened the way for small local autonomies within the autonomous whole. Usually groups desiring to form a village secured substantial grants of land from the company in Boston. Holdings were distributed among the individuals in proportion to their contributions, with special consideration for position and prestige.

The characteristic New England village evolved rapidly

for obvious reasons of mutual aid and protection. Local problems of boundaries, the use of common lands, plans for defense against Indian attack, school administration, the admission of new members made some sort of local control and administration necessary. The natural answer was a meeting of the freeholders of the colony since all were concerned with the common interest. The town meeting was born. Here was the germ of a portentous experiment in self-government, a working democracy unrecognized and unnamed. There were no prophets to foretell the day when Samuel Adams would make the Boston town meeting a powerful engine against governor and council with a revolution at the door.

There were other factors operating in New England. The establishment of schools was required from the beginning, each village of fifty houses being called upon to maintain an elementary school. When the fifty houses had grown to a hundred, a grammar school was to be added. When Harvard College was founded in 1636 to insure an educated ministry, the substance of a commonwealth came into being. Vexing questions arose in the relation of villages to the mother colony of Boston and, in 1631, Watertown refused to pay a levy of sixty pounds for the building of a stockade for defense against Indian attack from the north. The reason given for the refusal was that the consent of Watertown had not been secured in advance. The principle of no taxation without representation had been asserted.

The new land soon wrought changes in economic and social status and importance. The growth of wealth asked no odds of position or orthodoxy, and the sons of nobodies could and did become somebodies in shipbuilding and in trade. Men could and did move from the forecastle to the quarterdeck in a few years. The nice stratified English system that the founders had sought to establish in the wilderness could not withstand the pressure of new energies that were being released.

The great advantage of the Massachusetts Bay colony lay in their possession of the charter and the restriction of membership in the company to residents in the colony. These two facts, coupled with the unchangeable factors of time and distance, made Massachusetts virtually autonomous. The government was formed and, until 1680, remained on a completely local basis. The governor, deputy-governor, and assistants, elected by the "freemen," as the stockholders were called, were the executives and the judges, civil officers in a complete sense and not officers of a corporation as had been the case in Virginia. By 1644 the lower house, or "General Court," had appeared, and the bicameral form was established. This was genuinely representative government, although property and religious qualifications for voting continued to exist until well after the Revolution. Salaries were fixed and paid by the representatives, a fact which was to prove troublesome to kings and parliaments in due course.

The rapid increase in shipping and trading wealth brought a new force into the colony, also unknown in Virginia where status came only through the ownership of land. To the older heads of church and state these newcomers were disruptive and embarrassing. The Puritan theology regarded work as next to piety in the list of virtues, and the rewards of industry and enterprise were at least no indication of divine displeasure, but it was hardly possible to applaud success and at the same time deny prestige and power to the successful. The Puritan leaders had seen to it that only a shadow of power over them remained in the hands of the king. Now their own members were challenging the supremacy of the theocracy.

When the Massachusetts Bay planting was only five years old an offshoot of their planting was transferred to Connecticut. Thomas Hooker, minister of a struggling congregation in Newtown (Cambridge) on the outskirts of Boston, led his people through the wilderness to the Connecticut River, to found the towns of Hartford, Windsor, and Wethersfield.

Here, in 1639, the freemen of the towns adopted the Fundamental Orders, a genuine constitution. From the Puritan point of view this was a radical document since it granted a vote to those who had been "admitted inhabitants by the major part of the town wherein they live." This was not manhood suffrage, but it was close. The document also recognized the right of the general court to criticize or displace officers or magistrates called into question for any misdemeanor.

This right of a representative body, the general court, to control and, if necessary, to remove elected officers raises the question of the ultimate source of power in government. The Reverend Thomas Hooker had made his position clear on this point in 1638: "The foundation of authority is laid, firstly, in the free consent of the people . . . those who have the power to appoint officers and magistrates, it is in their power, also, to set bounds and limitations of the power and place unto which they call them." The Puritans in Parliament were claiming authority, but not in terms of democratic power. Their position was stated by John Winthrop, many times governor of Massachusetts Bay, in a letter to Hooker, expostulating "about the unwarrantableness and unsafeness of referring all matter of counsel or judicature to the body of the people, *quia* the best is always the least, and of that best part the wiser part is always the least."

The Connecticut cleavage had been accomplished quietly and, so far as the record shows, without open objection from Boston, but Roger Williams was not to find the going so easy. As minister of a church in Salem he had grown rebellious of the hard control exercised by the church heads in Boston through ministerial meetings and political pressures. He called attention to the cornerstone of the Puritan doctrine, the priesthood of the believer. Here was declared the necessity that lay upon every man to deal directly with God for his own salvation. Ministers might advise and explain; they could not mediate or forgive. To the stiffnecked leaders in Boston,

Williams' opposition was both heresy and rebellion, and Williams fled to the Indians of Narragansett Bay for refuge. The result was Providence Plantations. In the new colony complete separation of church and state was declared, with full liberty to the individual conscience in religious matters. The secular state was showing its head.

There were other colonies on the American mainland in which men of English origin were seeking ways in which they might live in a new land. From the point of view of the home government the differences among them might appear to be considerable and important. Charles II could hardly regard Virginia and Maryland as closely akin, nor could James II view Pennsylvania and Massachusetts Bay as merely different aspects of the same thing. Pennsylvania and Maryland were proprietary colonies, attempts to create feudal baronies in America. For a brief time, after it was wrested from the lax hold of the Dutch West Indies Company, New York was in the same category. Francis Parkman in *Montcalm and Wolfe* stated the case in curt fashion: "Pennsylvania was feudal in form, and not in spirit; Virginia in spirit, and not in form; New England in neither, and New York largely in both." In all these colonies the new environment warred with Old World concepts. The Calverts and Penns were the recipients of large royal bounties in lands which were theirs to rule or ruin. Maryland was never a success either as a feudal barony or as a refuge for oppressed and disfranchised Catholics and soon became a royal colony. The Penns took their task seriously and set about the business of settling and developing. Here to Englishmen were added continental Europeans, chiefly German, with a sprinkling of Welsh, Irish, and Scotch, with Swedes and Dutch in "the three lower counties on the Delaware," now the state of Delaware. No barriers of faith and creed were raised against the newcomers and strange sects appeared, Mennonite, Moravian, Dunkard, separatists and pietists of many sorts. All were moved by the same desire, a new chance in a new land. It was land that defeated the proprietors' dream of manorial wealth. Settlers wanted more than a quitrent title, they wanted land in perpetuity, for their heirs and assigns forever, and the land was there. So they took it. James Logan, agent of the Penns, complained that squatters interfered with the just and orderly collection of rents, but they kept coming. The wilderness was outwitting the proprietor.

Freedom to walk by the inner light that was in each man was more important to Penn than any system or philosophy of government. In presenting the Frame of Government to the first settlers in 1682 he referred to government of some sort as necessary to the orderly practice of religion. "Any government is free to the people under it (whatever be the frame) where the laws rule and the people are a party to those laws and more than this is tyranny, oligarchy, and confusion." Vague as these terms are they suggest possibilities far beyond anything envisaged in Massachusetts or Virginia. The form of government established was not unlike that of Massachusetts, a governor appointed by the proprietor and responsible to him, a council, and an assembly, the latter two elected by the freemen, still the landowners. At the beginning the council held the major power. After the granting of the Charter of Privileges by the younger Penn in 1701, the assembly became an independent legislative body with power to initiate legislation, while the council was concerned chiefly with administrative matters. From that time until the Revolution the assembly's power increased and there was much criticism of the radical proposals by members from the frontier districts. The newer lands were beginning to speak.

The political contributions made by the other colonies in the early stages were unimportant or were similar to those already mentioned. New York before the English took it in 1664 was a struggling post of a chronically bankrupt Dutch company. The local governors were petty tyrants, corrupt, bigoted, stupid, and stubborn. Tentative beginnings had been made in the fur trade and large land grants along the Hudson had been handed out to influential families in the hope of buttressing the feeble settlement marooned on the lower end of Manhattan Island. Capture by the English was little more than a formality, the lowering of one flag and the hoisting of another. The only trace remaining of Dutch occupancy was the patroon system anchored in the land grants. This hung on until near the middle of the last century, outmoded and antisocial. Partly because of this feudalistic survival the colony was strongly Loyalist during the Revolution and uncooperative for some time afterwards.

Carolina has an antiquarian interest for the student of political history. The territory was granted to a group of eight noblemen high in favor at the Stuart court in 1663 and 1665. The Earl of Shaftesbury, then Lord Ashley-Cooper, enlisted the services of John Locke in the drafting of an "Unalterable Constitution" for the organization and government of the province. The result was a fantastic scheme of counties, signories, baronies, and precincts, with an appanage of admirals, chamberlains, constables, chancellors, high stewards, and the like. The lion's share of the land was reserved for the noble proprietors. After a considerable allocation had been made for the "local nobles" who were expected to appear, the fragments remaining were to be set aside for small holders, of whom apparently only a few were anticipated. Lawyers were barred and it was forbidden to make comments or explanations which might obscure the clarity and justice of the Constitution. Unalterable or not, it never worked and, in 1691, Carolina became a royal colony. There was no room for feudalism in the wilderness.

The period from the founding of the earlier colonies until the restoration of the Stuarts to the throne in 1660 was one of comparative freedom for the new Americans. England was convulsed by the struggle between king and Parliament and, when Cromwell became Lord Protector after the execution of Charles I, he had his own troubles with Parliament. The Dutch and the Irish added to his difficulties, leaving him little time or energy for distant colonies. Charles II returned to an England that was weary of strife and willing to accept almost any regime that might promise quiet. It is to be written to the credit of Charles II that he at least saw something of the possibilities of colonial development and set about their realization. It was no fault of his that the new beginning was made under the spell of a politico-economic theory that was bound to work to the disadvantage of the colonies. This was mercantilism.

The theory of mercantilism was not a new one, and the laws of trade and navigation that issued in the next decade were only the implementing of a widely held belief. The purpose of trade was the development of national wealth. Hence care must be taken to see that Englishmen got none the worse of it. Colonies were important as producers of necessary raw materials and consumers of finished goods. Goods to and from the colonies must be carried in British ships, including those of colonial construction. Only those raw materials which England did not need or could not use were to be sold elsewhere. At the beginning the materials on which England asserted a monopoly were relatively few in number, tobacco, indigo, rice, sugar, and ship supplies of timber, hemp, pitch, and tar. This list of "enumerated articles" was extended steadily until by the middle of the next century it included practically all the important colonial products except fish. As colonial manufactures began to develop, the home government set about their restriction, particular attention being paid to such things as hats, woolen cloth, and iron, except in bars or pigs which were much in demand in England.

While the colonial leaders seldom questioned the reasonableness of mercantilism from the English point of view they sought to lighten the burden that the new laws laid upon their own development. In this they were aided by the incompetence and indifference of the agents sent to enforce the requirements. Where smuggling and evasion were so easy and profitable they soon became the regular procedure and fortunes so gained involved no loss of respectability. It was a time of low standards and the lines dividing piracy, smuggling, and legitimate trade were dim and easily crossed.

From 1660 to 1713 there was little reason for colonials or Englishmen to suspect a radical change in relations any time in the predictable future. Here and there were protests and signs of growing unrest on the colonial side, but these were seldom produced by trading frictions. The shortage of currency in America was in fact a more prolific source of dissatisfaction than were the laws of trade. In the mercantilistic practice, gold and silver were important forms of wealth and their control was essential to the success of a trading nation.

With the balance of trade steadily against them in spite of all their evasions, the colonists sought for substitutes for the sterling that England denied them. Massachusetts daringly experimented with colonial coinage, but the pine tree shillings soon came under the ban. Even if this had not happened the available supply of gold and silver was too small to give the colonial assemblies much hope in this direction. Bills of credit issued against tax anticipations, tobacco warehouse receipts, promissory notes, bills of lading on materials in transit to England, and other forms of commercial paper had considerable vogue. The home government frowned on land banks as means for the issuance of such bills, but Massachusetts especially made considerable use of this form of security, not always with good results. The Spanish dollar coming by way of the West Indies was widely circulated and became in some parts a substitute for sterling, although the uneven rate of exchange in the different colonies made its use awkward and uncertain.

In all of these matters the colonial assemblies took a prominent part and Massachusetts especially acquired a bad reputation at Whitehall for the pernicious activity of its general court. The royal governors were in general more good than bad, and many of them were intelligent, public-spirited men who strove to reconcile the irreconcilables. To add to their difficulties most of the colonies had kept the control of the purse strings in their own hands and assemblies were not slow to delay the payment of even the meager salaries that most of the governors received. England was slowly discovering that she could neither control nor ignore her American offshoots.

In the meantime the colonies were growing in wealth and in numbers. The older generations that had known England as home and viewed themselves as still Englishmen had died out and their places were being taken by the native born who knew only their own colony. While it could not yet be claimed that the new generations were Americans, they were at least less English than their fathers and grandfathers had been. They were thinking more and more in terms of their particular colonies and their individual and colonial interests. This in itself was a political fact of the first importance. They were still English subjects, but no longer Englishmen as their fathers had been, and their colonial assemblies and town meetings were of more importance to them than Parliament or the lords of trade and plantation.

The decade from 1680–90 was important not only in England but also in the colonies. James II had come to the throne on the death of his brother and was proceeding to overhaul England's relation with the colonies. Being a Stuart, he was no friend to representative institutions and the colonial assemblies were particularly vexing to him. As a first step he proceeded against Massachusetts and her charter in the High Court of Chancery and, in 1684, that body declared the old charter to be "vacated, canceled, and annihilated." In the three years following this act the colonies of New England together with New York and New Jersey were thrown into one great viceroyalty, under the governorship of Edmund Andros. Colonial assemblies were forbidden and all power was in the hands of the governor and his council. Tyrannical as this act appeared to the colonists neither James nor Andros attempted to play the role of tyrants and in general the steps taken were, from the English point of view, moderate. But governors must govern and Andros was an alien who could never understand the difference of feeling that lay between a man from Massachusetts Bay and one from the Jersey coast, and between them both and an Englishman, and, when he attempted to tax without warrant of legislative act, the fat was in the fire.

In the meantime James was having his troubles with Parliament. In 1688 he succumbed to the pressure from Westminster and slipped away to France under cover of darkness. Thus was the Glorious Revolution accomplished, a polite revolution if there ever was one. Quiet as it was, it was real. Other parliaments would quarrel with other kings, but it was soon to appear that England was done with absolutism. A successor to James was found in the joint persons of William and Mary of Holland. In the colonies the change was hailed as a triumph for the assemblies, and the dominion ruled by Andros fell apart overnight. In most of them royal governors remained, but their salaries came again under local control.

Another important happening in England soon after the Glorious Revolution was the appearance of John Locke's essays on government. Locke was an English philosopher who had collaborated with Shaftesbury in the concocting of Carolina's Unalterable Constitution which had proved to be anything but unalterable. But his reasoning on the origin of governments was sounder than his political planning and it was to be extremely useful to the radicals in America when it came to the final showdown, although it had been written as a refutation of the absolutist theories of Hobbes in his *Leviathan*. Here are his words:

> Men being, . . . by nature, free, equal, and independent, no one can be put out of this estate and subjected to the political power of another without his own consent, which is done by agreeing with other men, to join and unite into a community for their comfortable, safe, and peaceable living, one amongst another, in a secure enjoyment of their properties, and a greater security against any that are not of it. . . . When any number of men have so consented to make one community or government, they are thereby presently incorporated, and make one body politic, wherein the majority have a right to act and conclude the rest.

This was hard gospel for an English king, even mildly moderate William, but it was to be extremely useful for a colonial Virginian named Jefferson. Locke made another statement which was to become a part of colonial thinking: "I desire to know what government that is . . . where one man . . . may do to all his subjects whatever he pleases without the least liberty to any one to question or control those who execute his pleasure." Englishmen and colonials knew that the answer to Locke's rhetorical question was absolutism and most of them didn't like it. To take another look into the near future, the new Americans preferred their government with limitations. That belief had already been expressed in many of their legislative acts.

Another English date that may well be borne in mind is 1713, the signing of the Treaty of Utrecht. This marked the ending of the War of the Spanish Succession, Queen Anne's War to us, and the admission of England to a share in the slave trade with the Spanish colonies. English traders were not likely to neglect the market open to them in their own colonies, especially Virginia where the tobacco fields called loudly for labor. Around 1700 the Negro population of Virginia was estimated at a meager six thousand. Fifty years after the Treaty of Utrecht it had grown to nearly two hundred thousand. The basic economic difference between North and South, out of which such momentous political differences were to grow, was now beginning to appear.

The period between 1713 and 1763 was tranquil on the surface. The colonies were growing in numbers and in wealth, and trade with the West Indies and overseas generally was on the increase. Newspapers were appearing, especially in New England, although it was in New York that the press fought and won its first fight for freedom. John Peter Zenger, publisher of the New York *Weekly Journal,* had opened his columns to Lewis Morris for criticism of Governor Cosby, who brought suit for libel. Andrew Hamilton of Philadelphia, who defended Zenger, appealed to the jury in the name of English liberty and won his case, in spite of the narrow rigidity of the English law of libel. This was a case for freedom of the press even against a royal governor.

In England the Hanoverian kings had appeared following the death of Queen Anne. The first two Georges were more German than English, the first hardly bothering to learn the language, and affairs of state were left in the hands of the cabinet and parliament. The great figure in the English political sky was Robert Walpole, corrupt, dissipated, cynical, but an able, patriotic Englishman for all that. England's greatest need was time to rest from her long struggle between kings and parliaments, and he saw to it that she had the time. Even Spain's petty prodding failed to move him to retaliation in spite of charges of supine cowardice aimed at him. Likewise he turned a deaf ear to suggestions of taxes on the colonies, on the ground that he had half England against him already and had no intention of bringing his American subjects about his ears. Such laws for control of trade through taxes and monopolies as were passed were feebly applied and easily evaded.

There were proposals in both countries for colonial union. New England had tried it in the confederation for defense against the Indians and the French, and it had lasted from 1643 to 1680 with intermittent success. Special conventions of governors from several colonies were held: at Albany, to discuss treaty terms with the Iroquois; at Lancaster, Pennsylvania, in 1744, to consider the Indian problems of Maryland, Virginia, and Pennsylvania; at New London, in 1709 and 1711, to plan expeditions against Canada.

In 1754 a congress was called at Albany to discuss a general colonial union and Franklin presented his plan of union. This proposed a colonial parliament and a general colonial government, holding allegiance to the king, but supplanting the English Parliament in the control of colonial affairs. The plan was adopted by the congress at Albany and submitted to the colonies for approval. There it had short shrift, being rejected because it reserved too much power to England. The home government opposed it on the ground that it gave too much power to the colonies.

The tranquility of this half century was illusory as events were soon to prove, but it is not unfair to describe it as a period of rest and reorganization, a time of growth and, with the growth, a strengthening of the differences between the two countries. Meanwhile the old hostility between France and England was growing sharper. The reforms of Colbert had made France a trading power that was not to be ignored and the rivalry with England in America was becoming a growing menace. The end of it was the Seven Years' War. Colonial militia had fought in other English quarrels, but this one was nearer home. The outcome of the war and the events that followed it belong to the revolutionary period of our history rather than to the colonial.

What had the new Americans learned in the century and a half since Jamestown was founded? First, that their interests were not the same as those of Englishmen at home. While they accepted mercantilism in principle as a natural way for an ambitious nation to behave toward its colonies, they had also learned how to evade its impacts and had done rather well for themselves economically. They had discovered some of the weaknesses of absentee government and the stronger local governments among them had become centers of colonial loyalty. Their experience with royal governors had been more often good than bad, but good or bad they disliked powerful executives in normal times, a feeling their descendants have been slow to lose.

The colonial assemblies had been excellent training schools in political technique and convenient forums for the expression and crystallizing of opinion. Local governing bodies had spread this political education broadly through the population, the depth and intensity of it varying with the needs and circumstances of the time and place. The growth of small local industries and of overseas trade had given them a sense of economic self-sufficiency and a corresponding dislike of mercantilistic controls. The struggles over the charters, especially in New England, led them to attach special importance to contracts and covenants and to distrust such vague guarantees as lay in English common law and the constitutional rights of Englishmen. Finally, the more active leaders in the colonial assemblies had begun to feel an acute distaste for government that acknowledged no limitations in its control over individuals. Locke's reference to the "consent of the governed" required no explanation to them. They might call themselves Yankees or Virginians, but they were beginning to think and act as Americans.

CHAPTER II

Revolution and Confederation
(A. B.)

IT IS A SINGULAR ASPECT of the Seven Years' War that through it England gained an empire and lost her thirteen American colonies. When it began in 1756 France held all of Canada, except for the rather shadowy claims of the Hudson's Bay Company around Hudson's Bay, and had a rather better title to the Mississippi and its confluents and the land adjacent than anything that England could offer. When it ended in 1763 the only vestiges of French dominion remaining in North America were a share in the fishing rights of Newfoundland and the St. Lawrence and the small islands of St. Pierre and Miquelon off the Maritime Provinces.

To all appearances England held all that counted of North America, and only Spain in the Southwest and at the mouth of the Mississippi, far away and unconsidered in the American scheme, could hope to rival her. But it is one thing to gain an empire overseas, and quite another to organize and administer it. Two problems faced England in the new territories. First and most pressing was the control of the Mississippi Valley and particularly that part of it between the Great Lakes and the Ohio River and adjoining Pennsylvania.

Settlers were trickling across the Alleghanies, and the Shawnee Indians, whose hunting ground it was, were restless and resentful. Pontiac's conspiracy was a dangerous threat and the Indians hated the English and longed for the return of the French. A quick determination was essential and England had no ready answer.

In the hope of averting hostilities and to gain time for planning, Lord Shelburne issued the Proclamation of 1763. This drew a hasty line along the crest of the Alleghanies and prohibited any further settlement west of it. Trading with the Indians might continue but only under government license. Shelburne, a friend of the colonies and possessed of considerable understanding of colonial attitudes, was careful to make it clear that this was only a temporary measure and would be withdrawn as soon as a settled policy could be determined, but Shelburne left the cabinet soon after and his successor did nothing toward lifting the barrier. Naturally a feeling of resentment spread through the colonies. Meanwhile settlers continued to trickle over the mountains.

The other important Canadian problem was the manner of dealing with the French population rooted around Quebec and Montreal. The solution of this, too, was postponed and, when a plan was put forward in 1774, it did nothing to allay colonial fears. This was the Quebec Act which was both wise and foolish. Its wisdom lay in the declaration of a policy of toleration toward the Catholics in the province. Even this failed to impress the Americans, especially in New England where Catholicism was held in low esteem. The foolish part of the act was the extension of the boundaries of Quebec Province west and south to the Ohio River. This destroyed whatever chance the wise provision had of final acceptance in this country, and proved to the suspicious colonists the malign intent of the home government to ring them round with a power alien in both language and religion. It was not for this that they had fought the French and Indians. Another important fact ignored by the act was Virginia's claim to most of this area, based on her second charter.

Soon after the ending of the war other signs appeared in England of a disturbing change in the official attitude toward the Americans. The war which had been fought on the continent of Europe, and even in India, as well as in America, had left England heavily in debt. Government debts were a new thing. Kings might live beyond their means and often did, but wars were usually paid for through indemnities of treasure or territory capable of producing a quick return in profit or strategic advantage. The vast territories won in America were raw wilderness offering little immediate profit, whatever might be their future value. Government finance in England had been put on something like a modern basis with a budget, a bank as fiscal agent, and a chancellor of the exchequer. How was the debt to be paid? The acquisition of the new territories threw an added burden on the military establishment for the control of the resentful Indians and the guarding of the long frontiers. The total cost of the civil and military establishment in America which had been £70,000 a year in 1748 had climbed to £350,000 in 1764, and could hardly be expected to shrink. Empire is expensive.

In 1763 George Grenville became chancellor of the exchequer and set himself to the task of finding a way through the financial tangle. To his narrow, rigid, unimaginative mind the answer was easily found, taxes. And why not? The war had brought great relief to the colonies. No longer need the settlers in frontier New England, New York, Pennsylvania, or Virginia lie awake in fear of raids from the north. To be sure colonial blood had been shed in the war, but there had also been large profit for colonial merchants in military supplies, to say nothing of the contraband trade with the French in the West Indies. In reply the Americans pointed to their own debts incurred during the war, at least two and a half million pounds. Clearly this was a job for a diplomat rather than an accountant, and Grenville was no diplomat.

Unhampered by knowledge or fear of colonial resentment, he set about his program of revenue increase. The first item was the Sugar Act of 1764. Thirty years earlier a tax of sixpence a gallon had been levied on foreign molasses brought into the colonies, but little effort had been made to enforce it. The new act reduced the tax to threepence, but there was a catch in it. The tax was to be collected. The old game of imposition and evasion was over.

A year later another tax appeared as obvious to the English as it was hateful to the colonists. This was the stamp tax. This form of taxation had been common in England, but it was new in America and aroused a storm of protest. Nonimportation agreements were made by merchants threatened by heavy imposts on their bills of lading, contracts, bills of sale, promissory notes, all the documentary incidents to trade. Publishers of newspapers, broadsides, and pamphlets saw ruin to their business. Mobs attacked the offices where the stamps were for sale; the stamps were thrown into the streets, and the agents were threatened with worse treatment if they persisted. In staid Boston, Lieutenant Governor Hutchinson's house was broken into and the contents wrecked.

Virginia, proudest and most loyal of the colonies as she was the oldest, proceeded in a more orderly manner. Urged on by Patrick Henry the General Assembly after a brief debate passed a series of resolutions that were published widely through the colonies. The fifth of these crystallized the opposition and offered a principle of action on which the colonists might stand.

> The General Assembly of this Colony have the only and sole exclusive right and power to lay taxes and impositions upon the inhabitants of this Colony, and . . . every attempt to vest such power in any person or persons whatsoever other than the General Assembly aforesaid has a manifest tendency to destroy British as well as American freedom.

While Virginia spoke only for herself in this declaration, she voiced a general feeling. The sense of a common bond which had failed to develop in normal times was beginning to show itself in these days of adversity. Highly individualistic in the enjoyment of their advantages, the colonists were beginning to feel the companionship of grievance and resentment. The hated Grenville was producing a sense of a common cause where the trusted Franklin had failed.

A few months after Virginia acted, a town meeting in Braintree, Massachusetts, spoke up to similar effect. The resolutions drawn by John Adams opened with pointed reference to the drain of specie caused by the Stamp Act, prophesying that it would "strip multitudes of all their property and reduce them to absolute beggary." Then it called attention to the unconstitutionality of the act, violating "a grand and fundamental principle of the constitution that no freeman should be subject to any tax to which he had not given his own consent, in person or by proxy." The provision of the Stamp Act that cases arising under it should be tried in courts of admiralty aroused the wrath of Lawyer John. The power vested in a single judge to pass on questions of both law and fact struck at the right to judgment by a jury of a man's peers laid down in the Great Charter.

The position of the opposition in America was taking shape. If there was a single political idea or theory represented in the arguments it was no more than an assertion of the equal rights of the colonists with all English subjects anywhere. These rights they believed they had enjoyed throughout their history and, in the light of colonial practice, the case was a good one. The lawyers in the House of Commons laid emphasis on the rather bland assumption that all Englishmen everywhere were "virtually" represented in Parliament and that therefore the colonists had no need of actual representation. This argument the colonists largely ignored. It was hardly to their interest to raise the cry of no taxation without representation as a slogan for the election of colonial members. That would have destroyed their strongest case with no practical improvement in their relationship with Parliament. On this point their intent was clear; to pay no taxes except such as they themselves had imposed.

This was made still more clear in the resolutions of the Stamp Act Congress which met in New York, October 7, 1765, a week before the voters of Braintree had spoken their minds. The importance of this congress lies not so much in what it did as in the fact that it was held. Early in June, James Otis had proposed that the Massachusetts assembly send a circular letter to the other colonies asking that delegates be sent to such a meeting. Nine colonies were present, Virginia, New Hampshire, North Carolina, and Georgia sending no spokesmen. The resolutions were careful to express the "warmest sentiments of affection and duty to His Majesty's person and government," but this did not deter them from declaring that the Stamp Act and other acts were a subversion of the rights and liberties of the colonists. They also called the attention of the government to the fact that the tax would make it impossible for the colonists to buy English goods. These were not new statements nor were they particularly radical or extreme, but they were made by representatives of the American colonies in congress assembled. It was not union yet, but they were taking counsel together. Already they had hit upon a common road that presently they would travel again.

The opposition to the stamp tax was so violent, accompanied as it was by protests from British merchants who were feeling the loss of trade, that Parliament grudgingly repealed it early the following year, but they salved their injured pride—and still further revealed their political ignorance and ineptitude—by coupling with the repeal the sweeping Declaratory Act. This odious act made sweeping declaration that the colonies and plantations in America "have been, are, and of right ought to be, subordinate unto, and dependent upon the imperial crown and parliament of Great Britain" and that the king and Parliament together "had, hath, and of right ought to have, full power and authority to make laws and statutes of sufficient force and validity to bind the colonies and people of America, and subjects of Great Britain, in all cases whatsoever."

Four months after this statement of government intent Charles Townshend took Grenville's place as chancellor of the exchequer and, a year later, he forced through Parliament his revenue acts. He lived only a year longer, but he had used his short term in office to launch the series of extraordinary blunders by which the British made the loss of their American colonies inevitable. Even more than Grenville he saw only the need of revenue from the colonies and to that end instituted sweeping taxes on colonial imports and backed them up by the authorization of arbitrary search warrants, Writs of Assistance, without the limiting conditions imposed upon such warrants in customary British practice. Notice had now been served on the colonists that they were subordinate members of an empire and not self-governing dominions. They struck back with more nonimportation agreements, and the government retaliated by dissolving the assemblies of the prime offenders, Massachusetts and Virginia.

Both sides soon tired of this bickering and after that ridiculous scuffle that is sanctified in our history as the "Boston Massacre," the Townshend taxes were repealed in 1770 except that on tea. The next three or four years were a period of comparative calm. Merchants on both sides of the Atlantic welcomed the apparent return of harmony and prosperity, and tempers cooled. Only Samuel Adams, the Boston propagandist of revolution, distant cousin of John and czar of the Boston town meeting, took exception to this tranquility. To Samuel it smacked of spinelessness and subservience and he said so in the Boston *Gazette,* under such pseudonyms as

Publicola, Vindex, Determinatus, Candidus, and Cotton Mather. While merchants prayed for a continuation of prosperity and quiet he prayed too, in the *Gazette*.

> In this extreme distress, when the plan of slavery seems nearly complete, Oh, save our country from impending ruin. Let not the iron hand of tyranny ravish our laws and seize the badge of freedom, nor avow'd corruption and the murderous rage of lawless power be ever seen on the sacred seat of justice.

Samuel Adams deserves careful consideration in any study of revolutionary thought and planning. It is doubtful if any other colonial leader at this time meditated separation from England as anything but a remote and probably undesirable extremity, but Adams wanted it and worked for it. It is not clear from his writing when he first set his mind and will to a complete break, but it was surely much earlier than in the case of any other figure of importance. His skilful use of eighteenth century ideas on the rights of man and the nature and significance of the social contract are illuminating on this point. He could write as glibly as any other reader of Locke or Rousseau on the origin of society and the nature and significance of natural law. He knew Locke's second essay on civil government and he could appeal to the rights of the colonists under the British constitution, but it is difficult to find a single theory of government or of society in which he staked his faith. He used them all and discovered new ones as the need of the moment determined. One thing emerges clearly from a study of his writings from 1768 to 1774, his distrust and dislike of King George and his agents, whether in England or the colonies.

In all his moves Adams made skilful use of the Boston Town Meeting as his forum and his authorization. On November 20, 1772, he put through that body a set of resolutions that smell of revolution in every line:

> All men have a right to remain in a state of Nature as long as they please; and in case of intolerable oppression, civic or religious, to leave the society they belong to and enter into another. . . .
>
> When men enter into society, it is by voluntary consent; and they have a right to demand and insist upon the performance of such conditions and previous limitations as form an equitable original compact.
>
> Every natural right not expressly given up or from the nature of the social compact necessarily ceded remains.
>
> All positive and civil laws should conform as far as possible to the law of natural reason and equity.

Considered in the context of his other writings and his acts, these phrases can have only one meaning. Governor Hutchinson, also a colonial with a long American ancestry, at least had no misunderstanding when he wrote of Adams:

> I doubt whether there is a greater incendiary in the king's dominions or a man of greater malignity of heart, or who less scruples any measure ever so criminal to accomplish his purposes; and I think I do him no injustice when I suppose he wishes the destruction of every friend to government in America.

Hutchinson had ample reason for bitterness since he had been the target of many of Adams' sharpest darts. Cousin John summed Samuel up more calmly and probably with greater accuracy:

> Adams, I believe, had the most thorough understanding of liberty and her resources in the temper and character of the people, though not in the law and constitution; as well as the most habitual, radical love of it, of any of them, as well as the most correct, genteel, and artful pen.

Adams at least spoke for an increasing number of his fellow countrymen who were growing suspicious of England and resentful of absentee domination, whether harsh or tolerant. In a hundred and fifty years they had learned to think for themselves.

The brief honeymoon period came to an end in 1773, and for an absurd reason. The British East India Company found itself on the verge of bankruptcy with a tremendous overstock of tea on hand and no adequate market, the result of a bad speculative guess. The company appealed to the government for aid and the cabinet responded generously by granting a monopoly on all tea sold to the colonies. Incidentally the tea was to be sold through the company's agents, eliminating the profits to the retailer. In spite of the low cost of the leaf to the consumer the colonies rose in resentment of this ill-considered monopoly. In Charleston the tea was landed but was not offered for sale. Philadelphia and New York forced the return of the cargoes to England. Boston took the melodramatic course. Men disguised as Indians boarded the tea ships and dumped the packages into the harbor, the famous Boston Tea Party. The government had made the mistake of alienating the merchant class and had goaded a powerful colony to violence.

The "Intolerable Acts" followed fast in March, 1774. The first of these closed the port of Boston until satisfaction had been given for the lost tea. Two months later a sweeping reorganization of the government put the election and payment of all officers, judges, and assistants, all the lawmaking and law enforcing power of the colony of Massachusetts, in the hands of the king and his agents. A third act gave the government the power to transfer to another colony or to England the trial of cases that might arise out of charges of unlawful acts by any of the king's officers. Local government was as dead as governmental edict could make it. The Committees of Correspondence organized by Samuel Adams for the maintenance of communication among the colonies spread the tidings fast, and a hastily assembled group meeting in the Raleigh Tavern at Williamsburg, Virginia, issued a call for a Congress of all the colonies to meet at Philadelphia early in September.

In Albemarle County, Virginia, a set of resolutions drawn by Thomas Jefferson declared flatly that the colonies were subject to laws of their own making and to no other; that the Intolerable Acts had destroyed the natural and legal rights of British subjects. The official instructions of the Virginia convention to her delegates in the forthcoming Congress declared allegiance to the king and denounced the acts of Parliament as illegal. The action of the British in prohibiting all local assemblies in Massachusetts was branded as the most alarming that had ever appeared in any British government. Out of the tornado of words and charges that appeared, two facts stood out: colonial determination to stand by their long established rights of local governments, and a growing willingness to translate words into acts.

The Continental Congress had among its members some of the ablest men in the colonies, probably the most distinguished gathering that had been held anywhere up to that time. Few of them were radicals, but all were determined. From the British point of view this meeting was illegal, as it was in fact, but it was also of the first importance, which the British failed to realize. These men believed that they were speaking for all the colonies; the ferment of federated action was stirring in principle if not yet in form.

The action of this first Congress was firm but moderate. Galloway's draft of a compromise proposal which would have given the government an easy way out was rejected by a narrow vote and the meeting adopted a set of ten resolutions. These, while avowing allegiance to the king, charged Parliament with violating the rights of freeborn Englishmen guaranteed by charters and validated by the British constitution and restated in specific detail in British statutes. In closing they declared that the separation of the constituent branches of government was essential. There was to be no more combining of the powers of lawmaker, administrator, and judge in the hands of a single man or a group of men appointed by the king and subservient to him.

The Congress had been careful to avoid commitment to a fixed plan of government except as implied in their recital of grievances and rights, but some of the members went further in their writing. Prominent among them were James Wilson, John Adams, and Thomas Jefferson. In all three cases there was a general similarity of conclusion. The government they desired was a federation of colonies with a parliament of their own, independent of the British Parliament and having only the same relation to the king as that claimed by the body at Westminster. If Britain had accepted the result would have been something very like the present Commonwealth of Dominions, but Britain was not ready for anything so sweeping and so wise.

Some of Jefferson's statements were too strong for even his fellow Virginians, for example: "our ancestors, before they emigrated to America, were the free inhabitants of the British dominions in Europe, and possessed a right which nature has given all men, of departing from the country in which chance, not choice, has placed them, of going in quest of new habitations, and of there establishing new societies, under such laws and regulations as to them shall seem most likely to promote human happiness." This was strong medicine and there was no place for it in the British program, nor would there be for another century and more.

Now the stage was set for the big drama. The time for debating and compromising and rehearsing was at an end. The first act was to take place in Boston. General Gage held Boston under tight military control and the outlying militia began to assemble and gather munitions. Then came Lexington and Concord.

It is not too easy to find a single thread or theory running through the tangled course of events from 1763 to 1775, when the guns took up the argument. On the British side the position, if not the argument, is clear. The Seven Years' War plus the disturbing debt had brought the need of greater tax revenue to the fore. The capture of Canada increased the problems of administration and defense. Why should not the colonists help pay the bills? Guided by Pitt, the government saw an imperial future beckoning it. What had been chiefly a plan for trading outposts that should add to the wealth of the mother country now assumed the form of a territorial empire, worldwide and overpowering in its strength. To realize this ambition, the colonists must make due contribution of men and money. The desire of the colonists was of small importance and their local governments must give way to imperial demands.

On the colonial side there was no clear central idea or philosophy with which to oppose English aggression. This explains the rather bewildering shifts and turns in their attempt to rationalize a position which depended on their unwillingness to surrender rights which they believed that they had exercised. They were no longer English subjects in America, they were Americans, and would soon be calling themselves by that term. They had acquired long experience in government and were unwilling to sink back to a state of compliant subservience. The sparring with the English cabinet and Parliament over taxes and assemblies and writs of assistance and quartering acts and all the minutiae of political action had given them good training in legal and diplomatic footwork. Franklin in diplomacy, John Adams in legal technicalities, Jefferson in political philosophy could give odds to the best the British could put forward. In the new and difficult art of translating political ideas to the man in the street, in two words "propaganda" and "rabble-rousing," prosy old Sam Adams stood alone. Governor Hutchinson might hate him, General Gage hold him in contempt, Parliament and the king ignore him, but he was making a revolution and he knew it.

It is easy to rewrite this period of our history in terms of "if": *if* Franklin's Plan of Union had been adopted in 1754; *if* Grenville had been more of a politician and less of a bookkeeper; *if* Gage had recognized the narrow limitations of military power; *if* Parliament and the king had realized that these British subjects in America were citizens of a New World; *if! if! if!* It is easy but idle. One *if* leads to another and then to others in an endless sequence and the result is a futile rewriting of a long record that refuses to be changed. This was not a game in which one play might be changed and the final score altered. This was serious business. Men of English blood, with the same characteristics as other Englishmen elsewhere, the same virtues and weaknesses, the same political instincts, and the same stubbornness, had experienced a deep taste of governing themselves, of making their own mistakes, and of scoring their own successes. They liked the sensation and they wanted more of it.

Just what had the Americans learned about government in the course of their unavoidable experiments that they might carry with them into the storm that was now blowing up? Much about local government, the amount varying among them. Town meetings in Massachusetts had been useful training schools. John Adams wrote of his father: "He was an officer of militia, afterwards a deacon of the church, and a selectman of the town, almost all the business of the town being managed by him in that department for twenty years altogether."

The experience of the elder Adams was only one example of a schooling that was being enjoyed in all the colonies of New England. In Virginia it was the landholders who profited most. Below that level the numbers were few and unimportant as compared with New England, although by this time the settlers in the Piedmont were becoming vocal and assertive, with Patrick Henry as their chief spokesman. In Pennsylvania the power of the Quaker hierarchy around Philadelphia had been made aware of the presence of the newer population in the outlying districts.

When the colonists spoke of representation they knew what they meant. They had possessed it, not always evenly but usually effectively, in their assemblies. Here had been their principal defense against royal governors. Because of the governors they were suspicious of executive power, as they showed by the vigor of their protests against the Massachusetts Government Act in 1774. They were opposed also to the combining of executive, judicial, and quasi-legislative power in a single man or body. Montesquieu praised the British for their separation of the powers of government, but it was in the colonies that the lesson had been most clearly learned. Locke had stated the case against unlimited government, but the feeling had been growing among the colonists almost from the beginning that there was a realm in which the individual must be safe, a zone in which he was supreme. Their formulations on this point might not yet be very clear, but the new state constitutions were soon to clarify this belief.

Their greatest weakness was their failure to recognize more clearly the necessity of some kind of united action and authority. This was to handicap them seriously and almost fatally during the war. As matters stood, in spite of a general sentiment of sympathy and support for Massachusetts, when news came of Lexington and Concord, Americans still thought of themselves first as Yankees or Virginians. Federation was in the air, but not in the blood, and when the war began it was as states that they acted first. State constitutions were their first documents of government.

Virginia was among the states that acted early in the adoption of a bill of rights, being preceded only by New Hampshire and South Carolina. Nearly a month before the adoption of the Declaration of Independence the state convention of Virginia stated that "all men are by nature equally free and independent" and that they had no power to divest their posterity of the "enjoyment of life and liberty, with the means of acquiring and possessing property, and pursuing and obtaining happiness and safety." Other significant statements dealt with the separation of the executive, legislative, and judicial powers, free election of duly constituted representatives who alone should have the power to impose taxes, trial by a jury of one's peers, right to bear arms, and freedom of worship.

The third paragraph of the Virginia document is clear and impressive on the nature and purpose of government:

> That government is, or ought to be instituted for the common benefit, protection, and security of the people, nation or community; of all the various modes and forms of government, that is best which is capable of producing the greatest degree of happiness and safety, and is most effectually secured against the danger of maladministration; and that when any government shall be found inadequate or contrary to these purposes, a majority of the community hath an indubitable, unalienable, and indefeasible right to reform, alter, or abolish it, in such manner as shall be judged most conducive to the public weal.

Other states followed suit, not all as specific or detailed as was Virginia, but all agreeing in substance. By July, 1777, ten states had adopted constitutions and organized their governments. Massachusetts was slow, acting finally in 1780. The delay was due to no unwillingness but to the extreme care with which the constitution was discussed. Local meetings were held in towns and villages in which the proposed articles were threshed over item by item until final agreement was reached. Here was democratic action to the nth degree. Connecticut and Rhode Island alone took no action until after the end of the war, regarding their colonial charters as sufficient for immediate purposes.

The fourth article of the Massachusetts Bill of Rights sheds some light on the concept of sovereignty held in that colony and presumably in most others:

> The people of this commonwealth have the sole and exclusive right of governing themselves, as a free, sovereign, and independent State, and do, and forever hereafter shall, exercise and enjoy every power, jurisdiction, and right, which is not, or may not hereafter be, by them expressly delegated to the United States of America in Congress assembled.

All of the states were suspicious of executive power, having an active memory of some of their royal governors. New Hampshire, which was the first to set up a government of any kind, made no provision for a permanent governor or executive. All necessary civil officers were appointed by the legislature and were removable by the same body. In all the states it was taken for granted that the right to vote rested upon the ownership of property, usually of a hundred pounds value, and the holding of some form of religious belief. No claim of sovereignty appears in any of these documents, but the actions of most of the states make it clear that they claimed most of the rights of sovereignty, such as the issuance of bills of credit or other forms of money, the imposing of import duties, the control of trade both internal and external, and the fixing and collecting of taxes. It is a historical fact that the exercise of state rights in practical government preceded by ten years any attempt to form an adequate central government, a point which John C. Calhoun used to good effect after 1830.

While the states moved with speed in setting up their machinery of government, the Continental Congress, the only organ of central power, was struggling with the problems of continental war. The Declaration of Independence was a ringing statement of principles and an appeal to the European governments to regard separation as merely the legitimate termination of a contract that had become unbearable. But it was not a practicable instrument of government. Jefferson made it clear that governments rested on the consent of the governed, a point made by John Locke eighty years earlier, and followed close on the heels of Virginia in the assertion of the fundamental right to life, liberty, and the pursuit of happiness.

This was good revolutionary philosophy in the late eighteenth century as was the declaration of the right of the people to alter or abolish their government in such manner as they saw fit, but it did not create a government that could bring revenue into a national treasury or set armies in the field. The Congress was still a voluntary association of representatives of states. Voting was by states and not by individuals. The Congress could request, it could not command. It was an agent, not a chief. With the choice of George Washington as commander in chief it took a step in the direction of a national force, but it could not appropriate money from a nonexistent treasury. As Washington was soon to learn, his commission was little more than a blanket authorization to do the best he could to raise an army and fight a war. State militia were slow to enlist in the Continental Army from the beginning and mutinous tendencies appeared among the troops around Boston as soon as Gage evacuated the city in March, 1776.

Congress did borrow money and issue currency and bills of credit, but it lacked the power to lay a firm foundation on which national credit could rest. It was not until November 15, 1777, that Congress acted on the Articles of Confederation, and more than three years were required before the agreement was ratified by the necessary number of states. It could and did send envoys to the French, Dutch, and Spanish governments, the last as an ally of France, and it was able to conclude an alliance with France by February 6, 1778. If the British had prosecuted the war with vigor, particularly around New York and Philadelphia, it is doubtful that even Washington's stubborn integrity would have been enough to keep the cause alive.

The voluntary origin and nature of the Continental Congress condemned that body from the beginning to a relationship of subordination to the states, in effect a special agency charged with the responsibility for performing a special task, the fighting of the war with Great Britain. That fact conditioned all the acts and policies of the Congress. Article II of the Articles of Confederation makes this abundantly clear: "Each state retains its sovereignty, freedom, and independence, and every Power, Jurisdiction and right, which is not by this confederation expressly delegated to the United States, in Congress assembled." Article III refers to the tenuous union thus created as a "firm league of friendship." Obviously it was not intended to be anything more—as yet.

Most of the document deals with war powers. States are prohibited from the commission of acts which might trespass on the war powers of the Congress, such as sending or receiving embassies, making treaties or alliances with foreign powers or with each other, maintaining vessels of war, making war or peace "without the consent of the united states in congress assembled." The Congress had power to regulate coinage, fix a standard of weights and measures, regulate relations with Indian tribes "provided that the legislative right of any state within its own limits be not infringed or violated," establish post offices and postal service, and appoint and commission all officers in the service of the united states.

The greatest weakness of the confederation was in its lack of adequate power to levy and collect taxes. The funds in the common treasury were to be supplied by the several states in "proportion to the value of all land within each state, granted to or surveyed for any Person." The taxes for providing the stipulated amounts were to be levied and collected by the state legislatures. Considering the lack of power in the Congress the marvel is that the states paid in as much as they did.

As the war progressed more and more men were drawn away from the Congress to join the military forces or to take posts of importance with the state governments. The distinction and energy that had marked the early congresses diminished, and petty wrangles and intrigue increased. Supplies ordered were not paid for or were allowed to rot in warehouses or at roadsides for lack of a vigorous administration to enforce delivery. What was being demonstrated was a simple political axiom that a government lacking power lacks also integrity and efficiency. A thorough house cleaning was needed some time before it was supplied by the Constitutional Convention.

In general it can be said that the political lessons of the war lie chiefly in the light they shed on the colonial willingness to resort to the rule of trial and error in case of need, holding as firmly as they dared meanwhile to the lessons of previous experiments. They had not liked powerful executives in the past. *Ergo* they would pin their faith in their state legislatures. They believed firmly in the limitation of the power of government—any government—over them; hence they were chary in their grants of power. Hence also the Bills of Rights in the several states. For a hundred and fifty years they had wrangled over charter rights and had set them higher than the vague guarantees that might or might not be found in the somewhat misty British Constitution. To the rank and file of the people above the community or town meeting level, government was remote and probably dangerous. They had helped to beat the redcoats; now they wanted only to go back to their farms and their families. To most of them the boundaries of their own states represented the farthest limits of their political thinking. If a stronger government was to be achieved someone else would have to do it.

The manner in which the next important step was taken was in the pattern of all previous developments in this new country. Immediate problems pressed for solution; very well, they would deal with them, not according to any preconceived theory or general concept, but by the old familiar style of cut and fit. They would move forward from the known into the unknown, but cautiously as was befitting to prudent men in a world of reality with which they were astonishingly familiar. The immediate reality was thirteen "sovereign states" loosely bound together into a confederation which grew more impotent each year. According to the Articles, the Continental Congress was the court of last resort in boundary disputes between the states. There were many such arguments going on: New York and New Hampshire over Vermont; Connecticut and Rhode Island over Connecticut's eastern line; Virginia and North Carolina; Virginia and Maryland.

It was the last case, Virginia versus Maryland, that started something. The quarrel had its amusing features. In the Potomac River surveys, Maryland had somehow contrived to have the interstate line drawn on the Virginia side of the main channel of the river, thus giving control of navigation to Maryland. The quarrel had reached the stage where Maryland was threatening to close the Potomac to Virginia boats, which would have been a blow to the planters for whom it was an essential highway. Virginia knew the answer to that threat; she included in her borders both Cape Charles and Cape Henry, on opposite sides of the entrance to Chesapeake Bay. A line drawn from cape to cape would make inland communities of all the bay towns. Neither side appealed to the enfeebled Congress. Instead both states sent commissioners to the feet of a wise man at Mount Vernon and a prompt compromise was reached. That was in 1785.

The example was noted and the suggestion was made for another conference to be held at Annapolis the following year at which all intercolonial grievances would be aired. But the lesson was still imperfectly learned and only five states were represented at the 1786 meeting. It lasted long enough, however, to draft a request to the Congress to put out a general call for a meeting of all the colonies in 1787. On February 21, 1787, Congress drafted an appropriate resolution. The exact reading of the resolution is not without interest:

> Resolved that in the opinion of Congress it is expedient that on the second Monday in May next a Convention of delegates who shall have been appointed by the several states be held at Philadelphia for the sole and express purpose of revising the Articles of Confederation and reporting to the Congress and the several legislatures such alterations and provisions therein as shall when agreed to in Congress and confirmed by the states render the federal constitution adequate to the exigencies of Government and the preservation of the Union.

Note the cautious wording. This convention was for the *purpose of revising* the Articles of Confederation; no hint is there of a radical reconstruction of the foundations of government. They were clinging to that which they had and knew, and were reaching forward tentatively in the direction of "alterations" in the existing instrument. The rule of trial and error was being applied, but the result this time was sweeping, nothing less than the Constitution under which we still live.

CHAPTER III

The Great Compromises of the Constitutional Convention

(D. R.)

IN THE LIGHT of preceding history perhaps the most significant words of the Constitution drafted at Philadelphia were the three opening words: "We the People." The Articles of Confederation were a compact between sovereign states. The delegates to the Convention were appointed by the states for the specific purpose of "revising the Articles of Confederation." They took it upon themselves to propose the adoption of a "Constitution for the United States of America" by the people, to be ratified by conventions of delegates "chosen in each state by the People thereof, under Recommendation of its Legislature."

In this way it was to be made clear that the Constitution was the fundamental law of a nation established by the people who were citizens, not merely of the several states, but "of the United States"—although exactly who were citizens of the United States was not defined until the Fourteenth Amendment was adopted after the Civil War.

The Articles of Confederation did not create or recognize any national citizenship. They created only a confederacy of

THE GREAT COMPROMISES

sovereign states and not a government of the people of a nation. This might be proclaimed, as it was, a "perpetual union" of states; but it was not established by all of the people themselves, as a national government, supreme, within its granted powers, over the state governments which sections of the people had established separately as state citizens.

This creation of a national citizenry with rights and duties was an act of courage and necessity. The peoples of the colonial states, who had waged a war in the harmony of one objective, independence from Great Britain, but with considerable confusion as to other objectives and much discord as to methods, were far from united in their political desires and intentions. They wanted to gain the strength of union in dealing with foreign governments but, residing in communities remote from one another, meeting and communicating only through slow means of transportation, and being intimately concerned with local interests which were often in conflict, they were fiercely determined to retain state powers of local self-government.

It was an object of transcendent importance to preserve for the separate states the "exclusive right of regulating the internal government and the police thereof." This statement, quoted from the Maryland Constitution, expressed the opinion prevailing in all the states. Let it be noted that under the Constitution today protection against domestic violence can be extended by the national government only "on application by the Legislature or of the Executive (when the Legislature cannot be convened)." Without strong assurance that the governing rights of the states would be preserved, the Constitution could never have been adopted. Indeed, fears of an all-powerful centralized government almost defeated adoption, which was finally approved by such narrow margins as: Massachusetts 187-168; Virginia 89-79; New York 30-27 (the latter two only after final acceptance by the nine states necessary for adoption).

The supreme problem of the Constitutional Convention was clear: How to establish a strong national government and yet protect the individual liberties of the people and the governing rights of their established states against the potential tyranny of a national government. The solutions were found: First, in creating a national government with only expressly delegated and expressly limited powers; Second, in dividing national authority between separate legislative, executive and judicial officers; Third, in dividing the supreme legislative power between representatives elected directly by the people and senators chosen by the states; Fourth, in electing the supreme executive by the people for only a brief term of office (with the clumsy interposition of electors, whose functions have become nominal); Fifth, in the promised adoption of the first Ten Amendments, which made individual rights and the reserved powers of the states and the people expressly immune to derogation by the national government.

They labored long and hard, those founding fathers of a nation, to find compromises of conflicting convictions, and then to find just the exact words with which to write them into principles and processes of government. They accomplished the miracle of creating a government strong enough to serve the people but unable to master them. They welded local governments into a national state capable of serving their common interests but incapable of destroying their local powers to serve their separate interests. They wrote a constitution providing a way for the people to create a national government and to prevent the abuse of its powers, recognizing that its worth would depend on how well or poorly the people chose their administrators and exercised their own ultimate authority. They defined only a few qualifications for public office and avoided the sin of legislating in a constitution. In the words of Madison they chose "to rest all our political experiments on the capacity of mankind for self-government."

They sought to maintain the capacity of the people to govern themselves; issues immediately arose in the convention over how to prevent the abuse of power by either the lawmakers, or the administrators, or the courts. The members knew from history and from their own experiences how individual liberty could be destroyed if unlimited authority to make or to enforce laws were granted or permitted to any body of public officials. They were able quickly to agree upon the principle, written, for example, in the Virginia Bill of Rights, that "the Legislative, Executive and Judicial powers of government ought to be forever separate and distinct from each other."

They were not, however, misled into making these powers complete and independent in each branch of the government. On the contrary they made each branch somewhat dependent on the other and subject to check upon any abuse and unwarranted assumption of power. The Congress, as a body of representatives most responsive to public opinion, might come nearer to the exercise of a supreme authority, but its powers were carefully defined and limited to those expressly granted.

Furthermore, in the veto power given to the President, unwise or improper lawmaking by a bare majority was checked by requiring a two-thirds vote to override a veto. Finally, the Supreme Court was empowered to uphold the Constitution "and the Laws of the United States which shall be made in *Pursuance thereof*," as the supreme law of the land. This meant, as was well-understood, that laws enacted by the Congress in violation of limits upon its powers would be held invalid and unenforceable.

As Governor Johnston explained it to the North Carolina ratifying convention: "Every law consistent with the Constitution will have been made in pursuance of the powers granted by it. Every usurpation or law repugnant to it cannot have been made in pursuance of its powers. The latter will be nugatory and void."

Through its power over expenditures the Congress could exercise a definite check upon unwise or improper use of executive power—or judicial power. Specifically the Congress was forbidden to make appropriations for armies "for a longer term than two years." Thus the possible seizure of tyrannical power by a President, as commander in chief of the armed forces, would be made difficult.

In such ways the convention solved without too much difficulty or disagreement the mechanical phases of its problem of creating a strong government without opening the way to the exercise of any arbitrary authority by one group of officials. The skeleton structure of the new government and the division of powers met general approval. But the method of selecting its officers and the grants and limitations upon their powers raised issues so profound that for some time agreement seemed impossible. Even if the Convention could find compromises of conflicting views, the question would remain as to whether the peoples of the separate states would accept these compromises in sufficient numbers to permit ratification.

Foremost among these dangerous issues was the practically universal demand for the preservation of local self-government—commonly referred to as the preservation of "states rights." The Articles of Confederation had provided for legislation by one house composed of delegates from the federated states. The proposal of a legislature for the new government, composed only of representatives of the people apportioned according to population, would place the smaller states at a hopeless disadvantage. They would never consent. The irreconcilable differences between the so-called slave states and the others were of less importance than a widespread insistence upon the principle of local self-government which was clearly written into the constitutions of Massachusetts, New Hampshire, Maryland and Pennsylvania. On the other hand, a legislature composed only of representatives of the states would perpetuate many of the weaknesses of the existing confederation.

Late in June, 1781, with this problem unsolved, one delegate reported that the convention was "scarce held together by the strength of a hair"; and Benjamin Franklin proposed that each session should be opened with prayer. A committee was appointed to seek a compromise, but, so hot was the debate over its proposals, reported on July 5, that in the midst of it Washington wrote to Hamilton: "I almost despair of seeing a favorable issue and do therefore repent having had any agency in the business."

Happily, on July 16, by a vote of only five states to four, the great compromise was adopted of providing for representation in the House proportional to population and equal state representation in the Senate by two members from each state. Also the House was given the exclusive right to originate all bills for raising revenue—thus placing this vital power under control of representatives elected directly by the people.

There was nothing novel in the idea of having two houses in the legislature. The Parliament of England had been divided into two houses in the reign of Edward III (1341). But the device of having one house represent the citizens of the nation and the other house represent the states and their respective citizens, as a means of federating the states in a national union, was sufficiently novel that Lord Bryce, the most notable foreign commentator on our Constitution, described it as an American invention which made possible our federated union.

After the settlement of this momentous issue there followed intensive debates over many other issues where shrewd compromises were essential to reach agreements. As was inevitable these compromises were expressed in general phrases, in the interpretation of which controversies have raged throughout our history. The wisdom of the framers in creating a supreme court made possible the settlement of these controversies by peaceful adjudication in a court of final authority and the avoidance of armed conflicts between governments of the "sovereign" states and the "sovereign" authority of the national government. "Judicial supremacy" preserved the union from internecine warfare except in the one tragic conflict of interests that led to the Civil War.

An ultimate appeal from an unpopular Supreme Court construction of the Constitution was wisely provided in a cautious but practical provision for a careful and decisive determination of the will of the people by the adoption of an amendment to the Constitution by the action of three fourths of the states. In this way a defect in the Articles of Confederation, which required *unanimous* adoption of amendments, was remedied. But, at the same time, a minority of the states were protected in their powers of self-government, while the people as a whole were protected against being compelled to submit to an excessive exercise, or an undue limitation, of national authority imposed by an irrevocable ruling of the Supreme Court.

These protections afforded to the states and the people helped to induce acceptance of compromises in settling two of the major issues regarding the powers of the national government. The control of interstate commerce by the federal government and the creation of a federal power of taxation presented very difficult problems. Clearly it was necessary to give the national government the power to regulate commerce "that concerned more states than one." Clearly the national government must be able to raise revenue for its own support and to provide for the defense of the nation. But, an unlimited power to control commerce or to tax all the people would offer the means of a consolidation and concentration of government which would inevitably destroy local self-government.

The Virginia Plan, embodied in resolutions presented to the convention by Governor Randolph, would have given the Congress power "to legislate in all cases to which the individual States are incompetent or in which the harmony of the United States may be interrupted by the exercise of individual legislation." Various amendments were proposed to except from the national authority "any matters of internal police." These were not adopted; but in final action the convention chose to rely upon specific grants of power to the national government and a reservation to the states "or to the people" of powers not delegated to the United States, nor prohibited to the states. This intent was expressly written into the Tenth Amendment.

The debate over the commerce power to be granted to the Congress was vigorous and far-reaching. Fears were expressed of giving any power to the federal government to grant monopolies. Fears of interference with the slave trade moved many southern delegates who were nevertheless convinced the federal government must have power to make an end to state laws interfering with commercial intercourse between the states.

Eventually there emerged the present clause giving to Congress the broad power "to regulate commerce with foreign nations and among the several States." The states were not directly prohibited from regulating any commerce except by subsequent clauses which prohibited them from laying imposts or duties on imports or exports without the consent of the Congress, or from laying any duty on tonnage. But the Congress was also prohibited from laying any tax on exports, or giving any preference to the ports of one state, or requiring vessels moving to or from one state "to enter, clear, or pay duties in another." Then the slave traders were mollified by a special provision protecting from adverse federal legislation the importation or migration of persons acceptable to any state, prior to the year 1808.

In this connection it should be noted that the Constitution framers compromised another disagreement between, roughly speaking, Northern and Southern states by providing that three fifths of the number of slaves should be counted in apportioning both representatives *and* direct taxes. Thus Northern objections to undertaxation of Southerners and Southern demands for overrepresentation were both satisfied!

This was one of the less happy compromises adopted, but it undoubtedly encouraged ratification by Southern states—and, in view of the spreading sentiment against slavery in such states as Virginia, Maryland and even North Carolina, there was reason for hoping that time would eliminate discord between the states arising from this "peculiar institution." Indeed, prior to the adoption of the Constitution, delegates from Virginia, Georgia, South Carolina and North Carolina had voted for the ordinance establishing the Northwest Territory which forever prohibited slavery in that vast area.

Before leaving the commerce clause it should be again emphasized that it did not provide for regulation of *all* commerce *within* the United States (as it did provide for regulation of *all* commerce *with* foreign nations). On the contrary it was the grant of only a limited power to regulate commerce *"among* the several states." The states were apparently left free to regulate all internal commerce—giving to the national government only the power to regulate "that commerce which concerns more states than one." In the language of Chief Justice John Marshall, the great expounder of the commerce clause, "The completely internal commerce of a State, then, may be considered as reserved for the State itself." If this had not been the accepted limitation of the grant of federal power it is quite certain that the Constitution would not have been ratified by the necessary nine states.

Another need for wise compromise arose from the necessity of granting adequate power to the national government to levy taxes and spend money to meet national needs. The first grant of power to the Congress now reads: "To lay and collect Taxes, Duties, Imposts and Excises, to pay the debts and provide for the common Defence and general Welfare of the United States, but all Duties, Imposts and Excises shall be uniform throughout the United States."

Debate over the extent of congressional power thus granted began in the Constitutional Convention, has continued to this day, and will probably continue indefinitely. The power to levy taxes, to pay national debts, and to provide for national defence was clearly necessary. Otherwise the government would be impotent. But, what sweep of power would be granted in authorizing taxation in order "to provide for the general welfare"? A government levies taxes in order to spend. The power to tax must be granted to enable the national government to spend money for its necessary but specifically defined and carefully limited purposes. But, would there be any limit to a power that might be granted to tax (and hence to spend) "for the general welfare"?

Week after week the Constitutional Convention debated this conflict between the need on the one hand for a national government capable of protecting "the general interests of the Union" and of legislating in all matters wherein "the separate states are incompetent," and the dangers of creating a national power capable of destroying local self-government by the states. In seeking to draw this line between necessity and danger the convention first resorted to a specific enumeration of the legislative powers of the Congress, to which were ultimately added a power "to make all laws necessary and proper for carrying into execution the foregoing powers, and all other powers vested by this Constitution in the Government of the United States, or in any Department or Officer thereof."

Weeks after the convention had definitely embarked upon a precise limitation of national legislative powers by a specific enumeration of the subjects of congressional legislation, and had apparently turned away from any blanket grant of power, there occurred, on September 4, 1787, one of its most surprising and never adequately explained actions. In the course of approving a committee report the convention adopted the present provision for levying taxes to "provide for the common defence and general welfare"—*without debate!* Considering the far-reaching nature of this decision and this sudden end of a controversy that had created deep antagonisms and threatened the convention with the immediate or ultimate failure of its efforts, the subsequent charges of "trickery" and "precipitate" action may seem plausible.

There is, however, another explanation that is more creditable to the influential members who evidently engineered this great compromise. The strongest advocates of strictly limited national powers, such as Madison, had achieved their major purpose in having the objects of congressional legislation apparently confined to those specially stated. The strongest advocates of unlimited national power, such as Hamilton, had achieved their major purpose of having the national legislature expressly empowered to make all the laws that seemed to them essential to create a dominant national government. The vagueness of the grant to lay taxes "to provide for the general welfare" made it possible for both sides to quiet their respective apprehensions of subsequent construction of these words.

The Madisonians could say to themselves: We have listed all objects of legislation that involve the general welfare; and thus defined and confined any general welfare legislation. We are granting no additional power to make laws—just the supplementary power to raise money to administer the laws.

The Hamiltonians could say to themselves: We have covered everything we need by other specific grants of power, except the power to tax. Now we get that, and this welfare clause won't limit the other powers which are specifically given and it may add something that we have overlooked or couldn't get more plainly stated.

Both groups of leaders were profoundly anxious to establish a competent national government. They were worried with lengthy, tiresome debates and fearful of failure if they could not soon end the talking and reach agreement. Both could easily persuade themselves that, if they did not immediately win, at least they did not immediately lose by leaving the issue to be settled by posterity.

However, upon the submission of the Constitution for ratification, immediate and violent criticisms were made of this provision as one extending an indefinite and extensive power to the national government which could be made destructive of all powers of local state government. Typical of these is the letter written by Richard Henry Lee to Samuel Adams of Massachusetts and to Governor Randolph of Virginia wherein he said:

> But what is the power given to this ill-constructed body? To judge of what may be the general welfare; and such judgment when made the acts of Congress becomes the supreme law of the land. This seems a power coextensive with every possible object of human legislation.

Some of the fears of federal legislation under such a broad power were reduced by the promise of amendments, which were in fact immediately adopted by the First Congress, providing a bill of rights to protect individual rights against federal legislative destruction and also a specific declaration in the Tenth Amendment that "the powers not delegated to the United States by the Constitution, nor prohibited by it to the States are reserved to the States respectively, or to the people."

So, despite the opposition of such formidable opponents as Luther Martin of Maryland; Elbridge Gerry and Samuel Adams of Massachusets; Richard Henry Lee, George Mason and Patrick Henry of Virginia; Governor DeWitt Clinton, Melancton Smith and many others in New York; and dominant politicians in Rhode Island and North Carolina, the

Constitution was finally adopted and was followed quickly by the supplementary adoption of the first ten amendments.

Differences over the power of Congress to legislate for the general welfare smoldered for decades after 1787, but the prevalence of "strict constructionists" among the presidents and congressional leaders throughout the nineteenth century prevented the issue from bursting into flame. Jefferson denied the power of Congress to appropriate federal funds for anything but a clearly national purpose. Madison developed at length the doctrine that congressional power to promote the general welfare was confined within the boundaries of other powers specifically enumerated. Monroe and Jackson vetoed bills for public improvements of only local advantage. River and harbor bills were vetoed by Taylor, Polk, Pierce, Grant, Arthur and Cleveland on the grounds of the same unconstitutionality.

As a result of this self-restraint of the federal government the Supreme Court of the United States was never required to make an authoritative construction of this either very limited or almost unlimited power of the Congress until the year 1936, then the court rejected the "Madisonian construction" that the general welfare clause added little if anything to the otherwise "enumerated powers" in favor of the "Hamiltonian construction" that it added a grant of far-reaching power only tenuously limited by congressional judgment as to what is in aid of the general welfare.

Thus, what may be regarded as the last great compromise in the convention (chronologically speaking), which consisted of a grant of power in such broad terms as to be apparently but not surely limited by more precise grants, permitted the avoidance of a profound issue for nearly 150 years. Since avoidance of a clash of irreconcilable opinions is an art of statecraft, the success of this compromise indicates again the remarkable political sagacity of the principal framers of our Constitution.

THE GREAT COMPROMISES

The supreme compromise that insured the adoption of the Constitution was developed during the debates over its ratification. Here Madison and Hamilton joined forces in persuading their antagonistic followers that the miracle had been accomplished of creating a national government strong enough to sustain the national interest against all forces of foreign aggression or competition and against individual or sectional dissent, and at the same time so restricted in its powers that individual liberty and sectional self-government could be preserved.

The compromises with state government advocates were sufficiently effective so that opposition from the extremists of this order could be reduced to minorities in the state conventions which, being composed of delegates chosen for that purpose, were expected to ratify more readily than would the state legislatures which might be more jealously intent on preserving all their political authority. But, this appeal to the people themselves made particularly dangerous the argument that individual liberties could be seriously curbed by the laws enacted and enforced by a remote centralized government. The demand for a bill of rights to guarantee to individuals that their personal liberties could not be curtailed and that federal justice could not be administered arbitrarily and in disregard of time-honored safeguards could not be easily satisfied.

Arguments were first advanced to the effect that the powers of the federal government were strictly limited and that the accepted rights of a free people could not be overridden because their protection was implied. It was pointed out that all local affairs would be regulated by local governments which would be themselves restrained by local popular control and by local constitutions safeguarding individual rights and liberties. But it soon became apparent that the people wanted written, express guarantees. They were not inclined to trust implications and assumptions of protection, or the theoretical arguments of politicians.

So it became necessary to give assurances and to create a tacit understanding that the Congress to be established under the prospective Constitution would immediately propose amendments to meet these influential objections to the original instrument. This promise was promptly fulfilled when the First Congress proposed twelve amendments on September 25, 1789, of which ten (now called the Bill of Rights) were adopted with significant speed by the necessary three fourths of the states.

The ultimate compromise necessary to the establishment of the government of the United States was thus achieved. The founding fathers were now assured that their patient, courageous and tolerant labors had created a nation. But they were humble and wise enough to know that its future rested, not in the words that they had written, but in the hoped-for capacity of the people for self-government. They knew, as Washington expressed their thought in his first inaugural address, that

> The preservation of the sacred fire of liberty and the destiny of the republican model of government are justly considered as deeply, perhaps as finally, staked on the experiment entrusted to the hands of the American people.

CHAPTER IV

Creating a Federal Government
(D. R.)

DURING THE ADMINISTRATIONS of Washington and John Adams the structure of a federal government was built upon the foundations laid down in the Constitution. In outlining the growth of government during this period we can well omit any detailed discussion of the profound and difficult problems of the two Presidents of the infant nation in handling foreign relations and avoiding the ever-present dangers of our involvement in international warfare. Through the wise and often unpopular efforts of these early Presidents the nation was permitted for twenty-three years to work out solutions of its vital problems of self-government free from any demoralizing entanglements in foreign wars and from the disruptive effects of an armed attack upon our own country.

The executive departments of State, Treasury and War were immediately organized. A judiciary act provided for an administration of federal justice by the Supreme Court and inferior district and circuit courts. The necessary immediate amendments to the Constitution were proposed by Congress and soon ratified by the states. Many minor precedents were established which had long-range consequences, such as the refusal of the houses of Congress to have cabinet officers participate in their deliberations.

Then in the early days of 1790, Hamilton, as Secretary of the Treasury, submitted the first of his famous creative reports—the First Report on the Public Credit. Through these Hamilton, in Webster's classic tribute, "smote the rock of natural resources and abundant streams of revenue gushed forth." Of course his program for the assumption of the public debt and redemption of depreciated certificates was sure to arouse a popular opposition to this enrichment of speculators who had bought as low as twenty-five per cent and would now be paid the full face value of the debts.

Hamilton's program was frankly designed to appeal to the creditor-capitalist class and to gain their support of the government. It had also a definite appeal to the states which had incurred debts for defense of their areas and in aid of a common cause. Why should not the federal government, which had taken away their great source of revenue in tariff duties, use these revenues to relieve them of their debts? But this assumption proposal, favored by debt-burdened states, was naturally opposed by those which had contracted few obligations, or had paid them off.

At the height of controversy over "assumption" occurred one of the strangest compromises of our early history. Apparently the nation survived only through a succession of compromises of the type abhorrent to all extremists. Hamilton, in grave danger of congressional defeat, appealed to Jefferson, the newly appointed Secretary of State, so effectively that Jefferson invited him and a select group to a dinner at which —possibly under the mellowing influence of much food and drink—an effective but most peculiar agreement was reached: Jefferson was to secure the additional Southern votes necessary to approve the national assumption of state debts and

Hamilton's influence was to assure the location of the national capital on the banks of the Potomac River!

Thus Jefferson himself contributed heavily to bringing a "money power" support to the government (which he later decried), and also, happily, to establishing firmly the credit and financial stability of the government (which he certainly desired). But, it appears that thereafter Jefferson became more wary than before of advancing any Hamiltonian plan. His opposition to establishing a national bank persisted after passage of the enabling act by Congress. He and Attorney General Randolph strongly urged Washington to veto the bill; but Hamilton's argument prevailed.

Historians may differ as to whether Hamilton's measures, which included laying excise duties which were productive of good revenues, were the major cause of the increasing prosperity of the young nation, or whether expanding trade and commerce brought prosperity and made Hamilton's measures a success. But there can be no doubt that he served his country well and, in all probability, those who opposed him would have been poor financial guides in our national infancy.

However, the political division, which later developed the extraconstitutional system of party government in the United States, became inevitable in the conflict over Hamilton's financial policies. The fermenting conflict between creditors and debtors, between the well-to-do and the poor, between prospering men of commerce and struggling workers on the farms or in the shops—the old, old conflict of interests between the classes and the masses was beginning to have political effects on all enjoying or seeking political power.

No wonder that Washington, at the end of his two terms warned the people against "the danger of parties in the State" and "the baneful effects of the spirit of party generally!" He particularized his fears:

The spirit of party, he said, "serves always to distract the public councils and enfeeble the public administration. It agitates the community with ill-founded jealousies and false alarms; kindles the animosity of one part against another; foments occasionally riot and insurrection. It opens the door to foreign influence and corruption, which find a facilitated access to the government itself through the channels of party passion."

How true! How true! But the party spirit had begun to develop; and it would grow steadily until in time party government would impose itself upon the constitutional government of the United States and transform it to an extent that would have utterly disheartened George Washington.

The handling of foreign relations in Washington's first administration intensified the persistent conflict between Hamilton, Secretary of the Treasury, and Jefferson, Secretary of State. The Federalists, lining up behind Hamilton, inclined strongly toward England in its quarrels with revolutionary France. The opposition led by Jefferson, originally known as Democratic-Republicans, was definitely friendly to France.

The prospect of entanglement in European hostilities, with a suicidal division of our people in foreign relations as well as in domestic policies, was the decisive influence in persuading Washington to postpone his intended retirement and to accept election to a second term of office. He yielded, in his own words, because of the "perplexed and critical posture of our affairs with foreign nations." It was fortunate for the American people that he did.

For four years Washington had suffered with superlative patience the open struggle between Hamilton and Jefferson, privately begging them to work together, but without avail. Happily, although persisting in their antagonisms, they both urged their chief to extend his invaluable service; and both, thereafter supported his masterful settlement of what may be called the Genêt imbroglio.

Early in April 1793, Citizen Edmond Genêt, Minister from the French Republic, which was at war with England, arrived in the United States and began his boisterous ride from Charleston, South Carolina, to Philadelphia, through banquet tables packed with cheering partisans of the newest republic. If he were received and his government recognized we might be dragged into war with England, because of our treaty of alliance with France made in 1778. Washington, with the unanimous approval of his cabinet decided to receive Genêt, but also to proclaim our neutrality in the European war, which was done on the same day on which Genêt arrived in Philadelphia. Domestic discord over this proclamation was partly averted by the outrageous conduct of Genêt. Jefferson and Hamilton agreed that his recall should be requested; and a Neutrality Act was passed by Congress on June 5, 1794.

This act of Congress stilled a debate over the President's authority to proclaim neutrality; but this proclamation of Washington firmly established the power of the President thus to maintain peace, as distinct from the power to declare war which the Constitution granted exclusively to the Congress. Thus one of the most momentous of the implied powers of the chief executive became embedded in our law.

Of course, official neutrality did not prevent the private fomenting of differences between Federalists and Republicans, which boiled over into a raucous debate in the adoption by the Senate of the Jay Treaty with Great Britain in 1795. The close vote in the Senate and the year's delay of the House before voting, only 51 to 48, to appropriate money to execute the treaty, showed how deep was the popular opposition to what was, on the whole, a wise measure, essential to our domestic tranquility and to our commercial development.

With the conclusion, also in 1795, of a treaty with Spain, another sore spot in foreign relations with its menace to our westward expansion was removed so that, when Washington gladly turned over his office to John Adams, our relations with France presented the major international problem for which the second President must find a solution. Here Adams had to deal with an unstable revolutionary government and with one of the wiliest, most unscrupulous diplomats of history, Talleyrand.

For more than two years John Adams strove valiantly to maintain the dignity of the nation, despite indignities heaped upon its envoys, to resist international blackmail and extortion, and to keep reins upon the rising martial spirit of the American people, when Republicans and Federalists united in preparation for war. It was no easy task to preserve peace after a navy department had been created and new warships built, and the army expanded, with Washington called to its command and Hamilton named as commander in the field.

Indeed, although war was not declared, we were actually at war with France and our naval heroes were capturing scores of armed vessels flying the French flag. Then destiny, in the shape of Napoleon Bonaparte, sent doves of peace to the harassed President, who, as others long after him, was diligently preparing for war and desperately working for peace. And so, in the sunset hours of John Adams' difficult reign, a treaty with France was signed and the United States finally freed from the last foreign entanglement that menaced the life of the young republic.

It is unfortunate that the administration of John Adams is so well remembered for the passage of the oppressive Alien and Sedition Acts, which on their face violated the constitutional protections of free press, free speech, trial by jury, and unrestricted immigration (prior to 1808). These acts provided a major basis for the anti-Federalist campaign of the Republicans led by Jefferson, who after his resignation from Washington's cabinet in 1793 and throughout his service as Vice President in President Adams' term, was the pre-eminent and indefatigable propagandist of Republican policies.

In this work he was curiously abetted by Hamilton whose antagonism to Adams approached, if it did not equal, that of Jefferson.

Hamilton and other notable Federalists were opposed to the Alien and Sedition Acts; and President Adams, despite the pressures of extremists, did little or nothing to enforce them. But the curse of their enactment fell heavily upon the Federalist candidates in the presidential election of 1800. Jefferson's program of appeal to the "common people," to take governing power away from a mercantile aristocracy, roused a fear of his ascendancy which evidently warped the judgment and divided the councils of the Federalists. Indignities and injuries heaped upon our people and our commerce by both Great Britain and France brought violent criticisms of an administration that "truckled" to such oppressors.

But when the peace-seeking Adams persuaded General Washington to take command again of the armies of the United States, when he went forward with "vigorous preparations for war," including the enlargement of the navy, and when his conduct of foreign relations finally averted the threatened war, the Republicans made much political capital out of the high and "unnecessary" taxes with which the poor people were being burdened! Denunciations were poured upon the Federalist administration for "preparing for a war which does not exist, and expending millions which will have no other effect than bringing war upon us." This was the comparatively temperate language of James Monroe, then, as ever, a stalwart lieutenant of Jefferson.

The great significance of Jefferson's campaign for President lies in this first systematized program of appealing to popular emotions and prejudices and developing that "party spirit" decried by Washington, which since that time has dominated every general election in the United States. The phantasm of a nonpartisan electorate, which had appealed to Washington as a practical ideal, faded out like the grin of the Cheshire cat in the campaign of 1800. In later years that ghostlike smile has been recreated frequently to hover over local campaigns and at intervals over discussions of international relations.

The unreality of a search for a nonpartisan electorate is that the very purpose of voting is to decide disagreements, not to voice consent, but to register both consent and dissent. Thus we establish dominant force behind our representative rulers—and at the same time assure that the lesser force of a chastening opposition will not be ignored.

In recent years the farce of "one party" elections in a communist-ruled country has proved the evanescent nature of the nonpartisan ideal which was only made tangible by the extraordinary virtues of the First President of the United States. In Washington's administration the earthy differences of men as brilliant and combative as Jefferson and Hamilton made the President, who could tolerate both of them as his chief advisers, seem so angelic that history remade a splendid, attractive man into the image of a repellently angelic superman. But even the most idolatrous of Jefferson's followers never portrayed him as an angel.

The election of Jefferson was finally made possible by the triumph of an honest compromise over treacherous double-dealing, setting another precedent for the generations of politicians to come. When Aaron Burr, instead of throwing his votes in the House of Representatives to his co-candidate Jefferson (who was the obvious first choice of the electors), accepted for himself the support of Federalist representatives, he overreached himself. Hamilton regarded Burr as much worse than Jefferson and from previous experience knew Jefferson's capacity for compromise and his honorable fulfillment of his promises.

Jefferson, who had faith in federalism, but not in Federalists, could easily give assurances that the fundamentals of federalism, including the fiscal system, would be preserved, with no wholesale purge of Federalist officeholders. With the aid of Federalist votes he won, encumbered with the discredited Burr as Vice-President. This political compromise, combined with Jefferson's strong will to maintain the federal union, transformed the anticipated "revolution," so that it turned out to be only a shrewd popularization of the previous Federalist policies.

The Federal party never recovered from the peaceful absorption of its programs and many of its leaders into the Jeffersonian "democracy."

CHAPTER V

Jefferson and Marshall
(D. R.)

WHEN THOMAS JEFFERSON walked up the country road, Pennsylvania Avenue, to take his oath of office in the partly built structure which is now the impressive Capitol, he dramatically began the process of transforming the provincial formalities of Federalist administrations into the simpler forms which he deemed more appropriate to a people's government. He followed the same thought in sending his first message to Congress instead of delivering it in person, as a sort of "Address from the Throne."

But there was no undue modesty in his execution of the powers of the President, carefully confined by him where expressly limited by the Constitution, but broadly construed in the undefined domain of "implied powers." In his devotion to the principle of local self-government, he was rigidly insistent on the reserved powers of the states and the declared and reserved rights of the people. But where the nation must act in the interest of all the people, and the states were clearly incompetent, he was prepared to speak and act with a majestic disregard of cautious counsels that would have paralyzed the will of a less resolute head of a popular government.

In his use and development of the national government he had the unsolicited and often embarrassing aid of a great, politically minded judge with whom, at the very outset of his administration, he seemed destined to be in continual conflict.

John Marshall of Virginia, Secretary of State in Adams' cabinet, was appointed Chief Justice of the United States Supreme Court by President Adams on January 20, 1801, and speedily confirmed. But he continued to serve (without salary) as Secretary of State to the end of Adams' term. He administered the oath of office to Jefferson on March 4, 1801.

Immediately thereafter arose the famous case in which Chief Justice Marshall eventually laid what is well described as "the cornerstone of Constitutional law." James Madison, Jefferson's Secretary of State, had refused to deliver to William Marbury his commission as a justice of the peace, which had been signed by President Adams and sealed by Marshall as Secretary of State on the night of March 3, just before Adams' term expired. Marbury asked the Supreme Court to issue a writ of mandamus to compel Madison, the new Secretary of State, to deliver the commission to him.

After long delays the case was argued and Chief Justice Marshall delivered the opinion of the Court on February 24, 1803. In those days a Justice of the Supreme Court was not embarrassed to rule on a case which involved his own conduct in a previously held public office! Here was a ruling of momentous consequence. If the Court issued the writ and Madison refused to obey it, the authority of the Court would be seriously impaired. If the Court refused to issue the writ, it would apparently abandon its judicial authority under pressure of the executive. Public feeling ran high. The prestige of the Supreme Court and of the President were both at stake. The solution found by Marshall demonstrated his unique abilities both as a lawyer and as a statesman.

To summarize one of the most important opinions ever

handed down by a court, what Marshall decided was: First, that under the Constitution the Court had an absolute obligation to hold that any act of Congress which violated the Constitution was not a law and should not be obeyed and could not be enforced. Second, that the act of Congress, apparently authorizing the Supreme Court to issue a writ of mandamus in such a case as the one presented, violated the Constitution and was null and void.

The reasons for holding that the act of Congress was unconstitutional were based on a close, strict construction of the language of the Constitution which gave the Supreme Court "original jurisdiction" in only a limited variety of cases (within which this case clearly did not come). In all other cases the Court was given only "appellate jurisdiction." Hence the Court could not be given by Congress any authority to issue the writ as an "original writ" in a case which could not legally originate in the Court.

This dismissal of the case took away from the executive branch of the government any ground for complaint. It had won the case; the writ had been denied. But, the remainder of the opinion established "judicial supremacy" and the "supreme law" of the Constitution in no uncertain terms. That is what gives *Marbury* v. *Madison* its great place in the history of jurisprudence.

It was mere dicta (statements quite unnecessary to the decision) for Marshall to point out that Marbury had a right to his commission and that he had a right to an order (in a proper case) to compel the Secretary of State to deliver it to him. Since the Court later held that this was *not* a proper case, why discuss what the ruling should be in a proper case? But, Marshall as a judge and a statesman was determined to vindicate the right of the applicant and the authority of the judicial branch to give him a remedy for the violation of his right. Also he soothed the outraged feelings of those who resented an abuse of power by an executive officer in refusing to perform an official duty.

Then the Chief Justice proceeded to deliver a lecture on constitutional law, which was the basis for the decision that the Court had the authority and duty to refuse enforcement of a legislative act which was not authorized, or was prohibited, by the Constitution. This exposition of the authority of the Court to maintain the Constitution, as interpreted by the Court, as the supreme law of the land, was so closely reasoned and so persuasive that it has never been seriously challenged. Arguments have raged over whether this judicial power was intended to be granted, but the records of the Constitutional Convention answer these completely. Arguments against the need for such judicial power find their final answer in Marshall's opinion. Proposals to limit the power of the Court or to provide for some appeal from its rulings, other than the submission of an amendment to the Constitution, have never gained sufficient support to warrant their adoption.

In *Marbury* v. *Madison* the workability and enforcement of a written constitution met its first great test. Through that epochal opinion of the Supreme Court it was made clear that a people *can* adopt a fundamental law which *will* preserve their liberties and their institutions of self-government as long as the people continue to select and to support public officials who are faithful to their trusteeship under the document which grants, and at the same time limits, their authority to govern their fellow men.

In the same year that Chief Justice Marshall was establishing the supremacy of the Constitution—through establishing the judicial supremacy of the Supreme Court—President Jefferson was demonstrating the vast power potential in the chief executive. He was extending his authority, beyond all recognized and presumably constitutional bounds, by doubling the area of the country in one huge international bargain known as the Louisiana Purchase.

When Jefferson authorized his emissaries to negotiate with Napoleon a settlement of our vexatious controversies with France, he had no idea of proposing a complete withdrawal by France of its sovereignty in the vast area west of the existing United States. He sought only the purchase of New Orleans and perhaps West Florida. But Napoleon had no great interest in retaining this territory for French colonial expansion. His eyes were fixed on the great project of French domination in Europe. There lay the empire of his dreams.

In the treaty sent to him by his peace-seeking mission, Jefferson was suddenly faced with a grave dilemma. Napoleon proposed in brief the liquidation of all French claims and abandonment of its interests west of the Mississippi (and a dubious interest in West Florida) in exchange for what then seemed a large amount of money, about $14,500,000, but which today would appear trifling for the territory sold. By this "Louisiana Purchase" Jefferson would double the national area, obtain complete control of the Mississippi River, establish peace with France, and end all future rivalry on the American continent with the then strongest European power.

But, where in the Constitution had been granted any power to the President to make such an agreement and thus to increase the area subject to the jurisdiction of the United States? Jefferson, himself, was confident that no such power had been granted. He was at first convinced that he must withhold decisive executive action and propose a settlement of the entire problem through an amendment to the Constitution. Yet the dangers of that course were obvious. No one could be sure of the outcome. Domestic disagreement would at least insure protracted discussion and a doubtful issue. Napoleon wanted the bargain sealed at once. He might change his mind or lose his power.

Oppressed as he was with many doubts, Jefferson finally

decided that the risk of failing in a wonderful achievement was greater in cautious procrastination than in bold immediate action. He was the first of several Presidents to decide that the thing to do was to exercise a questionable power and then trust to eventual ratification of his act. That might come from either legislative or judicial authority, if therein could be found a power of ratification. Or an official disapproval might come too late to prevent the consummation of an act that posterity at least would approve. He sealed the bargain and the Louisiana Purchase became a fact.

Eight hundred and seventy-five thousand square miles of land, between the Gulf of Mexico and Canada and westward from the Mississippi River to the Rockies, was added to the domain of the United States at a cost of about three cents an acre! In addition Jefferson had provided a precedent for the use of executive authority which, in the course of time, would be followed by such diverse Presidents as Monroe, Polk, Lincoln, Theodore Roosevelt, and Franklin D. Roosevelt.

It has been said, with some justification, that the ability and willingness of American Presidents to exercise a dubious authority in national emergencies has given a flexible strength to our government of expressly limited powers which has been proved to be essential to the promotion and protection of our national interests. The specific grant of emergency powers, leaving the chief executive free to create an "emergency," would be clearly dangerous. But, when the President must take the risk of repudiation or impeachment for abuse of authority, there is a restraint imposed, which may be normally more effective than any written limitation of "emergency" powers that could be devised.

Of course the Louisiana Purchase was violently assailed by old and new opponents of Jefferson. But, with the speedy approval by the Senate of the clearly advantageous treaty with France, and the vote of funds to implement it by the House, the opposition was quickly overcome. The popularity of the purchase helped to insure the re-election of Jefferson, and the continuance of his party in power after the end of his second term. The newly acquired land became a "territory" of the United States, thereafter to be carved into separate states to be admitted one by one into the federal union. The legal machinery had now been provided for the extension of the government of the United States across the continent and eventually into Alaska and to island possessions in the Atlantic and Pacific oceans.

It appears in retrospect that Jefferson's Louisiana Purchase enlarged not only the geographical sovereignty of the United States but also the implied powers of the national government, with lasting consequences. It is an ironic fact that this outstanding opponent of "centralized authority" may properly be regarded as the Chief Executive whose influence in nationalizing our government is fairly comparable with that of the nationalizing Chief Justice, whose contemporary influence in developing the strength of the national government is more frequently recognized.

The difference between the sentiments that moved Jefferson and Marshall may be indicated by an oversimplified explanation: Both wanted a strong national government. But, Jefferson was restrained somewhat by his fears of the potential tyranny of centralized authority and by his abiding faith in the virtues of local self-government. Marshall, on the other hand, appeared to have few fears of concentrated power but a keen understanding of some of the weaknesses of local governments and the dangers of a divided control of national affairs. When he wrote an early opinion nullifying a state law he made these significant observations:

> Whatever respect might have been felt for the state sovereignties, it is not to be disguised that the framers of the Constitution viewed, with some apprehension, the violent acts which might grow out of the feelings of the moment; and that the

people of the United States, in adopting that instrument, have manifested a determination to shield themselves and their property from the effects of those sudden and strong passions to which men are exposed. The restrictions on the legislative powers of the states are obviously founded in this sentiment; and the Constitution of the United States contains what may be deemed a bill of rights for the people of each state. [He was *not* referring to the first ten amendments, which restrained only the federal government.] [1]

The conflict between Jefferson and Marshall persisted long after the nominally favorable *decision* and the definitely unfavorable *opinion* delivered for the confusion of the Jeffersonians, in *Marbury* v. *Madison*.

Although the issues were profound and the exponents illustrious, this was essentially a contest between rival politicians, each determined to shape the development of government in accordance with his convictions as to how the nation should be governed. Hamilton had been slain in a duel with Aaron Burr on July 11, 1804, but Marshall, from his powerful judicial office, carried on the Hamiltonian struggle with the President whom, strangely enough, Hamilton had helped to put in that high office because he regarded Burr as a much greater evil than Jefferson.

At this point it should be noted that an amendment to the Constitution resulted from Burr's unscrupulous effort to get himself elected President by Federalist votes, although he was in reality the vice-presidential candidate of the Republicans, whose presidential candidate was Jefferson. The original provision of Article II had provided for the choice of presidential electors in each state who would then vote for "two persons." On the count of their votes by the Congress the person receiving the most votes would be President; but if no one had a majority of all votes then the House of Representatives would elect the President; and "after the choice

[1] *Fletcher* v. *Peck,* 6 Cranch, 87.

of the President the person having the greatest number of votes of the electors" would be Vice-President; but in case of a tie the Senate would choose between those tied.

This cumbersome provision (intended to avoid a direct choice by the people) had fantastic results. From 1797 to 1801, the Federalist President Adams had to get along with the Republican Jefferson as his Vice-President. Then, when Jefferson and Burr, running presumably for the *two* offices on the same ticket, received, naturally, the same number of electoral votes, the election was thrown into the House. There Burr, conniving to get Federalist support, blocked the election of Jefferson as President for thirty-five ballots in all of which Jefferson carried eight states (each state voted as a unit) and Burr carried six, with two states tied in the votes of their Representatives and thus not counted. Finally the Federalists in Vermont and Maryland were induced to cast blank ballots, giving those states to the Republican voters, and Jefferson was elected by a vote of ten states to four—with the ineffable Burr as his Vice-President!

It is not surprising that after this discreditable affair the Twelfth Amendment was proposed on December 12, 1803, and adopted on September 25, 1804. This provided: That the electors should name their choice for President and "in distinct ballots" their choice for Vice-President; and in case of no majority there should be an election of the President by the House from the highest three and an election of Vice-President by the Senate from the highest two. There was a further provision that no one ineligible under the Constitution to be President should be eligible to be Vice-President. Thus the law remains to this day, plus the supplementary provisions made by the Twentieth Amendment, adopted in 1933.

When we realize that, after the immediate adoption of the Bill of Rights in 1790, and the minor restriction on judicial power made by the Eleventh Amendment in 1798, this electoral amendment of 1804 was the only amendment of the Constitution adopted until the first post-Civil War amendments of 1865, we must be impressed by the composite wisdom demonstrated by the framers of our supreme law. The structure of government which they fabricated was extraordinarily well devised to encourage a rapid growth of population and a tremendous development of man power and natural resources by the individual initiatives of a people kept singularly free from either the restraints or oppressions of government. The founding fathers were quite familiar with such restraints and oppressions. They sought and found ways to protect themselves and their posterity against them.

Returning now to the historic disagreements of Jefferson and Marshall it is pertinent to comment in passing on the similarities between the two antagonists.

Jefferson had a large variety of interests and talents. His amazing energies and fruitfulness in pursuits of politics, architecture, music, agriculture, education, diplomacy, and literature have been well publicized. His great public services in so many high offices, Governor, Ambassador, Secretary of State, Vice-President and President, make him widely known, not only as a public character but as an attractive man, resourceful, inventive, eloquent, profound and charming, shrewd and high principled, farsighted and painstaking, altogether one of the world's great men, who would be expected to be an overpowering opponent for even a giant of the law. But Marshall was much more than that.

In the first place Marshall had a very limited legal education—a few months' study at William and Mary College. He had less of academic instruction in the law, at Williamsburg under the eminent George Wythe, than Jefferson had. But Marshall had comparably a much better training in the active practice of the law. It was probably well for him and his future work that he was so thoroughly trained in all the arts of advocacy, in striving to win cases for clients, in employing every tolerable device of evading weak issues and concentrating on strong ones, of using reason, logic and emotion to advance his cause. He did not bring to the office of Chief Justice remote, disinterested, abstract concepts of a duty to discover and apply legal rules of metaphysical virtue. On the contrary he came obviously possessed by an intention to make laws, precedents, and dialectics serve the theories of government and the interests in government which he believed to be worthy of support.

Marshall was no scholarly recluse. He was as genially human as Jefferson. Both were fond of good living and enjoyed lively companions. As Professor Bates has pointed out, both men came from the same environment but "where the frontier taught Jefferson its dogmas of democracy and equality, it showed Marshall an example of individual conflict from which a natural aristocracy emerged. He admired efficiency, and he admired success." Here, pitted against each other, were two of the ablest strategists, debaters, and tacticians of their time, each resolved to make government serve the welfare of the people as *he* envisaged that service and that welfare from his angle of vision. Both were zealous men but neither was a zealot.

The impeachment of Justice Chase by Jeffersonians (in 1803) may have been justified by his intemperate misconduct, but it clearly menaced the life tenure of a judge who might make himself too offensive to a political party dominating the legislative branch of government. Marshall was obviously fearful of the results. He testified timidly; and he made the extraordinary suggestion in a letter to Chase that, instead of impeachment, it would "better comport with the mildness of our character" to have judicial opinions reversed by the legislature than to have the judge removed who had rendered them "unknowing of his fault"! Thus, more than one hundred years before Theodore Roosevelt shocked all conservative lawyers by proposing the "recall of decisions" (re-enactment of laws held to be unconstitutional), the greatest judicial expounder of the Constitution and expander of judicial power had offered the same suggestion. But this brief panic subsided when the able lawyers representing Justice Chase successfully disintegrated the prosecution with the argument that the only grounds for impeachment were those specifically listed in Article II, Sec. 4 of the Constitution: "Treason, bribery and other high crimes and misdemeanors." A Justice might be appointed to hold office only "during good behaviour," but he could not be impeached and removed for mere misbehaviour! Chase was acquitted. Marshall recovered his "intestinal fortitude" and resumed his belligerent opposition to Jeffersonian ideas.

Marshall's next conspicuous opportunity to embarrass Jefferson came in the trial of Aaron Burr for treason, over which the Chief Justice presided. His rulings made impossible the conviction of Burr, but he made a tactical and legal error in summoning Jefferson to appear in court with certain papers sought by the defendant, Burr. The President declined on the sound ground that the chief executive could not be made subject to the commands of the judiciary and to punishment for disobedience. With Marshall's abandonment of his assumed authority, the law became firmly established that the President is immune from such judicial coercion.

One of the consequences of the Burr trial was the proposal of an amendment to the Constitution approved by Jefferson limiting the tenure of all federal judges to a term of years and providing for their removal by the President on petition by two thirds of both houses of Congress. But this and other Republican attacks on a Federalist judiciary became less aggressive when it appeared that Jefferson would be able to make appointments to the Supreme Court which would give it a Republican complexion.

But the performance of his appointees was sadly disappointing to Jefferson. Under the ingratiating influence of

Marshall the Republican justices came more and more into general agreement with the Chief Justice. The members of the Court lived and ate in the same boarding house. They had long, convivial sessions of their most exclusive club, chatting for hours over their wine—the best brand of Madeira being labeled "The Supreme Court"! The persuasive charm of Marshall, gently molding their predilections, inevitably shaped their judicial opinions.

When the President, through embargo acts, sought to use an economic boycott as a peaceful substitute for, and a preventive of, war, he found himself thwarted by the very judges he had relied upon for support. The embargo acts were not held unconstitutional, but they were practically nullified and enforcement hampered by public opposition combined with judicial disfavor and antagonistic rulings from the Justices of the Supreme Court, including Jefferson's own appointees.

With the end of Jefferson's second term in 1809, his wrestling with Marshall in the official arena came to an end. He had to leave the Chief Justice and his Court in possession of an undiluted power to promote that centralization of political authority which Jefferson so distrusted. Then, in the years following his retirement from public office, the number and importance of cases presented to the Court increased and he must listen to the resonant voice of the Chief Justice, announcing and enforcing the supremacy of federal law as laid down in the Supreme Court, continually arousing bitter opposition from the sage of Monticello.

The Court of Appeals of Virginia denied the authority of the Supreme Court of the United States to reverse its decision which was intended to settle a title to land in Virginia. Chief Justice Marshall delivered a stern opinion of the Supreme Court establishing the supreme authority of the federal judiciary over that of the state.

The legislature of New Hampshire attempted to amend the charter of Dartmouth College. Chief Justice Marshall held that the state act was void on the ground that the charter was a "contract," and that the Constitution prohibited any state from "impairing the obligation of contracts."

The state of Maryland undertook to levy a tax on the Bank of the United States. This was the national bank, established by Hamilton over Jefferson's objections and re-established in 1816 under Madison, who had approved the bill despite his expressed "prejudices of a lifetime." Chief Justice Marshall first vigorously sustained the implied (but not "enumerated") power of the federal government to establish a bank. Then, with even greater vigor, he denied the power of a state to tax the operations of the bank, laying down his famous doctrine that "the power to tax involves the power to destroy." He held that even the acknowledged vital power of a state to tax could not be used to control an agency of the national government.

Jefferson's early solicitude for states' rights, his early antagonism to a federal judiciary, his distrust of John Marshall, his persistent fears of concentrated political power, were again inflamed. Sizzling attacks upon the Supreme Court issued from Monticello. Yet, contrary to later, quite common misunderstandings of his attitude, the major complaint of Jefferson at this time was directed against the action of the Supreme Court in *supporting the validity of federal laws* (as in the national bank case). His objections to the nullification of state laws naturally proceeded from his devotion to local self-government and his hostility to centralization of power in the federal government. But he thought it entirely desirable for the Court to use its power to keep the legislative branch of the federal government within constitutional bounds. He was particularly aggrieved that the Court had failed to do this, but, on the contrary, had supported new extensions of federal authority.

John Marshall remained in his high office until 1835, building up and strengthening the powers of the national government year by year while the nation was growing rapidly in wealth and population. Its national welfare was expanding from the largely localized interests of five million people, most of whom lived adjacent to the Atlantic seaboard, to the widespread interests of some fifteen million people scattered over a great expanse of land stretching from the Atlantic to the Rockies and from the Gulf of Mexico to the Canadian border.

Meanwhile the long triumphant Republicans had so completely absorbed the nationalism of the Federalists that after Madison's message to Congress in December, 1815, his program was described as having "out-Federalized Federalism." The Monroe Doctrine, defensive in its origin, had started the nation on its career as an aggressive protector of the North, Central and South American nations against European intervention and control of their affairs. It is not surprising that in the presidential campaign of 1824 a deep schism divided the Republicans. The nationalists became known as National Republicans. Their opponents revived the old name of Democratic-Republicans.

John Quincy Adams embarked upon his administration with the futile intention of gaining the good will of both factions while still advancing nationalistic policies. He only helped to prepare the way for the triumph of Andrew Jackson in 1828. In the meanwhile, Jefferson and his long-time, but respected, adversary, John Adams, had died on the same day, July 4, 1826. But, with his farsightedness, Jefferson could have seen before his death that Jeffersonian democracy was on the march again.

CHAPTER VI

A Time of Ferment

(A. B.)

THE PERIOD FROM 1800 to 1860 was one of rapid growth and unexpected change. When it opened the number of states had been increased by the addition of Vermont, Kentucky, and Tennessee. When it closed the states numbered thirty-three, and the present pattern of the continental United States had been completed. As the western boundary moved toward the Pacific, population followed, fast at first until the Misisssippi was crossed, then more slowly, leaping over the dry lands and the mountains to Oregon and California. In 1800 the census counted 5,308,483; in 1860, 31,443,321. Immigration accounted for some of this growth; Marcus Hansen, the most reliable authority, estimates slightly over 4,000,000 aliens in the country in 1860. Immigration grew rapidly in the fifties, but this first great westward moving wave was predominantly of native stock.

The general impression of these sixty years, seen in retrospect, is of vast energies suddenly released, an explosion of humanity spreading across an empty continent. It was more than a mere movement of human beings into new lands. New states came into being, sharp conflicts developed, strange faiths appeared, cities were planted, industries germinated, and new political practices were introduced. Humanity on the march creates new ways of life, takes on fresh forms, and sets up strange institutions. In essence it was unplanned, unexpected at least as to size and significance, and largely undirected. The American people were turning their backs on the known and the stable and pushing into the unknown in search of something. Why did they go? What did they want? What did they do? What do they mean to us of today, who are, in some part, their successors and heirs?

The beginning of it was land beyond the Alleghanies to be had for the taking. The English kings had been lavish in some of their colonial grants, especially to Virginia, Massachusetts, New York, Connecticut, the Carolinas, and Georgia. The extent of the territory beyond the mountains was unknown. Probably the western ocean was near. Early Virginians hoped to find in the Potomac or the James the gateway to the western passage. Whether the Pacific was near or far it cost the king little to toss a few thousand square miles into the pot for his plantations to set boiling. Boundaries were vague and grants overlapped. In places around the Great Lakes, Massachusetts, Connecticut, and Virginia claimed the same land and, in the south, the Carolinas and Georgia were in conflict. Colonies lacking such domains were jealous and watchful of their more fortunate brothers.

Maryland felt herself particularly aggrieved, especially by the claims of her Virginia neighbors, and hesitated to approve the Articles of Confederation. In consequence the Continental Congress passed a resolution on October 10, 1780, expressing a willingness to accept "the unappropriated lands that may be ceded or relinquished to the United States." The resolution stipulated that the lands so ceded should be "settled and formed into distinct republican states, which shall become members of the Federal Union, and shall have the same rights of sovereignty, freedom, and independence as the other states." An amusing condition was added that the new states so formed "shall contain a suitable extent of territory, not less than one hundred nor more than one hundred and fifty miles square." New York and Connecticut promptly expressed their willingness to make the cessions suggested and Virginia followed suit in 1783. Georgia was slow to act and did not release her claims to the land lying between her western border and the Mississippi River until 1802.

By this simple process of agreement among equals the first problem of the new lands was solved, but this was only the beginning. There were many problems still to be faced. United action had been a fact of wartime, but a limited fact. The power of the Continental Congress scarcely went beyond the minimum that was necessary for the waging of a war, and had been sometimes short of that. The Union was an alliance of sovereign states, seeming sufficient for the purposes of the moment, but having no vitality or reality of its own. Nevertheless the wild lands had been "relinquished to the United States," vague and ephemeral as that entity might be. By this act a dignity and reality had been conferred upon the Union, giving it an existence and a power apart from and within the western area superior to that of any state, or even all of them combined, except as they acted through Congress. When the Congress guaranteed to the new states "the same rights of sovereignty, freedom, and independence as the other states" the existence of something national having authority of its own right had been recognized.

The new lands at least had potential value and the title was held by the United States. The instrument that opened the way for a realization of this value was the Land Ordinance of 1785, passed by the Continental Congress. If the Congress had done nothing more than this it would have justified its existence by this act. The ordinance was brief but pregnant. Its chief purpose was to provide for a simple comprehensive survey, in which the basic units were prescribed.

Townships six miles square were to be laid out, each township containing thirty-six sections, and the system of numbering the sections was fixed. The effect of this plan was to facilitate the identification and location of holdings, thus preventing the confusion of boundaries and overlapping of claims characteristic of the informal local surveys of the older regions and simplifying titles and transfers. This was the act that fixed the section as the basic unit of land titles from the Alleghanies to the Pacific.

Four sections out of every township were to be reserved for future sale by the United States, a provision that was of little meaning after settlement began in earnest, and one section for the maintenance of public schools within the said township. Thus was the cornerstone laid for free, tax-supported education in the new states. A third reservation that was allowed to lapse through failure to use was of a third part of the gold, silver, lead, and copper mines. Uncle Sam was at least a considerable landowner and was preparing to put his lands on the market.

Two years later Congress enacted the Northwest Ordinance which made wise provision for the political organization of the territory of the United States northwest of the Ohio River. By this time, July 13, 1787, the Constitutional Convention was grinding its slow way through a rather sweeping "revision" of the Articles of Confederation. Soon another Congress would take the place of the shadowy body that still survived, but the dying government erected here another great monument to itself. By the Northwest Ordinance our system of territorial government was set up, and this, too, has lasted throughout our history. The chief power was vested in Congress, but provision was made for limited autonomy. More important was the arrangement by which the area should be divided into states, not less than three or more than five, as soon as the area in question had reached a population level of sixty thousand.

The framers of the Constitution took little account of the possibility of new states appearing in the near future, except to belittle their probable importance, but the new century was only three years old when Ohio came in. The Northwest Ordinance had a twofold importance; it provided for a form of temporary local government, and it pointed the way to statehood. It was clear at least that the relation of the newer regions to the old was to be that of equals and not of colonies to empire.

It was obvious from the beginning that the only way the government could realize anything on its huge real estate project was through the sale of the land. George Washington had been a shrewd operator in land from the time of his service as a county surveyor at the ripe age of eighteen. He was active, along with Governor Dinwiddie, in the Ohio Company, and his first trip into the Indian country that lay northwest of Virginia was that of a landlooker. He was not the only speculator in the field. Benjamin Franklin bought shares in a company of which his son William was a member, and Robert Morris, the treasurer of the Revolutionary government, was so heavily involved that he finally saw the inside of a debtors' prison. Land companies were common and their shares were popular, if shadowy, investments. Several of the framers of the Constitution held them, to their later regret.

The government hoped that much of the land could be disposed of in large lots to groups of settlers as well as through companies. It was expected that such groups would be able to buy in township lots—thirty-six sections. A similar plan had been followed in the case of villages in Massachusetts. The smallest unit to be sold was a full section, 640 acres, at a price of a dollar an acre, less to the larger buyers. The year of the Constitutional Convention the Ohio Company bought 2,500,000 acres north of the Ohio at a price of less than nine cents an acre.

But all this brought little lift in the pace at which settlers moved in on the land. The country was still suffering from the disorganization caused by the war and the depression which followed it. The currency was disordered and inflated and few people were interested in taking on a township or even a section of raw western land so far in advance of the simplest law and order. The Revolution had broken the power of the Iroquois who for so long had guarded the way west that ran through New York to the Lakes, but the Shawnees still held the Ohio Country.

The settlers who did drift across the Alleghanies by Pittsburgh or those who followed Boone's path through Cumberland Gap into Kentucky or down into eastern Tennessee were not interested in the enticing offers of speculators. Most of them lacked even the small amount of capital needed to pay at the cut rates offered. They were the displaced, dispossessed sons of fathers who were themselves pioneers, and they knew little of down payments and land titles. Born in a raw, new land, they took land where they could find it, built cabins, and settled down to cutting away the dense forests so that they might at least plant corn among the stumps. This was the advance guard of the squatters who were to be among those present until the Homestead Act gave form and legality to squatting for the payment of a fee of ten dollars after five years of continuous occupancy and improvement.

Scattering and few in numbers compared with the mass movement that was to set in after the War of 1812, the squatters led the way and in considerable measure were indicative of the attitudes and conditions of the people who made up the westward drift. Compared with them the Puritans who came into Massachusetts after 1630 were people of substance. Generally speaking, the moderately well to do are slow to abandon the known and secure for the unknown and the hazardous. Besides, the Shawnees were still there until Harrison broke their resistance at Tippecanoe in 1811. Three years later Jackson scattered the Creeks who had blocked the southern way from Georgia through Alabama to the Mississippi, and the land law of 1820 authorized the sale in smaller units as low as eighty acres at a minimum price of $1.25 an acre. By this time the tide was beginning to run in earnest.

By 1840 there were 6,330,000 people west of the Alleghanies, thirty-seven per cent of the population. In 1850 the center of population was twenty-three miles southeast of Parkersburg, West Virginia, nearly three hundred miles west of where it had rested in 1790. Now the West had arrived. Before 1820 six new states had been added to the Union east of the Mississippi. The purchase of Louisiana had added an area of unknown but overwhelming extent west of the Mississippi, and the Mexican War coupled with the Oregon treaty and the settlement of the northwest boundary dispute with England set our continental pattern in its present dimensions.

This rapid movement of people after 1815—twenty thousand new farms north of the Ohio every year from 1830 to 1850—is bewildering and intoxicating to the chronicler viewing it in restrospect. For the first hundred years of our history we had crawled back from tidewater at the caterpillar rate of a mile a year. Suddenly the caterpillar developed race-horse speed. It is dangerously easy to become sweeping and dithyrambic in contemplating it. Surely this was a new America, at least a radical change in the form and purpose of the American experiment.

Where had these people come from and what did they seek? Part of the answer is simple. They were hungry for land and the new chance that land could give them. The combination of people and land is a powerful social force. Most of them were poor, without capital or credit. Their worldly goods were easily packed in a Conestoga wagon. They were crude in their ways and their speech. Most of them were young, inured to hard work and simple living. They knew little of European culture or its colonial equivalent, and most of them cared less. They had turned their backs on the Old World and acknowledged no debt to it. There was no room for Chippendale furniture in a wagon or a flatboat. Their educational standards were simple but definite. Illiteracy was a badge of poverty and inferiority; hence they would have schools for their children. Being poor, they were in debt, and the lack of specie in that raw land turned their minds to the need for currency expansion. The irritating debtor-creditor conflict between West and East grew with the growth of the West, and is still a political fact of considerable magnitude.

Whatever the number of their shortcomings, and in the eyes of the older East they were many, these extremely plain people faced tasks of the first importance, not only to clear land and build homes, but to create communities and commonwealths. The meaning of the Northwest Ordinance was clear. The territories were to blossom into states as soon as the people in the territory were ready to bring it about. Frederick Jackson Turner stated the case in a phrase that has become classic: "American democracy was born on the frontier. It was not part of the freight of the *Susan Constant* or the *Goodspeed.*" The second part of this eloquent statement is not quite true. The possibility of democratic procedure is always present wherever people of whatever sort must fend for themselves, even in Virginia in the days of King James I. The fact is put more clearly in a statement in one of the early petitions for statehood: "A fool can sometimes put on his clothes better than a wise man can do it for him." There was no colonial office, no lords of trade and plantations, no army to establish and maintain law and order. They must do it for themselves.

What stock of political ideas had they? It would be a mistake to underestimate their political understanding although many of them in the early waves had been unable to qualify for the votes in the older communities where property qualifications applied. Questions of rights, of representation, of status, of citizenship were much in the air during the Revolution and the early days of the Republic. It was men like these who had fought the battles and been paid with depreciated paper or land warrants. Some of them had read Thomas Paine's *Common Sense* and could understand his plain speech on the duty of government to serve the greatest good of the greatest number. Every Fourth of July the Declaration of Independence was read and the belief that governments derive their just powers from the consent of the governed meant just that to them. Pennsylvanians were aware of the struggle between radicals and conservatives over the injustices suffered by the backwoods settlers. The ideas of Thomas Jefferson had meaning to such men as these.

The conditions under which they lived had produced a strong sense of equality. The land belonged to all, and each man was entitled to a chance as good as that of any other man. Since they recognized no superior governing class, this was easily translated into political equality. In point of fact it was impossible to avoid such translation, and manhood suffrage was the rule from the beginning. Distinctions existed of course. The most marked was the amount of land held by an individual. Land represented present debt, but it also held the promise of future wealth. A less lovely plant which grew well in the forest clearings was the desire for political office. That was the other form of distinction. Andrew Jackson's principle of rotation in office found receptive ears.

The qualities that the frontier demanded of the men who got on were sometimes irritating to Old World visitors, Mrs. Trollope, in particular. Frontier conditions required men to be buoyant, self-confident, self-assertive, if they were to survive, and these necessary virtues easily grew into unpleasant forms which seemed graceless and mannerless to people bred in older and more leisurely ways. Sharp practices developed in land deals and the man who could not protect his own hand was bound to lose. The sense of individualism was strong and there was little sense of obligation to older thought and tradition.

It was a place and a time of violence and crudeness in religion as in other things. The revival and the camp meeting were characteristic forms. Ritual of service, an educated clergyman in the pulpit, prayer book and hymnal were meaningless and repellent to the frontier. Peter Cartwright, all his life a circuit rider and revivalist, tells the story as well as it can be told. The historic instance is of the great camp meeting in Bourbon County, Kentucky, where twenty-five or thirty thousand people listened to continuous preaching through the full round of the clock from one or another of seventeen pulpits occupied by relays of exhorters. Hysterical manifestations of repentance and conversion were many, as were shouting, falling in convulsions, punctuating the exhortations with shouts and hallelujahs.

What kind of "republican" governments did these new states set up? At the time of the Constitutional Convention the reputation of the states was not too good among the conservatives who largely controlled that body. The acts of some of the state legislatures, notably those with a considerable backwoods representation as in Pennsylvania, had not endeared them to the solid middle class sentiment of the men from Boston, Philadelphia, New York, and the other seaport towns where overseas trade was the prime interest. "Democratic licentiousness" was a favorite phrase of characterization of these new democrats. Now the newcomers beyond the mountains, fresh out of covered wagons and flatboats, younger sons of small farmers crowded out of tight New England, New Jersey, Virginia, and the rest, artisans, common laborers, run of the mine human beings, lacking capital, credit, and political experience, were building states. If democratic licentiousness was more than a phrase, here was the chance to learn.

Now a curious fact appeared. The new state constitutions in general followed the pattern laid down by the older states. Ohio was no more radical than Massachusetts had been. Her constitution set up the same guarantees of civil rights and showed the same solicitude for the rights of property. The form of the government was identical in all important respects, the same clear separation of powers, the same bicameral legislatures, the same limitations of the power of government over the individual. Two new things were manifest, manhood suffrage and the responsibility of the state for the maintenance of free schools. Roger Sherman, the wise man from Connecticut, who had begun life as a cobbler, had foreseen it when he declared in the Constitutional Convention that the settlers in the new lands would be largely the sons and grandsons of the people making up the bulk of the existing population and would build the new after the manner of the old.

The Westerners might be crude and sometimes turbulent, wearing rough clothes, speaking in loud voices, boastful, swaggering, with offensive manners, as Mrs. Trollope said they were, but they were not political radicals except in the minds of conservative Easterners who saw political power slipping out of their hands. True they were separatists in many of their tendencies. Trade developed early down river to New Orleans and overseas bypassing the Eastern ports. Flatboats, keelboats, rafts carried their wheat, pork, lumber, barrel staves, and hoop poles down river rather than across the mountains. Slow as the trip was upriver on the return trip to Marietta, Pittsburgh, Wheeling, Louisville, and St. Louis, the cost was low and the traffic paid well. Both Marietta and Pittsburgh built ocean-going sailing ships that cleared from obscure river towns for the West Indies and the Mediterranean. Their gaze was westward and down river and their minds looked the same way. Burr may or may not have dreamed of an empire in the Mississippi Valley; many

Westerners were ripe for such a step. Even Jackson was something less than an ardent nationalist, but not after 1824. From then on his gaze was fixed increasingly on Washington and with his election in 1828 the risk of political cleavage between East and West dwindled. Instead of withdrawing from the Union, the West moved in and took over. With the election of Lincoln, a son of the pioneer days who knew little of the East came into the White House and his administration was made up largely of fellow Westerners.

Important as the westward movement was in our national growth and change, it was not the only force operating in this dynamic period. While the West grew in numbers and in wealth, the East shifted away from shipbuilding and overseas trade and turned to industry. The Napoleonic wars had cut the supply of overseas goods, hence ironworks and textile mills multiplied rapidly. New England with many streams for water power became a region of mills before her leaders knew what was happening. Embargo, nonintercourse, and war had closed American ports to European cotton goods and in eight years the total number of spindles in the mills of the United States had increased from eight thousand to more than half a million, most of them in New England. With the ending of the Napoleonic wars European textiles came back on the market and prices dropped with unhappy results for New England. The tariff of 1816 was aimed largely at the protection of the infant cotton mills of the country which were standing on the brink of bankruptcy. In spite of New England's urgent need, her leaders were unable to forget their Federalist traditions and their hatred of Jefferson and all his works and his successors. They opposed the tariff violently while the South, wiser in the political needs of the hour, supported it.

The process of industrialization of the Central Atlantic and northeastern states ran concurrently with the growth of the agrarian West and South and both presented new problems with marked political implications. The West, when it was not separatist, was vaguely nationalist. Clay's American system with its emphasis on internal improvements and assertion of purely American interests appealed to the restless West, jealous of the more static and prosperous East. The flamboyant hopes of Canadian conquest had fanned this flame, while New England at the Hartford Convention came dangerously close to declaring for secession from the Union. Wiser counsels at the eleventh hour overcame the arguments of Pickering, but enough of the old Federalist spirit remained in 1846 to keep New England lukewarm to the Mexican War. Easterners, including many from New England, swelled the human tide that began to run west after 1815, but the hopes and sympathies of New England did not go with them. It was Virginia rather than Massachusetts that gave the West such agrarian political philosophy as it possessed.

Shortsighted as she was in 1816, New England soon learned that her old dream of ships and overseas trade was a fading one. England was showing the way in iron and textiles and the minds of Eastern Americans turned in the same direction, and the effects were soon apparent. Individual fortunes increased in size and multiplied in numbers, largely in new hands. Howells in *The Rise of Silas Lapham* has pictured the impact of this new wealth in the older centers and the same story might have been written any time from 1820 on. These newcomers had no knowledge of the Federalist doctrine expounded by John Adams and acknowledged no obligation to it. Proud of the things that they had built and sure of their power, they were concerned only to build bigger and stronger things.

There were other effects of industrialization that offered less cause for pride. Mill towns were unlovely blots on the beautiful New England countryside, and the workers were in danger of becoming a race apart. In the small shops of colonial days master and men worked side by side, hardly distinguishable in dress, in way of life, and in ideas. Now it was impossible to confuse them. Power and machines had furnished the means for building great institutions, but they had also set a wall within the structure that was not easily penetrated. Masters thought as masters and workers more and more as workers.

This change began to show itself in the form of tentative and rudimentary labor organizations. These had existed in a few skilled trades before the end of the eighteenth century, Philadelphia shoemakers in 1792 and New York printers in 1794. Hatmakers soon followed suit and carpenters, stonemasons, painters, and bricklayers not long after. These were local, poorly financed, and had little power, but they early learned the techniques of the strike, the closed shop, and the boycott. In a few cities, notably Philadelphia, local unions of the different trades attempted the formation of local trades councils with representation of all the unions, but little was accomplished. The courts were unfavorable to this new development and applied the old English common law doctrine that the existence of an organization which might conspire was prima-facie proof of such an intent and hence unlawful. There are two cases which bear on this point. In 1835 in the case of *The People* v. *Fisher,* the New York State Supreme Court held to the common law doctrine:

> Without any improper and officious interference of the subject, the price of labor or the wages of mechanics will be regulated by the demand for the manufactured article, and the value of that which is paid for it; but the right does not exist either to enhance the price of the article, or the wages of the mechanic, by any forced and artificial means.

Seven years later another labor union case came before the Supreme Court of Massachusetts in *Commonwealth* v.

Hunt. In his decision Chief Justice Shaw denied the universal validity of the assumption that the existence of an organization that might conspire was prima-facie proof of intent, in the absence of specific evidence. He declared also that such an organization might be not only legal but desirable:

> We think, therefore, that associations may be entered into, the object of which is to adopt measures that may have a tendency to impoverish another, that is, to diminish his gains and profits, and yet so far from being criminal and unlawful, the object may be highly meritorious and public spirited.

Here was a clear assertion of a social and public stake in labor controversies, not admitted in previous decisions of record. It is to be noted that these cases ended with the supreme courts of the states. Labor questions, if they reached the courts at all, which they seldom did, were the exclusive concern of states, and so remained until the next century opened.

What was the political significance of this infant labor movement? On the surface little. The demands were mostly for shorter hours and higher wages, plus the closed shop here and there. But it is not easy to separate the political from the purely economic. The fact of associated action by a group with a sense of common interest and desire was a portent in itself. To call it a rudimentary form of the class struggle that Marx was soon to develop into a slogan for far-reaching revolution would have been extreme and mostly untrue. As long as raw land waited in the West the mill hand or the artisan was hardly likely to feel that he was unescapably committed to his calling, and that is the first essential in the establishment of class consciousness and a sense of community of grievance. Few will die in the last ditch for a special cause when the ditch can so easily be avoided.

But as unions began to seek the first simple goals they found themselves moving into a field where political action was necessary. In 1827 the Mechanics' Union of Trade Associations in Philadelphia sponsored an attempt to organize a workingmen's party to campaign for changes in laws and in procedure that went a long way beyond wages and hours. The eight objectives as stated by the convention were: 1) Ten-hour day; 2) Restriction and ultimate elimination of child labor; 3) Abolition of prison labor in competitive products; 4) Free and equal public education; 5) Abolition of imprisonment for debt; 6) Exemption of wages and tools from seizure for debt; 7) Right of mechanics to file liens covering overdue wages; 8) Abolition of sweatshops. The campaign lasted five years and three of the goals were reached, the ten-hour day, abolition of prison for debt, and free public schools. The principle involved in these demands was that of status. These were special citizens seeking the removal of handicaps that kept from them the enjoyment of the full and equal rights of citizenship.

This set of demands was symptomatic of a ferment of humanitarianism and millennialism that marked the period from 1830 to 1850. The struggles of labor, spasmodic and fragmentary as they were, aroused the sympathy and support of humanitarian agitators who saw in the movement something more than a game of grab and bluff between master and worker. Horace Mann worked side by side with them in the demand for free public schools, using the Massachusetts Board of Education as his laboratory and forum. In New York Governor DeWitt Clinton brought his great influence to bear in the same direction. William Cullen Bryant, through the editorial pages of the New York *Evening Post,* fought what he regarded as unjust decisions in labor cases with all the fire of his Puritanical liberalism. When in 1836 a New York judge laid heavy fines on a group of journeyman tailors for "a conspiracy injurious to trade and commerce," Bryant lashed out at the court:

> Can anything be imagined more abhorrent to every sentiment of generosity and justice, than the law which arms the rich with the legal right to fix, by assize, the wages of the poor? If this is not slavery, we have forgotten its definition. Strike the right of associating for the sale of labor from the privileges of a freeman, and you may as well bind him to a master, or ascribe him to the soil.[1]

The Puritan in Bryant kept him from going farther in his espousal of labor, but his friends William Leggett and Parke Godwin acknowledged no such restraint. Leggett especially was charged with setting class against class and seeking to destroy orderly government. When Chief Justice Marshall died Leggett struck back at his critics, also on the editorial page of the New York *Evening Post,* by charging Marshall with seeking to destroy "the great principle of human liberty." Both Bryant and Emerson distrusted and disliked the growing power of industry as tearing down the older, simpler ideals and using government for the furtherance of their own selfish ends, but Emerson with his continuing emphasis on the self-reliance of the individual was a doubtful partisan. Cooper, dreaming of the old manorial day of the great landowner whose house was a nursery of gracious living and the high arts of elegant leisure, was bitter against the sordid ways and standards of the *nouveau riche* that industry was spawning, but he, too, had little to say for labor. Horace Greeley, the radical from backwoods Vermont, with the ready sympathy and the disordered thinking, found a formula for all social ills in his slogan, "Go west, young man, go west, and grow up with the country." In such a confusion of counsel no clear leadership appeared

---

[1] Allan Nevins, New York *Evening Post,* p. 165. Quoted by Parrington, *Main Currents of American Thought,* II, 245.

for labor and the attempt at a national party with a definite social program faded out early in the thirties. The economic turmoil of the time continued to be a ruthless struggle for wealth and power, with the political powers enlisted on the side of what appeared to be the established order. Elements of the Northern Democrats, "Locofocos," and Van Buren's "Barnburners," held some who were friendly to labor chiefly because they feared the hard power of wealth, but labor platforms and candidates were far in the future.

Much of the humanitarian activity of the time ran into narrow utopian channels and aims. Belief in the special destiny of the United States was strong, but the aims by which to achieve it were vague and obscure. George Ripley and his little band of faithful followers sought to create a center of influence of Fourieristic communism at Brook Farm, but the plain living grew irksome and the high thinking produced nothing but talk as Emerson foresaw. Robert Owen thought he had found the way through cooperation at New Lanark, but his American version at New Harmony failed to take root in the harsh soil of frontier Indiana. The Shakers found a formula for righteousness and social peace through celibacy and the holy dance, but drew more derision than applause. Millerites saw the coming of the Kingdom close at hand, but their pathetic waiting through chilly nights on windy hilltops brought them nothing but colds and rheumatism. Spiritualism was popular for a time, as it always is in periods of uncertainty and fear. Temperance societies sprang up and flourished, although brewers and distillers still slept soundly o'nights. In spite of the debacle at New Harmony, Robert Dale Owen, the son, had courage to call a world convention at Boston in 1845 "to Emancipate the Human Race from Ignorance, Poverty, Division, Sin, and Misery."

It was a time of vague hoping and ineffectual dreaming of which Emerson wrote in *New England Reformers:*

What a fertility of projects for the salvation of the world! One apostle thought all men should go to farming, and another that no man should buy or sell, that the use of money was the cardinal evil; another that the mischief was in our diet, that we ate and drank damnation.

Out of this confusion of tongues and welter of panaceas two movements destined to have large national significance appeared. One was the Woman's Rights Convention at Seneca Falls, N.Y., in 1848. This was the first meeting of its kind held anywhere in the world and out of it came the famous "Seneca Falls Declaration of Sentiments and Resolutions." In form and phrasing it follows close on the Declaration of Independence, but the tyrant in question is King Man and not King George. The catalogue of grievances opens with these significant items:

> He has never permitted her to exercise her inalienable right to the elective franchise.
>
> He has compelled her to submit to laws, in the formation of which she had no voice.
>
> He has withheld from her rights which are given to the most ignorant and degraded men—both natives and foreigners.
>
> Having deprived her of this first right of a citizen, the elective franchise, thereby leaving her without representation in the halls of legislation, he has oppressed her on all sides.
>
> He has made her, if married, in the eye of the law, civilly dead.
>
> He has taken from her all right of property, even to the wages she earns.

It was over seventy years before this declaration bore fruit in the form of the Nineteenth Amendment to the Constitution, but here was the beginning.

The other weird mixture of religion and utopian social planning which succeeded was the Mormon Church. Fourierism and Cooperation had more respectable ancestry and origin than had this product of religious hysteria among obscure and ignorant backwoods people near Palmyra, N.Y., but under the able leadership of Brigham Young, a statesman if we have had one, Mormonism built a commonwealth and nurtured an able and public spirited people. It has been a common practice to deprecate or ignore Mormonism as something alien and a little shameful, which it assuredly is not. Minus polygamy, an exotic and unworkable institution, few of our political and social experiments have been more characteristically American and successful than this.

Behind all these shifts and probings, these wild aberrancies and experiments, these attempts to make fantastic and pathetic dreams come true, was a common force the component elements of which were people and land. Radek, the Russian anthropologist long since purged, declared that the great waves of civilization are the result of the struggles of human beings for a place to stand. This part of our history is an illustration of this epigram. The framers of the Constitution had distrusted people in the mass. In a moment of angry frankness Hamilton burst out, "The people, sir, is a great beast!" The Constitution sought to build a hedge to keep them from their full power. The Electoral College was a device to this end as was the election of senators by state legislatures. Reluctant as they were to concede the right of manhood suffrage, the delegates were unable to agree on conditions governing the vote and left the control in the hands of the states. The new states were quick to establish the rule of one man one vote and the older states unwillingly fell in line.

Democracy was a word attaint in Philadelphia and even Jefferson avoided its use. The French Revolution had intensified the conservative fear of popular rule and the excesses of the Jacobins were proof of the untrustworthiness of the people. It was difficult to refute the logic of the Federalist position and none of the leaders attempted it. It was the irresistible logic of circumstance that upset the arguments of Hamilton and Adams. As population grew and spread into new lands, the American democracy made manifest its tangible and powerful presence.

There was an ironic humor in the formation and growth of political parties that was one of the important signs of the times. The founders hoped that their new government would be spared the factionalism and discord that would inevitably attend the organization of parties. In his first inaugural address, Jefferson referred to the differences of opinion that had arisen during Adams' administration and announced that the contest having been decided, "all will, of course, arrange themselves under the will of the law, and unite in common efforts for the common good. . . . We have called by different names brethren of the same principle. We are all Republicans, we are all Federalists."

It was not quite that simple, as Jefferson well knew. The differences between himself and Adams ran deeper than mere opinion of the moment. The Sedition Law had revealed a dangerous power of government which ran directly counter to the principles held by Jefferson and the Kentucky and Virginia Resolves had raised a question that had to do with the essential nature of the new government. Jefferson's attitude toward these measures was far more realistic than the unctuous phrases of his inaugural speech. The answer was sixty years in the future but the question had been asked. The Constitutional Convention had hedged and compromised on this point and what they had produced was contradiction and confusion. What was the form of the government and where did the final power rest, in the states, in the national government, or somewhere else? Madison, who had been the busiest and most influential in the Convention, with a wide knowledge of political theory and practice, gave a definition that failed to define:

> The proposed Constitution . . . is, in strictness, neither a national nor a federal Constitution, but a composition of both. In its foundation it is federal, not national; in the sources from which the ordinary powers of the government are drawn, it is partly federal and partly national; in the operation of these powers, it is national, not federal; in the extent of them, again, it is federal, not national; and finally in the authoritative mode of introducing amendments, it is neither wholly federal nor wholly national.

What was it then? Nothing easily understood. The American experiment again, cut and fit, contriving a government that might somehow cover a body that already existed but was difficult to measure or describe. Meanwhile government went on within the existing framework, an experiment within an experiment. Seen in perspective the process seems to have begun in the selection of the President. The Constitution assumed that the electors meeting in their respective states would somehow divine the better candidate and, if they failed to read the signs in sufficient agreement, then the House of Representatives would solve the riddle. Congress, however, was not long content to leave the choice in that somewhat mystical realm, and voluntary caucuses appeared, groups of members who selected a candidate and made his identity known. State legislatures caught the idea and joined in with their selections.

These caucuses were far from being political parties. Generally they were nothing more than groups of individuals with special interests to advance, axes to grind. By virtue of their composition and purpose they lacked continuity, power, and responsibility. While congressional caucuses predominated, King Caucus presented a façade of nationalism, but there was little substance behind that imposing front with which to meet the regionalism of the state legislatures when the latter entered the lists, as they soon did.

It is the easy, postprandial attitude to name Thomas Jefferson as the founder of the Democratic party, but not many after-dinner speakers have time or inclination to be historians. Jefferson destroyed the Federalists largely by stealing their ideas and changing the words. Perhaps Hamilton would have ventured to stretch executive authority as far as did Jefferson in the Louisiana Purchase, and the Lewis and Clark Expedition which he sponsored was a long way beyond the imaginative powers of New York and New England. His embargoes were at bottom pure executive fiat as in a negative sense was his refusal to enforce the Sedition Law. The liquidation of the Federalists was made easier by the latter's inability to understand the potentiality of the new forces of land and people that were beginning to be felt. The political visibility of New England did not extend beyond the Hudson River and that of New York was scarcely longer. To both regions the new states spelled only weakness and disruption. In consequence the frontier wrote off the Federalists and turned increasingly to Jefferson whose agrarian faith they shared. This shift unquestionably cleared the ground for the Democratic party of Jackson's time, but it is doubtful if even Jefferson saw it coming.

The election of Jefferson in 1800 ushered in a regime which endured for twenty-four years—Jefferson, Madison, Monroe. The sequence of Presidents was almost dynastic in its regularity, in each case the Secretary of State playing the role of crown prince and hereditary successor. After his retirement in 1809, the founder became in large part the elder statesman for his successors. By no means all of his advice was followed, but in general the political philosophy of the time was of his making.

New England, once the nursery of revolution, sulked in political obscurity and found what satisfaction she could in pointless criticism and futile opposition. The attempt of Massachusetts and Connecticut extremists, led by Timothy Pickering and his friends of the "Essex Junto," to use the

Hartford Convention in 1815 to press for a revision of the Constitution as an alternative to the secession of New England was defeated by Harrison Gray Otis and the moderates and nothing worse came out of it than a severe condemnation of the commercial policy of Madison and his conduct of the war and a suggestion for seven amendments to the Constitution. Of the latter the most significant were: 1) a proposal that only free persons should be counted in apportioning representatives and direct taxes among the states; 2) two-thirds majority in Congress for the admission of additional new states; 3) the barring of naturalized citizens from seats in either house of Congress or any civil office under the authority of the United States; 4) the President to be ineligible for re-election, "nor shall the President be elected from the same state two terms in succession." A year later saw the third Virginian in direct order take his seat in Washington.

The report from Hartford might well be called the last words of the Federalists. Individuals might continue to speak and write, but what they said had little backing and less force. Marshall was to carry their banner in the Supreme Court for another twenty years, but what might have been a party was ended. What followed? Something less than a party, scarcely a coalition even. Voters were increasing in numbers, especially in the newer states. Out of the total population of 9,600,000 shown in the census of 1820 more than 2,200,000 were west of the Alleghanies. All but some ninety thousand of these were in states admitted prior to 1820. Kentucky, Tennessee, and Ohio with a combined total population of more than a million and a half were no longer negligible factors in national elections and it was in those western states that the political yeast was working.

The election of Monroe in 1816 ushered in what was long called the Era of Good Feeling. Era of Uncertainty and Change would be a better term. In the Electoral College

Monroe was practically unopposed: in 1816, 183 votes against 34 for Rufus King and, in 1820, 231 against one for John Quincy Adams. The Jeffersonian momentum was still working and Monroe moved on easily from the State Department to the Presidency, as had Madison before him. It was the election of 1824 that showed the caucus system at its most ridiculous extreme. The congressional caucus chose William H. Crawford; Massachusetts with the rest of New England behind her put forward John Quincy Adams, Monroe's Secretary of State, son of John but no Federalist; Kentucky offered another obvious candidate, her favorite son through most of his life, Virginia-born Henry Clay, beloved of the warhawks of 1812.

It was Tennessee that really troubled the waters with the name of Andrew Jackson. Here was something new in presidential timber. Any one of the others could be chosen without greatly altering the pattern of precedent, but not Jackson. His victory at New Orleans had endeared him to the violent haters of the British of whom there were many, especially in the Mississippi Valley, but his appearance on the national political stage had been insignificant, a single term in the lower house in 1796–97, after which he announced his retirement from public life, followed by a short period of service in the Senate, succeeding William Blount. His resignation after appearing at a single session ended this part of his experience as a national legislator. His record in 1824 seemed made to order for purposes of attack—land speculator, race track gambler, duellist, frontier bravo, "half horse half alligator"—it seemed almost pathetically easy to dispose of him in a presidential contest. The votes of the electors showed him startlingly less vulnerable than his enemies had preferred to believe, ninety-nine votes to eighty-four for Adams, forty-one for Crawford, and thirty-seven for Clay. There was no majority and the contest moved on into the House of Representatives where Adams won by virtue of

Clay's withdrawal in favor of the man from Massachusetts. When Adams made Clay his Secretary of State the cry of corrupt bargain arose on the Jackson side. The truth of the charge is unimportant now. The obvious reason required no long search for proof. Clay hated and feared Jackson more than he disliked Adams. Adams had served well as Secretary of State for Monroe and was therefore in the logical line of succession, but the cry became stock ammunition for the Jacksonians.

It is difficult to analyze this election in terms of issues. In essence it was a contest between individuals representing widely separated regions with no clear boundaries between them. Adams was a son of the older East, but could hardly be described as a supporter of either the older commercial interests or the newer industrial hopes of that region. His experience had been heavily on the diplomatic side and in most ways he knew the Old World better than the new. Crawford, Virginia-born but now a citizen of Georgia, represented a state that was sharply different from the tidewater regions farther north. Georgia had clung longest to her western claims and the growing need for new lands for cotton turned her attention sharply to the west. Clay, the shrewdest politician of them all, held Kentucky in his hand. His American system with its emphasis on the home market and internal improvements gave his candidacy a stronger coloration of political principles than could be found in any of the other three. How then explain Jackson's near success at the polls? If he had political principles they were unknown, except in the vague generalizations of stump speeches to frontier audiences. He gave no sign of larger political understanding or interest. To state it bluntly, he was an ignoramus in the fields of political history and theory, subjects in which both Adams and Clay were well grounded. But he ran ahead of them all in the voting. Why?

There is one answer to this question which has at least

the virtue of seeming true and applicable. Jackson more than any of the others had the support and spoke the thoughts and prejudices of the new voters in the industrial East as well as in the agrarian West. Perhaps there was an issue behind personalities here. As a result of the defeat of Jackson and the bitterness engendered by the contest, his followers closed more closely around him and set themselves to organize for victory. When did the Democratic party appear with Jackson as its standard bearer? Dates are seldom clear in matters of this kind, but it was certain that his candidacy had raised new questions on which it was possible to take sides. Factions had appeared despite the hopes of the framers of the Constitution, and the era of good feeling had given place to a feeling of partisanship. The election of Jackson in 1828 was still a personal contest, but it had narrowed in range to Jackson versus Adams. The lines were forming and the way was being cleared for the first nominating convention of 1832, which was at least a christening party for a newcomer in American political experience.

At the risk of repetition in summarizing the political aspects of this period of rapid change and chaotic ferment on the surface, it is necessary to stress the basic underlying political fact, more people spread over much more land. By 1820 the western boundary of the United States was beyond the Mississippi. The framers of the Constitution and other wise men after had disputed the possibility of a single government ruling over this huge extent of territory. John Quincy Adams as late as 1820 foresaw at least two independent republics if not three and welcomed the possibility if it might take the North out from under the growing shadow of slavery. But the people were there and more were coming fast, new states were organized, and the flag still flew. Wise men are not always good prophets. Strange as it seemed to many critics, these unknown and unconsidered persons were governing themselves and on the whole doing it not badly.

While they lacked the strong sense of allegiance to the state as a primary alliance, which had marked the people of the older states, they could not be called ardent nationalists. Government to them was the town or the state. The United States as anything more than a vague and distant entity was hardly present in their minds. If Uncle Sam protected their titles to land, brought their infrequent mail, and policed the Indians it was as much as they asked. For the rest they could take care of themselves. Next to and along with land they valued personal freedom, but this too was not the result of a philosophical process, a visualization of an abstraction made a human reality. The eighteenth century's discovery of Man as Man with natural rights was unknown to them. Their freedom was the right to have and to use concrete things, definite powers. All of them wanted land and at a price they could pay. For many of them public land meant land without cost except their own labor to make it productive. In 1852 this feeling was put into words by the Free-Soil Democrats: "That all men have a natural right to a portion of the soil, and that, as the use of the soil is indispensable to life, the right of all men to the soil is as sacred as the right to life itself."

As a corollary to land ownership or without it they wanted the freedom to vote, to hold office, to have an equal share in the business of government. From the time voting began in the colonies the suffrage had been linked to property, in most cases a freehold of at least a hundred pounds value or its equivalent in some other form. The price of office was higher, in North Carolina five hundred acres and ten slaves; in South Carolina seats in the assembly called for a thousand acres. The result had been large disfranchisement, varying with the proportion of smaller freeholders. In New England where small farmers were numerous the number barred from voting was small. In New York and eastern Pennsylvania where artisans, small shopkeepers, and laborers were numerous perhaps nine tenths of the adult males were without political voice. It is difficult to estimate the number of voters who took part in the choice of delegates to the conventions which ratified the Constitution and hence may be said to have voted for or against it, but it was probably less than half the adult male citizens. Political power was in the hands of the property owners in young America as in Old England. Before the new states began to knock at the door there had been growing demand for a liberalizing of the franchise and the practice of the new states speeded up the pressure, but in such planter states as Virginia and North Carolina the lords of the land were slow to relinquish their advantage.

The result of gaining this freedom was not in all respects a thing of beauty as the era of Jackson was to show. The new voter was crude, noisy, and bumptious. He was quick to assert that he was as good as the next man, if not a little better, and the old formalisms and decorums were pushed aside. De Tocqueville, observing American democracy in action in the mid-thirties, saw this as a land of somewhat graceless equality rather than freedom, and he found too little appreciation of superior excellence, too little realization that mere political equality does not produce equality in all other respects. Much as he admired a great deal of what he saw, he saw also the danger that standards of taste and canons of behavior would sink to a common denominator of mediocrity. There is abundant evidence that this danger still exists, best selling novels and million dollar Hollywood successes for example.

Having slight philosophical base in the common mind our political life reflected the mass materialism that had spread to the Mississippi and beyond. There was little thought of unselfish public service in the minds of the new representatives whether they spoke for agrarian interests or industrial.

Both groups were greedy for power and were not slow to make their weight felt at both state and national capitals. Where agrarians held the upper hand, laws favorable to debtors began to appear in the statutes, and Hamilton's Report on Manufactures had made clear declaration of the duty of the government to serve the national interest by aiding and protecting industry. But good or bad King Demos was crowding the older horseman for a seat in the saddle.

Mention has been made of the spread of free, publicly supported education. Here was another concrete freedom that was sought and gained against conservative opposition. Literacy was a necessity for complete freedom and equality of opportunity. With education, freedom of religious belief and worship must be coupled. In the colonies church and state had stood side by side with varying success. In Massachusetts and Connecticut Puritanism was the state church and the political power of the ministers was great. Anglicanism was the rule in Virginia until Jefferson forced his Statute for Religious Freedom through the Assembly during the Revolution. The Great Awakening of 1740 and after had shaken the grip of orthodoxy, but it was in the newer regions of the West and South that revivalism had and used a clear field. The settlers liked their religion raw and they took it that way, but the Constitution had made government secular and the new citizens made no move to change it.

Colonial practice in the inheritance of land in general followed the English model of primogeniture, exceptions being Massachusetts, New Hampshire, Connecticut, Pennsylvania, and Maryland. This bastion of aristocracy was also broken by Jefferson, who met Randolph's plea for at least a larger share to the older son by inquiring for proof that that son could eat more, or wear more clothes, or had other personal need for a larger part. Without a rule of primogeniture de Tocqueville saw no reason for the anticipation of an aristocracy in America. Such names as Astor, Vanderbilt,

Whitney, Rockefeller, and others of less fame may suggest that a way has been found.

All summaries of summaries must come to an end. Perhaps it can be said as of 1824 that about that time the People had announced their arrival. Henceforward, for good or ill, the last word would be theirs. In 1828 came the Jacksonians to illustrate some of the meanings.

CHAPTER VII

Jackson in the White House
(A. B.)

THE ELECTION of 1828 was in itself a political change of the first order. The six Presidents who had preceded Jackson had been natives of two states, four from Virginia, two, father and son at that, from Massachusetts. So far the hopes of the framers that political control might rest in the older and more stable states had been realized, although the political complexion had altered considerably from Washington to the second Adams. Jefferson had broken the power of the old Federalists and had indicated lines of cleavage along which party fronts might form. But even Jefferson had been unable to accept the full measure of popular control. Democracy was still a dangerous word and the anonymous population mass regarded as too ignorant and violent to be trusted with a strong political voice. At the best they were a reserve from which recruits might be drawn by a process of educational selection.

With the election of Jackson the old seaboard monopoly was broken and a new kind of human being appeared in the White House. The men of the Mississippi Valley still looked westward, but they had ceased to dream of a separate government. Instead they turned back and took over the one that many of them thought they had left behind. Most of them were landowners, but they were not the rich and wellborn in whom Hamilton had pinned his hopes. All of them were voters with a considerable amount of political experience in the establishment and operation of state and local governments. In dress and manners they seemed all that the orthodox East had said they were, loud voiced, swaggering, boastful, assertive. Contemporary accounts of the presidential reception at the White House—men with muddy boots standing on velvet chairs, breaking china, crowding to see or perhaps to shake the hand of their candidate—may have been exaggerated, but the material for exaggeration was there. The People had arrived and they were determined that no one should overlook that pregnant fact.

What would they do now that they were there? For Jackson, their chosen leader, it must have been a doubtful triumph. His wife, brokenhearted by scandalous gossip, had died soon after her husband's election and he was a lonely, old man facing new problems and a stupendous task. Little was known of his political ideas, largely because he had none, summing up his purpose in a single harmless and unrevealing sentence: "The Federal Constitution must be obeyed, state rights preserved, our national debt must be paid, direct taxes and loans avoided, and the Federal Union preserved." His bitterest opponent could hardly have disagreed with any of the items in this obvious list. His first choice of a cabinet was not promising. The only member of known ability and political experience was Martin Van Buren as Secretary of State, the son of a tavern keeper at Kinderhook, New York, and a leader of upstate anti-Federalism, one of the shrewdest political leaders of his day. Jackson's choice of men for the cabinet and his control of them after they were chosen was never among his more distinguished achievements. As a result he relied more and more on the counsel of unofficial advisers, especially Amos Kendall and Francis P. Blair, both of them honest and pugnacious newspaper writers with a flair for politics, but little apparent desire for office. The policies and decisions influenced and often shaped by the kitchen cabinet counted for much more in the Jackson regime than did the opinions of the official advisers.

The practice of rotation in office, later to be known as the "spoils system," did not originate with Jackson, but he was the first to state it as a principle. Jefferson had dismissed a larger proportion of appointive officers than did Jackson, but it was the latter who sought to give it an odor of sanctity. The right to hold office, declared the new incumbent, was akin to the right to vote. Furthermore, most official duties were comparatively simple and within the ability of the average citizen. What he did not make so clear was that here was a means of rewarding humble followers and making the fruits of victory tangible and palatable. Whatever the justifications in Jackson's time, the practice rapidly became fixed and vicious.

It was not until the election of 1832 that the party process became visibly established in our political activities. That year the Democrats held the first national party convention, openly proclaiming themselves THE Democratic party. Caucuses were things of the past and party machines had taken the field. The process of indirect and extralegal amendment of the Constitution in the manner of electing the President had begun. The Electoral College might continue to exist, as it still does, and occasionally its action would run counter to the popular will, but now the voter felt himself to be choosing the President.

The appearance of the Democratic party under the leadership of Jackson posed a problem for the opponents. What were they and what should they call themselves? Through the first decade of our life as a government the powerful landowners allied with the mercantile and shipping interests of

New England and the Middle Atlantic states had held the reins. The Federalists had the advantages of position; they were led by men of political experience with a solid intellectual understanding of the problems. Hamilton had funded the debt, thus establishing our credit on a sound foundation, and his Bank of the United States provided a fiscal agency of undoubted ability and power. Thanks to Washington's great reputation for integrity and patriotism and to John Adams' courageous stubbornness we had at least postponed entanglement in the European war. But the Federalists had failed completely to understand that government is something more than an intellectual process, involving as it does the interests and the desires of the whole population. The voice of the people may or may not be the voice of God, but it is dangerous to ignore it. This highly important political fact the Federalists failed to note. Their hatred and fear of the French Revolution led them to confuse popular opposition and outcry with the excesses of Jacobinism and to listen to the resounding rhetoric of Burke on the subject about which he was least informed and most mistaken. Discredited and half-forgotten Thomas Paine could have taught them better.

It is not easy to trace a clear course of political change through the twenty-eight years after 1800. National Republican was the name given to the followers of Jefferson, the party that was not a party. The events and acts of that tumultuous time give us little help. The purchase of Louisiana, the embargo, the admission of new states, the increase of population, the beginnings of immigration, the shift from trade and shipping to industrial production, combined with Chief Justice Marshall's emphatic assertions of national supremacy, can be seen clearly as a dynamic process, but the political characteristics are hard to identify.

Now that democracy, labeled as such at least in name, had taken over, the opposition faced the task of finding clear issues and a name. The latter was provided from England. The proponents of Parliament during the struggle between King and Commons late in the eighteenth century had called themselves Whigs. So "Whigs" these Americans became. Imported though the word was, the English Whigs had contained undoubted friends of the colonists among their leaders, so it was also patriotic. As to issues the name helped them there as Jackson began to apply executive power, especially in his war with the Bank. Here was an American tyrant to fight, merely a substitution of Andrew for George.

Not all the questions that were beginning to press for answer permitted such easy solution. For example there was industry. The existence of this new interest had been recognized in the tariff of 1816. New England had fought it then, but by the thirties they had begun to see the light. What would the Whigs do about it? While they groped and fumbled for phrases and slogans, Henry Clay from Kentucky had stolen the ball with his American System. His arguments for the protection of industry and the development of the home market were acceptable to the friends of industry, but internal improvements were something else. Turnpikes and canals leading westward speeded up the westward drift that was draining off labor wanted for the growing factories.

Public lands offered another bewildering tangle. A proposal to limit the sale of lands in order to slow down the draining off of needed labor gave Webster a chance to pull out all the stops of his powerful voice in behalf of the national union, but how much of his famous reply to Hayne was relevant to the problem of a party in search of a principle? "When my eyes shall be turned to behold for the last time the sun in heaven, may I not see him shining on the broken and dishonored fragments of a once glorious Union..." was a godsend to generations of college declaimers and filled pages in patriotic textbooks, but did it mean that the Whigs were claiming the monopoly of Union sentiment! If so, the Democrats could make effective counterclaim with Jackson's decisive action against South Carolina nullification. The President's famous toast, "Our Federal Union! It must be preserved!" was as good as anything that Webster offered. New England now saw the merit of protection, but the oratorical possibilities of a new schedule on cotton goods were limited.

The Whigs were in a tight spot, too, in the case of the Bank of the United States. Webster fought for the recharter of the bank along with many others, but as an advocate rather than a statesman. He was both borrower and paid attorney, a relationship discouraging to careful analysis and sound argument. There is no need to inquire here into the merits of the case of Jackson versus Bank. The bank had handled its affairs wisely and well on the whole up to the opening of the struggle with the President but, as the war grew, Biddle, its head, unwisely let himself be drawn into a vicious course of threat and blackmail which damned his cause beyond all hope. The demand for the immediate redemption by the state banks of all their notes held by the Bank of the United States, the calling of all outstanding obligations, the reduction of discount rates were political boomerangs, calling open attention to the political power in the hands of the Bank. The final step taken by Jackson in ordering the withdrawal of government deposits from the bank did present a political issue of a new and highly important character. Here was executive discretion written very large. When one considers that to accomplish this it was necessary to dismiss two reluctant secretaries of the Treasury it becomes evident that the Constitution was being interpreted in very broad terms indeed, when it suited the presidential purpose.

What did the Whigs get out of it? Little in the way of basic political ammunition except sore heads and a desire for revenge. In the popular estimation they had lost probably more than they had gained. So far as their support of the bank was a party matter they shared in the opprobrium that the shifty and unscrupulous attitude of the bank during the closing months of the struggle had incurred. Two issues had come into the open, the relation of the national government to banking policy and procedure and the nature of the speculating medium. Banks had been closely associated with the speculative boom in public lands and when Jackson issued his Specie Circular in 1836 prohibiting the acceptance of paper money for the purchase of public lands the whirlwind broke loose. Van Buren was to reap the bitter harvest of the collapse that followed, but the currency issue had been injected into the political realm.

Certain facts began to be clear, all of them arising out of economic and political change, and the necessity of finding constitutional and legal warrant for dealing with unavoidable situations. Beginning with the case of *Marbury* v. *Madison,* Chief Justice Marshall had established the supremacy of the Court as the final judge of constitutionality, but considerable latitude for individual cases and actions remained within the general enumerations of the supreme law of the land. What, for example, was the exact meaning and limitation of the power of Congress "To coin money, regulate the value thereof, and of foreign coin . . . ," or whence did Congress derive the power to charter a "Bank of the United States"? Hamilton had found it in the fact that every power of government is in its nature sovereign, "and includes, by force of the term a right to employ all the means requisite and fairly applicable to the attainment of the ends of such power." A week earlier Jefferson, then Secretary of State, had restricted the powers of Congress to those clearly delegated by the Constitution and had warned that a single step beyond that definite limit was "to take possession of a boundless field of power." Hamilton's view had prevailed and the bank had been chartered and rechartered twenty years later.

Now the question of a second recharter was coming up and Congress finally passed the bill only to have it vetoed by Jackson. In the bitter debate Jackson had declared the bill an unconstitutional and monopolistic invasion of state rights, but his final act in withdrawing the government deposits from the bank was an assertion of executive power for which it was difficult to find warrant in the fundamental document. A similar instance occurred in connection with the threatened removal by the state of Georgia of Cherokee Indians from lands within the state boundaries granted to the tribe by the United States. In the case of *Worcester* v. *Georgia,* Marshall found for the Indians and held that they occupied land over which the state of Georgia had no control. Decisions of the Supreme Court are not self-enforcing and the President refused to execute the decree. Here was executive dicrimination among laws to be enforced. The only counter action by Congress, if any were contemplated, was presumably impeachment, and this was not proposed.

And yet Jackson was not a complete states rights man, as his attitude toward Calhoun revealed. The only safe conclusion to be reached is that at this time it became clear that a strong President, secure in his popular support, can assert powers and declare policies that lie in the domain of the previously undetermined and unused. Justification of a sort can be found in Hamilton's argument that a government must have the power to use all powers that are necessary and applicable for the maintenance of itself as a government. Questions had been raised for which there was no ready answer; some of them are still unanswered. The business of governing was by no means so simple and clear as the framers of the Constitution had hoped that it would be.

By the end of Jackson's second term the stage seemed set for further tests of power in which the reserved rights of the states might play a part. Calhoun's new theory of the right of a state to pass on the constitutionality of an act of Congress if it seemed contrary to the interest of the state had been sidetracked by Clay's compromise tariff which allayed the fears of South Carolina, but the question had been raised. It was to be Van Buren's part to write the sequel to the disordered and disorderly drama of Jackson's administration, but it turned out to be an anticlimax of depression and bankruptcy. Real estate speculation had overextended credit beyond the safety point and the disruption of the bank was the occasion, though not the cause, of the collapse. Van Buren did nothing to slow down the widespread liquidation and his order that only specie should be accepted in payment for public lands increased the confusion.

The election of 1840 was a slapstick comedy, in which the issues were chiefly remarkable for their unimportance. Van Buren had the support of the more liberal elements of the new democracy, known in derision as Locofocos and Barnburners. The Whigs chose General William Henry Harrison as their candidate. His only known claim to fame was his breaking of the Shawnees at Tippecanoe, a name which figured prominently in the campaign. By this time the Whigs had decided that it would serve their purpose best to denounce Van Buren as a pampered aristocrat dining from gold plate and flavoring his food with French wines, while Harrison lived in a log cabin and drank hard cider. In the debates that preceded the election it was never learned what his political principles, if he had any, were, nor did anyone make a serious attempt to discover them. The Whigs set themselves to outdo the Democrats in their appeals to the "plain people." Their candidate's popular majority was only 146,315 in a total vote of slightly more than two and a half million, but he had 234 electoral votes for Van Buren's 60.

The confounding of confusion was not yet ended. The Whigs had chosen John Tyler of Virginia for Vice-President by way of presenting a "balanced" ticket and when Harrison died a month after inauguration they learned to their dismay what they might have known much earlier, that they had set a Virginia Democrat with a strong states rights inclination in the White House. This was of a piece with the political confusion of the time, but it helped to indicate the extent to which the popular will had become a political force to be reckoned with. The final liquidation of the Federalists had been accomplished, Andrew Jackson had become a symbol and a synonym as well as a party god, and nationalism had become a political fact, although the exact nature of the Federal Union was as yet undetermined.

What were the political ideas of this new American who had appeared on the new farms beyond the Alleghenies? By inclination and experience he was an extreme individualist with a narrow range of political vision. The government had sold his land to him and carried his infrequent mail. Roads and canals were important and if the national government could provide them he was appreciative, but most of the time he did the best he could with roads of his own contriving. He wanted more money, but was indifferent whether it was of national or state issue so long as it was acceptable.

His nationalism was largely emotional, growing out of his belief in his own competence and his vague sense of limitless area and boundless possibilities. This feeling of inexhaustible resources, coupled with the moving of the Indian menace farther west, contributed to his belief in his own security. Invasion was an obvious impossibility to him and the wars and the rivalries, as well as the ideas, of the Old World were dim and far away. He needed no process of philosophical rationalizing to arrive at the concepts of the inevitability of progress and the infinite perfectibility of Man. Material evidence for such conclusions was inherent in his own experience and in the endless environment around him. If he looked beyond his national boundaries it was with the serene belief that the example of America would soon be felt overseas to the great embarrassment of the effete aristocracies and corrupt monarchies of the Old World. It was this bumptious nationalism, even more than our bad manners, which annoyed the distinguished and thin-skinned Mr. Dickens.

The American of this period, as well as later, has been labeled lawless, and with reason. The human wave traveled faster than organized government with statutes and courts and orderly process, but it must not be forgotten that they made considerable law as they went. Desperadoes plied their trade in scattered instances, chiefly along the Ohio and Mississippi rivers, but in general Western America had an exaggerated idea of the infallibility and the effectiveness of "the Law." To "have the law" on someone was a common phrase for bringing a dispute to a final issue. It was a time when men believed firmly in a universal moral law of which man-made law was a reflection. The churches which dotted the new lands were severely plain, as were the services which were held in them, but even the newest county court was punctilious in its observance of the ritual of court procedure, opening often with the old Norman-French cry of "Oyez! Oyez! Oyez!" (usually pronounced "Oh, yes!")

Belief in a millennium was widespread, as has been noted, but the efforts to aid in its coming were private and voluntary. Political procedures were repetitions and adaptations of those which prevailed in the older East and utopian experiments were confined to particular groups and sects. The breaking up of the Mormon colony at Nauvoo, Illinois, was precipitated by rumors of a Mormon plot to take over the state government. In most regions the important center of political activity and power was the county seat. Feeling over its location ran high and county seat "wars" occasionally boiled over in violence.

It is not easy to reconcile this sense of localism with the consciousness of nationalism. Since the citizen asked little from the distant government in Washington why bother to call himself an "American"? The reasons are intangible but real. The Constitution and the government which it created were the final expressions of law, the ultimate center of power and the court of last resort. Individuals and localities might differ and bicker and protest, it was in Washington that the last word was spoken, the course of destiny determined and declared. If status and prestige were needed, what more could be said than "I am an American"? State boundaries were easily crossed, but after 1846 the western limits of the United States were a long way off, somewhere just short of the setting sun, and all the way the seeker was an American. "Civis Americanus sum!" It was a proud boast, and it had political meaning.

Now the rather vague and sweeping concept of a special American destiny had form and substance on a large scale. There were still doubts of the possibility of governing a territory of such continental extent. As late as 1832 John Quincy Adams recorded in his diary his gloomy prophecy on the future of the Union: "I now disbelieve its duration for twenty years, and doubt its continuance for five. It is falling into the sere and yellow leaf." Fourteen years later the settlement of the northwest boundary dispute with Great Britain brought Oregon and Washington into the Union and two years after that the Treaty of Guadalupe Hidalgo added Texas, New Mexico, Arizona, and California. The Constitution was only sixty years old but already it had been stretched over an area nearly four times the size it was in 1787. By 1850 six states had been organized west of the Mississippi. In the rest of the Western area, territorial governments existed or were soon to be established. Whatever the nature and competence of the national government it had taken on a sizable job. These new political tasks were not clearly visible or urgent in Jackson's time, but they were in the making and were already coloring the sense of nationhood.

Was Jackson a great President? It depends on standards and canons of judgment. Measured against the stature of any one of his predecessors, except perhaps Washington, he was a pigmy in knowledge of political history and thought. The realm of philosophical concepts through which Jefferson moved so easily did not exist for him. He lacked the hard logic of the elder Adams, the fine distinctions and definitions of Madison, and the hard, realistic diplomatic understanding of Adams the younger. But in 1828 he received nearly 56 per cent of the popular vote to Adams' 44 per cent, and in 1832 he repeated the feat against Clay. He had achieved popularity at least.

This fact is not without political significance, in spite of a widely prevalent belief that popularity is easily won by a series of clever tricks. Jackson had dramatized the presidency; he had made the government seem important to many. In 1828 more than three times as many votes were cast as in 1824. Some allowance is to be made for increase in population and for the four-cornered nature of the contest in 1824, but there still remains a wide margin that can be accounted for only as votes cast by men who were concerned over the outcome. Between 1828 and 1848 the population slightly less than doubled, while the popular vote increased threefold. The right to vote was not a negligible right. Jackson had at least given the presidency a personality and an importance beyond the point reached even by Jefferson.

By the time the new republic was sixty years old, still in its callow youth as the life cycle of government goes, the expectations of the framers had been disappointed in two important respects. The first great change was the one just noted, the sweeping extension of our boundaries. The possibility of such a happening had been held so lightly in the Constitutional Convention that there had been little discussion of the admission of new states. Williamson of North Carolina had brushed the subject aside as of little importance.

"They [the new states] would be too poor—would pay little into the common treasury—and would have a different interest from the old states." The final draft of the Constitution said only, "New states may be admitted by the Legislature into the Union." In 1850 California raised the grand total to thirty-one. This was anything but the union that the framers had contemplated and their Constitution must be made to cover them all.

The other new force to confound the expectations and plans of the constitution makers was the rapid growth in population, approximately a third each decade, with a corresponding increase in potential voters. In the presidential election of 1852 the total vote cast was 3,138,301, a far cry from government by the wellborn and well to do of Hamilton's hope. Not only was population growing, but changes were appearing in it. Industry had appeared and while the major interest was still agrarian Capital and Labor were making themselves heard. The political response was slow and difficult to analyze and classify. The old Federalist elements in the new Whigs were slow to turn away from their traditional preoccupation in land and commerce as the basic interests. The younger Whigs with Webster as their chief spokesman allied themselves with Capital and generally supported tariff increases for the protection of home industry.

Labor found little support in either of the larger parties, although the labor vote went largely to Jackson. In 1828 only New England, New Jersey, Delaware, and Maryland stood by Adams. The characterization of Jackson as the champion of the common man requires interpretation. By inclination and interest he stood by the property-owning class. He had been both debtor and creditor and during the depression of 1819 he had opposed relief proposals in Tennessee and pressed as hard as the most grinding of landlords for the payments due him. Nothing that he said or did reveals him as the leader of the proletariat, or shows any awareness of the existence of wage earner problems. His campaign against the bank was waged in behalf of the small against the large, the landowner against the rapacious mortgage holder, the state bank against the petted octopus in Philadelphia. Apparently the issue that he saw most clearly was the struggle of the small capitalist against the large, the man who hoped to be rich against the man who had already arrived. Even his support of state banks against the Bank of the United States was halfhearted, a choice of what he regarded as the lesser of two evils. In one of his few relatively amicable conferences with Biddle over the possibility of recharter he confessed to a dislike of all banks.

In way of life, association, activity, and interest Jackson was a landed proprietor, a self-made Southern gentleman, member of a class common at that time almost anywhere south of the Ohio. Such support as labor gave him can be explained more on the ground of a common fear of entrenched capital than because of any positive program that he offered. To those among the workers who hoped soon to become small scale enterprisers, capitalists on their own account, he spoke a language that was easily understood.

Meanwhile another issue was rising into view, one that had to do with the basic form and nature of the government, and was soon to overshadow all other political questions and change party alignments and purposes almost beyond recognition. That, of course, was Slavery, which requires a chapter to itself.

CHAPTER VIII

Cotton Threatens the Union
(A. B.)

There is a cryptic remark in John Fiske's *Old Virginia and Her Neighbors:* "It is curious now to look back and think how Marlborough and Eugene at Blenheim were unconsciously cutting out work for Grant and Sherman at Vicksburg." The sequence, however, is clear. Blenheim cleared the way for the Treaty of Utrecht which gave England the lion's share in the slave trade to the Americas. English shipowners pursued this advantage with vigor and the black population of the South grew rapidly. The South still put its faith and its money in tobacco, rice, and indigo. Cotton was grown, but the separation of the seed from the lint by hand labor was slow and expensive.

In 1792 a young Yankee tutor in South Carolina, Eli Whitney, produced a working model of the first mechanical cotton gin and transformed cotton from a long chance to a sure thing. The year before the first gin appeared, the South had exported 200,000 pounds, about five hundred bales; by 1803 the export figures had climbed to 40,000,000 pounds. In 1860, the last year for the old economy, the value of the cotton export was approximately $200,000,000, two-thirds of our total exports of that year.

Young Whitney's invention set King Cotton on the throne and gave new value to the slave. As cotton culture spread, talk of gradual emancipation and the preparation of the slave for freedom ceased in the South. Freedmen had been fairly common in Virginia. Slaves of special competence were given opportunities to earn money with which to purchase their freedom. Manumission might be accomplished by the owner's will, as in the case of Jefferson. Schools for negroes were permitted, at least to the extent of teaching them to read and write. These ameliorations disappeared after 1830.

At the same time prices rose on the auction block from $500 for a prime field hand in 1832 to $1,800 on the eve of the Civil War. Owners of wornout land in Virginia who were finding their slave property an expensive burden discovered a profitable and growing market for surplus labor in the Deep South. The effect of the improvement in the processing of cotton was not only a sharp rise in Southern wealth but also an increase in Southern confidence. Now they were producing a staple of worldwide use and limitless possibilities. Two years before the war began Senator Hammond of South Carolina declared that war against the South was unthinkable. Without cotton England would fall and the rest of the world with her. Cotton *was* king, and the king could do no wrong.

This swift growth of cotton from swaddling clothes to giant stature mirrors a process of economic change calculated to strain the political ingenuity of any government, even of one aware of the need and the danger of political action. The new government was unprepared to deal with such a problem and was forced into a course of postponement and compromise. The milestones along the way are illustrative of this process. The first marker was the admission of Missouri in 1820. New states had been coming in steadily, nine of them before that date. Vermont had been admitted almost simultaneously with the setting up of the government as a means of settling a quarrel between New York and New Hampshire and can hardly be described as a newcomer. The remaining eight were evenly divided between North and South, thus holding the balance even in the Senate. When Missouri knocked at the door, Congress found itself facing a knotty problem. The senatorial balance was preserved by transforming Maine, formerly a "province" of Massachusetts, into a state, but this did not answer the question of slavery. Did the admission of Missouri, a slave state, but not a cotton grower of importance, give warning of the spread of slavery in the states that should presently appear to the west and north? Henry Clay, with his genius for legislative compromise, found a by-pass by proposing the condition that no other slave states be admitted north of Latitude 36° 30′, the southern boundary of Missouri.

A crisis was averted, but slavery had made itself felt as a political issue. There was also a constitutional question involved. Could special conditions be attached to the admission of future states? The Constitution was silent on this point, but in the forming of previous states there had been a tacit assumption that admission was of an equal into the company of equals. And what about the prohibition of slavery in the Northwest Ordinance? Could this be maintained or extended? Evidently general provisions and prohibitions require careful tailoring if they are to fit special cases.

By this time the spread of cotton in the South had shifted the political dominance of the region from Virginia, where it had rested so long, to the black belt of the newer South where cotton was more profitable. The slave economy spread steadily westward to the Mississippi and across it, and Southern opinion moved with it. While industry grew rapidly in the North, Southern thinking was geared more and more to slavery. Two spokesmen of the older day saw the danger. John Quincy Adams wrote in his diary apropos of the Missouri Compromise: "I take it for granted that the present question is a mere preamble—a title-page to a great tragic volume." At the same time Jefferson wrote from Monticello: "This momentous question, like a fire-bell in the night, awakened and filled me with terror. I considered it at once as the knell of the Union."

The new South had an able spokesman in the person of John C. Calhoun. Here is one of the most powerful and tragic figures in our whole political history. Born in South Carolina of Scotch-Irish ancestry, a plantation owner by inheritance and by marriage, he spent forty-two of his sixty-eight years in public life. It is an impressive record. He was elected to the South Carolina legislature at the age of twenty-five and from that time until his death in 1850 he was out of office only one year—state legislature, three years; House of Representatives, six; Secretary of War, eight; Secretary of State, two; Vice-President, seven; Senator, sixteen.

The early part of Calhoun's career found him on the side of the nationalists in both theory and practice. He supported internal improvements as a national policy and as Secretary of War under Monroe was responsible for the reorganization of the army to put it on a genuinely national basis. This was the time when New England still put her faith in state militia and saw the germ of tyranny in a national military establishment. In 1817 he urged a liberal interpretation of the Constitution: "I am no advocate for refined arguments on the Constitution. This instrument was not intended as a thesis for the logician to exercise his ingenuity on. It ought to be construed with plain common sense."

It was the tariff of 1828, the "tariff of abominations," that aroused Calhoun's fears for his section and especially for his beloved South Carolina. Another of Clay's compromises enabled both sides to save a reasonable amount of face, but not until Calhoun had put forward his theory of the nature of the Union. His doctrine of a "concurrent majority" which underlay South Carolina's Nullification Ordinance has often been described as an instrument of secession. This it was not, at least in Calhoun's mind. To him it was the only way in which a powerful majority could be prevented from oppressing a minority located in a region having a special interest. Thus and thus only could the Union be preserved. The right to secede had been asserted fifteen years earlier and in New England of all places.

To him majority decision was a deception and a danger. A minority representing the special interests of a particular region, as in the case of the planters of South Carolina, must be protected against the tyranny of a national majority not greatly concerned about South Carolina cotton. The danger Calhoun saw undoubtedly existed, but the cure proposed in the ordinance was worse than the disease and if broadly applied would have destroyed the federal union as an effective government.

The Nullification Ordinance was not an act of secession except as a last resort, but it did mark the appearance of a new kind of issue and a new political alignment, this time an increasingly sectional one. Economic change had brought into sharp question the meaning of the Constitution and the nature and extent of the Union that had been created. Leaders of Northern opinion hedged and evaded, but Calhoun went straight ahead.

The next ten years saw Calhoun developing his theory into a complete system of society based on a classical concept of civilization whose only fault was its unreality. Before Marx and Engel had produced their Communist Manifesto, he saw society as a class struggle in which one part lived on the labor of another. It had always been that way and always would be. As between the wage slavery of the North and the chattel slavery of the South, he saw all the advantage on the side of the South. The slaves were better housed and better cared for than were the millworkers of the North. The owner must care for his slaves in sickness as well as in health, in infancy and in old age; he housed them in quarters that compared favorably with the crowded quarters of mill hands.

To cap it all the negro was by nature a menial bound to serve and content withal, while the industrial worker was equally bound to be restless, resentful, and rebellious. Drawing his proof from classical times Calhoun saw a cultured leisure class, interested in the arts, and with time and competence to rule resting securely on a basis of contented slave labor. An enduring civilization was possible in no other way. Unfortunately for his logic, the Southern art, literature, and political skill of his time gave little backing to his thesis. Such artistic and intellectual promise as mid-century America offered was Northern and not Southern. When a Southerner, Hinton Rowan Helper, pointed this out in *The Impending Crisis,* the South answered him by proscribing his book and exiling the author.

The change in Calhoun's attitude involved more than a shift from broad to strict in his interpretation of the Constitution. It might better be described as from general to particular. The minority which he proposed to save by his concurrent majority rule was in reality a vested interest within a region rather than the general interest of the region concerned. As Calhoun became more and more the philosophical defender of the rights of the states and the exponent of a rather misty concept of a civilized society, he narrowed the range of his vision to the plantation owners. The nonslave owning families outnumbered the slaveholders at least two to one, but no place was found for them in the philosopher's ideal state. The concurrent majority for which he sought recognition was in reality a minority group within the region which it purported to represent, although it held the major part of the wealth. As the price of slaves rose, the small farmers found themselves priced out of the labor market and driven to the poorer lands of the Piedmont and the clay uplands of Georgia and Alabama. Even the most rigid Federalist could hardly have gone further in the direction of an aristocratic control.

The role ascribed to slavery required the defense of the institution as a positive good. If this were true then the widest possible spread was not only permissible but highly desirable, and the perfect society would consist of an association of benevolent-minded masters. The fact that he once contemplated the possibility of an alliance of planter aristocrats and industrial capitalists as a governing elite indicates how far his inexorable Scotch-Irish logic had led him from the realities of the time. Absorbed in the construction of an impregnable and philosophically correct bulwark for the defense of his abstract society, he failed to perceive the dynamic character of the industrial growth of the North. The master class to which he once proposed to appeal there was largely nonexistent. What he missed was a broad upheaval in which middle class workers were becoming bosses and workers becoming landowners and in many cases small scale industrial capitalists. Industry was growing fast, but not in the ways Calhoun imagined. Cruel and greedy as it often was, it had broken down old barriers between classes. New wealth was appearing in new hands, and they were not the hands of sons of former landowners or merchants. The dispossessed were acquiring possessions.

Calhoun died in 1850, but by that time he had set the pattern of the case for the South. The process of evasion, ignoring, and compromising was to go on for a decade while the gulf between North and South widened and deepened. The terms on which Texas was admitted had permitted the division of that vast area into five states with ten senators. The North, with John Quincy Adams as its spearhead, fought the admission as it was to oppose the Mexican War. New England abolitionists denounced Webster for his speech of March 7, in support of the compromises of 1850 with their strengthening of the Fugitive Slave Act. Whittier branded him "Ichabod"—"the glory is departed from Israel"—although this was perhaps the most courageous act of Webster's glittering career. Douglas sought a by-pass in his "squatter sovereignty" for Kansas and Nebraska, a political device that pleased no one but Douglas and was to destroy him in 1860. Finally, in the Dred Scott decision, Chief Justice Taney announced that "no word can be found in the Constitution which gives Congress a greater power over slave property, or which entitles property of that kind to less protection than property of any other description." The next acts in the drama were staged at Sumter and Bull Run.

While Calhoun was building his case for slavery and the South, the North hesitated and fumbled. On the politico-economic side one thing was clear, the duty of the state to minister to the well-being of the citizen. This was no mid-nineteenth-century version of the "welfare state." Hamilton's Report on Manufactures had prepared the way for a state that should encourage the development of a variegated economy as distinguished from Jefferson's simple agrarianism. Under this standard the protective tariff had appeared, culminating in the Tariff of Abominations. The patent office offered protection to inventors and the joint stock limited liability corporation gave wide opportunity for investment. The risks of new enterprises were considerable, of course, but the total amount of the risk of the individual was clearly defined, which was not the case in the old individual or partnership type of organization.

The economic theory of this time has been described as *laissez faire*, but it was far from that of Adam Smith. As the Whigs began to take the place long left vacant by the liquidation of the Federalists under Jefferson, they found in the Hamiltonian precept a reason for their existence and a hard core for their otherwise vague and shaky platform. Government was to aid the development of industry and protect the tender plant against foreign competition. Beyond this point *laissez faire* prevailed. If the upper levels of industry were well served a due share would filter down to the lower in spite of the "iron law of wages." The state was no longer a passive umpire, but it was not yet a watchful policeman. Vernon Parrington (*Main Currents in American Thought*) has described this attitude as "a curiously ingenious scheme to milk the cow and divide the milk among those who superintended the milking."

Dubious and shabby as were many of the things that were done in the name of progress, the plan did give forced draft to the industrial power plant. By 1850 the cotton mills of New England had 3,614,000 spindles and were producing $76,000,000 of cotton cloth annually. Between 1820 and 1850 the cotton mills of Lowell, Massachusetts, had grown from nothing to 300,000 spindles and an English competitor wrote of Lowell in 1840: "The factories of Lowell produce a greater quantity of yarn and cloth from each spindle and loom (in a given time) than is produced in any other factories without exception in the world." [1]

Cotton was not alone in this bewildering transformation. Shoemaking, flour milling, and the meat industry were moving up from the original individual and local level toward a corporate and national plane, not yet the giants of later days, but promising youngsters. Before 1850 the new western city of Cincinnati, Ohio, had been renamed Porkopolis, a sobriquet that was revealing. Railroads had largely overcome the old fears and prejudices that hampered them before 1840 and the dim outlines of some of the great systems were beginning to appear in New York and Pennsylvania. Foreign goods were forced to scale a tariff wall of increasing height but foreign labor found a warm welcome in mills and mines. The newcomers who had numbered 8,385 in the fiscal year of 1820

---

[1] This quotation and the figures cited above are from Edward C. Kirkland's *History of American Economic Life*, pp. 324, 327.

were 369,980 in 1850. The industrial revolution was in full swing.

Such a change in the economy of the country necessitated a reshuffle of political ideas and attitudes. The case of Webster is typical. In the beginning of his career he had been a staunch defender of the free trade so natural and profitable to New England's shipowners and overseas traders. He had favored a metallic currency and distrusted bank paper of all kinds. His defense of the Bank of the United States against Jackson is the measure of his shift on this point. No longer a friend of free trade he saw in the growth of industry a force for national unity as contrasted with the isolationism and particularism of the agrarians.

When he replied to Calhoun's compact theory of the Constitution, he rested his case primarily on the claim that sovereignty was inherent in the people and that it was the people who ordained the Constitution. His strongest arguments, however, were that the Constitution acted directly on the people and not through the states and, as an executed contract, it was not subject to revocation, only amendment. In the space of a few years economic change had brought a head-on collision between two diametrically opposed theories on the nature of the Union. Webster's doctrine found favor with Northern industry. Calhoun's was soon to become the gospel of the plantation lords. If the argument had been left on a strictly constitutional basis there was still a possibility of compromise and adjustment within the limits prescribed by the Constitution. Slavery was not yet the peculiar and cherished institution that it was soon to become, and gradual, compensated emancipation after the manner of England was finding supporters.

One man made this impossible, William Lloyd Garrison, the fiery advocate of immediate and compulsory freeing of the slave. His contribution lay wholly outside the political and the economic field. Slavery was a sin, Garrison declared, and those who compromised with sin were sharers in the guilt. Compensated emancipation was to reward the sinner and colonization, urged by Benjamin Lundy, was an unchristian dodging of the issue. From the beginning he rejected the idea of a constitutional settlement, writing in the *Liberator:*

> We affirm that the Union is not of heaven. It is founded in unrighteousness and cemented with blood. It is the work of men's hands, and they worship the idol which they have made. It is a horrible mockery of freedom. In all its parts and proportions it is misshapen, incongruous, unnatural. The message of the prophet to the people in Jerusalem describes the exact nature of our "republican" concept; "Hear ye the word of the Lord, ye scornful men that rule this people. Because ye have said, we have made a covenant with death and with hell are we at agreement."

This was strong medicine for the busy North, and abolition societies grew slowly; in 1830 there were only a hundred in the country, none of them in New England. Southern trade was profitable to the manufacturers and cotton brokers of New England and New York. Garrison was threatened with lynch law more than once. Churches barred him from their pulpits and newspaper editorials denounced him as a fomenter of subversive ideas. But he persisted and his followers grew. The obvious result of the growth of abolition sentiment in the North was the inflaming of tempers in the South. A price was set on Garrison's head and abolition literature was forbidden to circulate below the Mason and Dixon's line. The reconciliation of the conflicting interests and ideas of the two sections, difficult enough at the best, became impossible. It was not that the Constitution had failed, it was the tempers of men that broke.

The political story of the decade before the Civil War is easily told. In the South it was a tale of rising passions and determination. The acid test of legitimacy was one's position on slavery. There were numbers of Southerners who disliked slavery for various reasons. Others, not a few, were opposed to secession. Alexander H. Stephens, later a member of the Confederate cabinet, fought secession until it became a fact, declaring that the people who clamored for it were mad. James L. Petigru hated secession and refused to change his opinion or keep silent even in war-mad Charleston. But these courageous voices fell on deaf ears. For most of the literate and vocal there was only one issue, slavery, and only one party, that which defended the institution. These found Douglas too lukewarm for their taste and split the party in 1860, thereby insuring the election of the candidate of the new Republican party.

In the North the record is a shabby one of mediocrity fumbling with futilities. The great leaders in both sections, Calhoun, Webster, Clay, John Quincy Adams, were dead and they left no successors. The Northern Democrats were at their wit's end to chart a course. The Whigs were even worse confused. They faced the new day following the Mexican War by nominating and electing Zachary Taylor in 1848, a general, guiltless of political ideas and experience. In 1852 they put forward another war hero, Winfield Scott, only to see him beaten by Franklin Pierce, a respectable nonentity. In 1856 Buchanan from Pennsylvania, a Democrat, was chosen. It was to be his peculiar lot to sit helplessly in the White House in the closing months of his term and receive the resignations of Southern sympathizers while arsenals and forts in Southern states were undefended and many of them came openly under the control of the secessionists.

The support given the newly born Republican party in 1856 was an indication of the extent of Whig political defalcation. The candidate, John C. Fremont, had little to recommend him for the presidency except his wise choice of a father-in-law, Benton, of Missouri. Even so, he received 33 per cent of the popular vote to Buchanan's 45 per cent, the remainder going to Millard C. Fillmore who was the candidate of a party calling itself by the eminently safe but unrevealing name of American. In 1860 the Republicans, seeking a candidate not too cursed by either Whig vagueness or Abolition extremism, chose Abraham Lincoln. He was well known in Illinois and he had served a term in Congress. His birth in Kentucky might reassure the South, and southern Illinois was doubtful and hence important territory. Furthermore, nothing was known to his discredit. The platform was a cautious one. Declaring that freedom was the natural state of mankind, it spoke approvingly of the right of the states to determine the character of their own "domestic institutions." On the need for a more effective handling of the unorganized territory and a sounder public land policy, it spoke with more assurance.

It was too late in the day to appease the South with carefully phrased conciliatory promises and arguments, and the announcement of Lincoln's election was followed fast by ordinances of secession, Calhoun's state leading the procession. When did secession become inevitable is a question that is still sometimes asked, at least in college classrooms. The answer is unsure. Perhaps when Garrison convinced a large number of people that slavery was a sin and that its eliminaion was a moral and not a political issue. A case might be made for the conclusion that peaceable solution was out of the question when John Calhoun put the last stone on his neoclassical social structure with the slave at the base of it. It is certain at least that when philosophical absolutes are brought into political discussions the chance of adjustment and compromise grows dim. For more than two hundred years we had lived, and not too badly, by rule of thumb experiment. Political experiment requires patience and a willingness to accept half loaves. Passion will not wait, and it admits of no compromise. Its rule is all or none, so the war came.

CHAPTER IX

Taney to Lincoln and Civil War
(D. R.)

Roger B. Taney had the unique experience of being refused confirmation by the Senate when appointed a Justice of the Supreme Court and then being appointed and confirmed as Chief Justice in the following year. Because of his most noted opinion in the Dred Scott case he was for half a century commonly regarded as a narrow-minded illiberal supporting states' rights and slavery. Yet until the Supreme Court became practically impotent in the closing years of the Civil War, Taney's influence, except upon slavery issues, was exerted largely in support of economic and political liberalism.

The Marshall Court had increased and strengthened the power of the national government. But, at the same time the "vested rights" of property had been strongly maintained against political interference. The Taney Court moved in the opposite direction to uphold not only the power of the states against the national government, but also their police power to subordinate individual property rights to legislation to advance the safety, morality and general welfare of society. However, the conservatism of the Court in protecting slavery obscured for many decades after the Civil War the political liberalism elsewhere manifested by the Chief Justice and his associates.

Taney's own attitude toward slavery was a curious mixture of hatred for the institution and a contemptuous valuation of Negroes as potential citizens. As a noted lawyer, when forty-one years old, he defended the free speech of an antislavery crusader with a bitter attack upon slavery, saying:

> A hard necessity, indeed, compels us to endure the evil of slavery for a time . . . while it continues it is a blot upon our national character, and every real lover of freedom confidently hopes that it will be effectually, though it must be gradually, wiped away. Until the time shall come when we can point without a blush to the language held in the Declaration of Independence, every friend of humanity will seek to lighten the galling chain of slavery, and better, to the utmost of his power, the wretched condition of the slave.

Yet, this is the same Taney who, as attorney general, aged fifty-five, wrote an unpublished opinion (exhumed in 1935 by Carl Swisher) holding that:

> The African race in the United States, even when free, are everywhere a degraded class, and exercise no political influence. They were never regarded as a constituent portion of the sovereignty of any state. But as a separate and degraded people to whom the sovereignty of each state might accord or withhold such privileges as they deemed proper. They were not looked upon as citizens by the contracting parties who formed the Constitution.

But, before we proceed from this foreshadowing opinion of Attorney General Taney to the opinion of Chief Justice Taney in the Dred Scott case, it may be wise to look at the more liberal opinions which he contributed to the growth of the American government.

State authority in restricting pauper immigration, and in authorizing a state bank to issue bank notes, was upheld. State police powers were sustained wherever not clearly restrained by the Constitution. But, on the other hand, the admiralty and maritime jurisdiction of the national government beyond tidewaters over thousands of miles of inland lakes and rivers was sustained. When, however, a state-authorized bridge over the Ohio River was held by a majority of the Court to be an unlawful obstruction to navigation, Taney joined in a vigorous dissent against this judicial assumption of legislative power. Thereupon the Congress passed an act declaring this bridge to be a lawful structure and the Taney Court held the act to be constitutional. Thus the congressional authority to overrule the Supreme Court in determining what are obstructions to commerce was happily and firmly established.

One of the most notable liberal decisions of the Court was delivered in the famous Charles River Bridge case. To break a monopoly of transportation over the Charles River between Boston and Charlestown, enjoyed by an old chartered toll bridge, the state authorized another bridge with toll rights for six years and then a reversion to the state. The old bridge brought suit to prevent this competition as an "impairment of contract." Judge Taney's opinion was a treatise of economic liberalism, demonstrating how progress would be halted by establishing such a right of property which would block the development of new highways. "This Court is not prepared to sanction principles which must lead to such results."

Justice Story filed a lengthy dissent, the tenor of which was: "I stand upon the old law, upon law established more than three centuries ago." The eminent Chancellor Kent and other outstanding lawyers inveighed against this destruction of "a great principle of constitutional morality." But Taney had laid down a doctrine of economic progress in the interpretation of the Constitution that, for better or for worse, was bound to endure.

It is unfortunate for the consistency of Taney's position that when a question later arose over the repeal by state law of a special privilege granted to a state bank, Taney headed a bare majority of the Court in upholding the contention of the state bank that its "contract" could not be thus "impaired." Thus he roused a demand in *Northern* states for a reassertion of states' rights, and particularly their right to overrule decisions of the Supreme Court! Ohio incorporated the repealing statute in an amendment to the state constitution—and the Court, over vigorous dissent, struck that down. The judicial stage was now set for the tragic drama of the Dred Scott case; for the entrance of Abraham Lincoln; for the Lincoln-Douglas debates; for the Civil War and the resulting major transformation of our government from that which had been established under the original Constitution.

The details of the Dred Scott case present a confusion of facts and legal arguments which may be avoided by a summary, which may be objectionable to technicians but helpful to an effort to explain the importance of the decision.

Dred Scott was a slave whose master had taken him from Missouri to live with him for two years in the free state of Illinois, then for two years in the free territory of Wisconsin, and then had returned with him to Missouri. Thereafter Scott, an illiterate old man, learned that he had been "free" for four years and brought suit to establish his freedom. The Missouri Supreme Court held that he was still a slave, following a fairly recent decision of the Supreme Court of the United States.

Meanwhile Scott's master had died, his widow had married an abolitionist and transferred Scott's ownership to her brother, a Mr. Sanford, of New York. This opened the door to a suit by Scott in the federal court as a "citizen of Missouri" against Sanford a "citizen of New York," who was unlawfully holding him in slavery. Like many a future case involving "civil rights" the suit was intentionally framed to force a judicial decision. Of course, Sanford could have set Scott free without going to court, but the sham battle was a preliminary skirmish which served effectively to bring on a real war.

In the Circuit Court it was decided by a jury that Scott was still a slave under Missouri law, and the case moved on to the Supreme Court. It was argued there early in 1856, and a majority agreed to affirm the decision of the lower court. Unfortunately some of the justices decided to play politics and to withhold a decision until after the presidential election that fall. They saw a chance after the election of Buchanan to shift the issue and thus to find a ground for holding that the Missouri Compromise, which was detested in the South, was unconstitutional.

The Missouri Compromise of 1820 had made possible the admission of Missouri without restriction as to slavery, but had provided that slavery should be forever prohibited in all of the Louisiana Purchase territory lying north of latitude 36° 30′ (the southern boundary of Missouri) except in Missouri. For thirty years this compromise had aided mightily in preserving the Union from the "irreconcilable conflict" between the slaveholding and nonslaveholding states. But the tension had mounted steadily since the "Compromise of 1850," and the passage of the Kansas-Nebraska Act of 1854 had nullified the great Compromise of 1820. Now, pressing upon a sympathetic majority of Supreme Court justices, was a demand from the irreconcilables of the South to demolish forever such a legal barrier to the spread of slavery—by a judicial holding that Congress had no power under the Constitution to determine whether slavery should be permitted or prohibited in territories acquired after adoption of the Constitution, or in any state. That was a power only to be exercised by a state government.

Two days after the inauguration of President Buchanan in March 1857, the fateful opinion of Chief Justice Taney was delivered. The worst feature of the opinion from the viewpoint of a lawyer was that it was a political disquisition, largely irrelevant to the decision made. What the Court actually decided was that a Negro could not become a citizen; hence the Court had no jurisdiction to entertain his suit. The argument in support of this decision was Taney's old one—that Negroes had always been regarded as "beings of an inferior order, and altogether unfit to associate with the white race either in social or political relations." Historical facts did not strongly support Taney's conclusion, but there was enough basis for his contention that Negroes were not thought of as the "citizens" to whom rights were given, in 1787, so that he might have rested his decision on that ground.

But, Taney went on to achieve his desired destruction of federal power to exclude slavery from either states or territories. Here he was forced to extremes of misconstruction of such a provision of the Constitution as that of Article III, Section 4, which explicitly gives Congress the power "to make all needful rules and regulations respecting the territory or other property belonging to the United States." He held that this applied only "to the territory which at that time belonged to, or was claimed by, the United States and was within their boundaries as settled by the treaty with Great Britain." Hence, the prohibition of slavery in the Missouri Compromise was unconstitutional. Hence a master could not be deprived of his property (a slave) just because he took it into a territory.

Finally, he held that, since under Missouri law Dred Scott had been held to be a slave, he was not a citizen and could not bring his suit.

It is painfully evident that Taney's opinion was a purely political document, written in aid of the struggle of the slaveholding states to maintain slavery and "white supremacy" against the continuing threat to their political power and their economic welfare from the increasing political power in the national government of the representatives of an increasing number of free states. The most charitable excuse for this misuse of judicial authority is that Taney, and his concurring associates, had the mistaken opinion that by nullifying the power of Congress to interfere with the spread of slavery—as attempted in Kansas and as might be possible in the Southwest—they could maintain such a balance of power as would protect the interests they favored until perhaps, in time, a peaceful separation of the Southern states from the rest of the Union would end the "irreconcilable conflict" between them.

It must be recalled that at this time the Democratic party was still the dominant party. Buchanan had been elected by 174 electoral votes to 114 for Fremont and not even his inept and weak administration could reduce the Democrats to a minority. Although Lincoln was elected by a majority of electoral votes in 1860, his popular vote was only about 40 per cent of the total and over 300,000 less than the total for the two Democratic candidates, Douglas and Breckinridge. The political blunder of Taney's opinion in the Dred Scott case was soon revealed as it became a major issue between Lincoln and Douglas in their famous debates. The Supreme Court had drawn a battle line between the Democratic party and the new Republican party; the rising leader of the Republicans quickly occupied the higher ground from which he could rake the disadvantaged Democrats with verbal shot and shell.

If the Taney opinion had been confined to supporting a decision that a slave remained a slave even after being taken temporarily into a free state there would have been no great issue developed. Even the denial of rights of citizenship to Negroes would not have raised a storm. Lincoln himself, at Charleston, said he was opposed to Negro citizenship, but he thought the judicial ruling that a state could not make a Negro a citizen was wrong. But the gratuitous ruling by the majority of the Court, that neither Congress nor a territorial legislature could exclude slavery from a territory, created a conflict that could only be decided by majority force either victorious in political struggles or in the battlefields of civil war.

The new and rapidly growing Republican party could not accept that ruling as the supreme law of the land. Lincoln wisely took the position that the decision of the Supreme Court must be obeyed while it remained the law. But the decision must be reversed. He returned to the positions of Jefferson and Jackson that the Congress was an independent branch of the government and in the exercise of its constitutional powers, as interpreted by it, could and should reverse a bad decision. The bitter attack of Taney on the Negro as a degraded person, without the protections and rights of a citizen, aroused an emotional opposition that reinforced and helped to make popular legal criticisms of his opinion.

Douglas, still the outstanding Democratic leader, was in a serious disadvantage in the debates with Lincoln. He could not maintain his following in the North by supporting wholeheartedly the Dred Scott rulings. His theory of "popular sovereignty" gave to the people of a territory, as well as of a state, the right to determine for themselves whether slavery should be permitted or prohibited in their domain. Yet here he parted company with his following in the Deep South. He could justify the repeal (and the judicial annulment) of the Missouri Compromise on the "popular" ground that Congress had no power to force people to live under an antislavery or a proslavery law. But he could not harmonize this theory with the new law laid down by the Supreme Court in a case which he could not afford to criticize.

Douglas attempted adroitly to straddle the issue, but Lincoln, against the advice of some of his best friends, insisted on forcing him to alienate his Southern supporters, although thereby aiding him for the time being to retain Democratic support in Illinois which gave Douglas victory in the senatorial contest with Lincoln.

There may be more legend than fact in the story that Lincoln deliberately sacrificed his chances to be elected senator in 1858 in order to insure the defeat of Douglas in the presidential contest of 1860. But, even in the shorter view, Lincoln's judgment was soundly based on his need to split the Democratic party in Illinois and widen the rift between Douglas and the Buchanan Democrats. So, he impaled Douglas on the point of his celebrated Freeport question, which was:

> Can the people of a United States Territory, in any lawful way, against the wish of any citizen of the United States, exclude slavery from its limits prior to the formation of a State Constitution?

Here was the old issue of states rights in a new form. If a territory could not be settled by slaveholders, obviously a state constitution would be adopted by "free state" voters—and new antislavery votes would be added to the Congress. On the other hand, a steady influx of slaveholders, even though originally a minority, might develop a majority vote for eventual statehood as a slave state.

Douglas answered the question as he was compelled to do in line with his previous arguments:

> I answer emphatically, as Mr. Lincoln has heard me answer a hundred times from every stump in Illinois, that in my opinion the people of a Territory can, by lawful means, exclude slavery from their limits prior to the formation of a State Consitituation.

Douglas then attempted to square himself with the decision of the "abstract question" by the Supreme Court as to whether slavery could go into a territory, by asserting that slavery could not exist anywhere "unless supported by local police regulations." In other words, if the territorial legislature could not pass a law directly excluding slavery it could by "unfriendly legislation" (or the lack of supporting legislation) make it impossible for slaveholding to be practically enjoyed.

The attempted evasiveness of this position served Douglas temporarily, but, with the rising strength of extremists in the South, encouraged by the Buchanan administration, Douglas lost the national voting strength that might have won him the presidency in 1860. The Democratic party was now on its way to the convention division which resulted in two presidential candidates and made possible the election of Abraham Lincoln. The assurance of "states rights" for the inhabitants of territories ironically provided the final impetus for inducing the secession of the states which were most insistent upon their "states rights." "Popular sovereignty" finally defeated its most eloquent advocate.

The growth of the powers of the national government was fast and furious in the Lincoln administration. The necessities of war always bring a centralization of authority and the extension of implied powers. Judges may solemnly proclaim that "emergencies do not create power." But the hard fact is that emergencies create conditions under which new powers not only are granted, or justified as "implied," but also are seized and exercised by common consent.

The Constitution provides that "the Privilege of the Writ of Habeas Corpus shall not be suspended unless when in cases of Rebellion or Invasion the public Safety may require it." This means that anyone can appeal to a court to end an imprisonment without lawful authority, as by mere executive action without judicial process. Lincoln suspended the privilege of obtaining a writ and a judicial decision, and thereby left the military free to imprison officers of the army or civil government who were actively supporting the Confederate cause. Chief Justice Taney held, correctly, that only Congress could suspend this privilege. Lincoln disregarded the decision and Congress later ratified his action, in a sense, by authorizing him to suspend the privilege.

Soon another tough question arose—the legality of the blockade of Southern ports because Congress had not declared war. Fortunately for President Lincoln he had by this time filled three vacancies on the Court; thus the legality of the blockade was upheld by a vote of five to four, with Taney and his three collaborators dissenting. Shortly thereafter the Court was increased to ten justices, solidifying the Lincoln majority. From then on the Court functioned as a silent partner of the administration. It declined jurisdiction of cases involving the legality of military commissions and of paper money as legal tender. Taney wrote two unused opinions holding the Conscription Act and the Legal Tender Act to be unconstitutional. He protested in vain against a tax on judicial salaries. This tax was held unconstitutional several years later and a refund was made of the taxes paid by judges.

If the Emancipation Proclamation had ever been made an issue in the Supreme Court there can be little doubt that Taney would have held it to be an unconstitutional exercise of executive authority and a deprivation of property without due process of law. Indeed the Court which handed down the famous opinion in *Ex parte Milligan* in 1866, holding that Lincoln's military tribunals were unconstitutional, would probably have held the Emancipation Proclamation invalid on the same ground that "The Constitution of the United States is a law for rulers and people, equally in war and in peace, and covers with the shield of its protection all classes of men, at all times, and under all circumstances."

But the passage of the Thirteenth Amendment settled the slavery issue and provided ratification for this most notable of Lincoln's many unprecedented and, strictly speaking, unauthorized exercises of the war powers of the President and Commander in Chief, in a war which was never officially declared to be a war!

Specific and far-reaching changes in the government of the United States were not made under Lincoln, but were brought about by amendments to the Constitution which followed the Civil War. It is, however, worthy of note that some of the most profound developments of our nation and its government were actually initiated and made inevitable by the exercise of executive powers invisible in the original Constitution, first by Thomas Jefferson and then by Abraham Lincoln. The tremendous influence of a strong President in a critical period has been made fearfully evident again in recent years. Judicial power and legislative power have had their day. Judges have erred, and legislators have blundered, and their mistakes have been repaired. But the fears of the founding fathers of the powers which a resolute executive might assume and exercise have not been laid at rest. A President, with the ever-expanding powers of his office and party leadership, may yet lead us to irretrievable disaster.

CHAPTER X

Reconstructing the United States
(D. R.)

By 1865, the extremists of the South had managed to destroy the institution of slavery which they had sacrificed everything to preserve. After 1865, extremists of the North, having sacrificed everything to preserve the Union, managed to drive the nation into a disunity and misgovernment that kept the wounds of civil war open and bleeding for decades. Infected with political poisons, they still fester, more than ninety years after the end of the war.

It is not a mere figure of speech to say that the worst victim of the assassin's bullet that killed Lincoln was the South. If Lincoln had lived to carry out his program of re-establishing the harmony of the Union he would have had a bitter struggle with the Northern extremists. Even if he had overcome their opposition, the demonstration of his wisdom might have been long obscured. His death let loose evil forces that soon proved the sagacity of his counsel.

During the war Lincoln had begun to make effective his benign policy. He took the position that the states had not left the Union, because they could not lawfully secede. Hence it would not be necessary to readmit them. Whenever their representatives were chosen by adherents to the Union they would be entitled as of right to participate in the federal government. Lincoln, during the war, recognized the loyal minorities in Virginia, Tennessee, Arkansas, and Louisiana as entitled to exercise governing power. Following Lincoln's death, President Johnson endeavored to carry on his program, by appointing provisional governors of Alabama, Florida, Georgia, Mississippi, South Carolina, and Texas who were to call conventions promptly to revise the state constitutions and re-establish loyal governments.

According to the Lincoln-Johnson theory the President could pardon all those engaged in rebellion, on suitable conditions, and restore their rights of national citizenship. And so President Johnson proceeded shortly to proclaim amnesty and to offer pardon to all demonstrating their new loyalty, by taking an appropriate oath. As a result, with certain limited exceptions, most of the states complied with the requirements according to which their senators and representatives became entitled to participate in the Thirty-ninth Congress assembling on December 4, 1865. Most unhappily the Republican leadership in the Congress was violently opposed to this executive handling of reconstruction.

To some of the extremists, the Southerners were not dissentient fellow citizens whose unyielding concept of their rights of self-government had been overcome by force of arms. They were hateful rebels who had tried to overthrow the lawful government. Other fanatics, insisting on the right of Negroes to immediate political and civil equality, were outraged by the continued maintenance of "white supremacy" in the Southern states. The Thirteenth Amendment had been proposed before Lincoln's assassination and was proclaimed adopted shortly after the Congress met. But it was evident that the mere abolition of slavery would not elevate Negroes to a citizenship for which they were obviously unprepared, but which both vengeful and utopian Northerners were determined to grant them.

In a calamitous decision the House and then the Senate ignored the credentials of those elected by the Southern states. A joint committee was appointed to determine whether any of the "so-called Confederate States of America" were "entitled to be represented in either House of Congress." In this manner the healing policy bequeathed by Lincoln and ineptly applied by Johnson was cast aside. A swift and curative reconstruction under a benevolent executive was rejected. The debilitating vengeance of malevolent legislators was begun.

To be fair, however, to the anti-Johnson leaders of Congress the passions that moved them must be recalled. The war had only actually ended in April. The victorious President had been, in that same month, assassinated. Over 350,000 Northerners had died of wounds or disease, fighting against the Confederacy. The cry for vengeance was natural. The hatreds aroused in millions of people did not suddenly expire. It was asking a good deal of human charity to expect "loyalists" to welcome the return of outstanding leaders of the "rebellion" to the seats of the mighty in the house of government which they had tried to destroy. Yet, naturally, it was just such leaders whom the "reconstructed" states would choose to send. And, naturally, the legislatures of the South would seek to prevent the newly emancipated slaves from lording it over their former masters.

It is not surprising that many of the victorious Unionists were determined to see the Confederate states made over as "conquered country," under governments made over to carry out the will of the conquerors. Against this malevolent policy the opposition was led, not by the broad-minded, now silent, Lincoln, but by a narrow, maladroit, impolitic little man whose good intentions were completely obscured by his bad methods. President Johnson could not rally even one third of either House to his support.

The Civil Rights Act, granting citizenship to Negroes, was passed over his veto. The Fourteenth Amendment was reported by the joint committee and approved by the required two-thirds' vote in both Houses. However, the mere proposal of the amendment could not overcome the inevitable opposition in the Southern states. They would not agree to cut their own political throats. Representatives of a white minority electorate would not vote political equality to a potential black majority.

But, in the fall elections of 1866, the tactless, exasperating President led the moderates to inevitable defeat by the radical reconstructionists. Now the Congress was prepared and willing to reorganize the government of the South to carry out the program of vengeful reformation. The "pretended State governments" were abrogated; five military districts were created under command of U.S. Army generals—Sheridan, Ord, Pope, Sickles, and Schofield. Under their direction, the Reconstruction Act (passed over Johnson's veto) provided for the registration of Negroes and disqualification of whites (for participation in rebellion) and then for new constitutions, assuring Negro suffrage. After congressional approval of these constitutions, the election of legislatures, and the necessary adoption of the Fourteenth Amendment by three fourths of the states, the reconstructed Southern states would be admitted to the Union. The glaring inconsistency of counting the votes of the states for ratification of the amendment prior to admitting them as states did not bother the Congress. But the compulsory nature of such ratification certainly justified the strictest possible construction of the amendment. When states were compelled to revise their constitutions and to grant new powers to the national government in order to be allowed to function as states, they could not be expected to approve of any "liberal" construction of the powers thus granted.

The Fourteenth Amendment, even strictly construed, made a fundamental change in the character of the government of the United States. Prior to its adoption the federal government had little control over the lawmaking powers of state governments. A few laws were forbidden, such as laws impairing the obligations of contract. Some laws could not be enforced if, or so far as, they interfered with federal authority, in such matters as the regulation of interstate commerce. But, the powers of self-government, in the matter of civil rights and the exercise of the police power, remained largely in the states.

After the amendment no one could tell how much power of self-government was left to the states. Citizenship was no longer under state control. "All persons born or naturalized in the United States, and subject to the jurisdiction thereof are citizens of the United States *and* of the State wherein they reside." Thus for the first time national citizenship was defined, and all national citizens were made state citizens.

"No State shall make or enforce any law which shall abridge the privileges or immunities of citizens of the United States." How far the federal government could go to create "privileges and immunities" for its citizens, in conflict with state laws, was a question that immediately arose and has not yet been fully answered. How far could individuals go to abridge "privileges" claimed as a right of American citizenship? That question has not yet been answered.

"Nor shall any State deprive any person of life, liberty or property, without due process of law." Here the door was opened to indefinite and far-reaching assertions of federal authority. Under this prohibition the states were, time after time, to be shackled by the Supreme Court in their attempt to enact "social welfare" laws.

"Nor deny to any person within its jurisdiction the equal protection of the laws."

Eighty years after this law was laid down cases of vast importance were still on their way to the Supreme Court seeking a federal edict to nullify a state law or to enforce a federal law against the will of the people of a state. The antisegregation decision of 1954 is a harsh example.

In the foregoing clauses of section 1, the remodelers of the federal government had managed to make the self-governing powers of the states subordinate to an indefinite veto power of a centralized national government.

Section 2 of the amendment proceeded to establish universal male suffrage by the curious indirect method of providing that if suffrage were denied by a state (except for "participation in rebellion, or other crime") to any male inhabitants the number of representatives should be reduced proportionately. The subsequent adoption of the Fifteenth Amendment denied the power of a state to deny suffrage because of "race, color or previous condition of servitude." Thus the states were to be prevented from denying votes to Negroes, even at the cost of reduced representation. They might still make illiteracy, or lack of property, or failure to pay taxes, a disqualification of whites and Negroes alike.

Section 3 sought to disqualify "rebels" from holding office, but authorized Congress by a two-thirds' vote to remove this disability.

Section 4 established the validity of the public debt of the United States but forbade the assumption of any debt of the Confederate states, and denied any liability for loss or emancipation of slaves, by the United States or any state.

Section 5 granted to the Congress power to enforce the provisions of the amendment.

The Reconstruction Act and the enforced adoption of the Fourteenth Amendment were designed to reduce the secession states to complete subordination to the federal government. In long-range results they perpetrated a sectionally conscious and unreconciled South and made certain an ever-spreading subordination of *all* state governments to federal lawmaking, and the nullification of many state laws by the federal judiciary.

The first reaction against this sweeping restraint, intentionally imposed on local self-government, came, surprisingly, from the federal judiciary. For several years a conflict between the Supreme Court and the Congress failed to reach a decisive issue, by virtue of several evasions by the Court and the constantly changing complexion of the Court. During this period the Court firmly asserted the judicial authority and the supremacy of the Constitution in *Ex parte Milligan*,[1] and then wobbled away from an adverse decision in the Legal Tender cases.[2] Finally, however, came the crucial decisions in the Slaughterhouse cases and then in the Civil Rights cases.

In the Slaughterhouse cases [3] the majority of the Court, in the opinion of Justice Miller, undertook to sustain as the fundamental purpose of the Fourteenth Amendment a program of anti-discrimination against the Negro and at the same time to maintain as unrestricted the reserved police power of the states, which was upheld.

In the Civil Rights cases [4] the Court went further in its strict interpretation of the Fourteenth Amendment. It denied the power of Congress to enforce equal treatment of Negroes in hotels, places of amusement, and public conveyances. The Fourteenth Amendment, the Court held, was directed against *state* action—not against the action of private persons. The Congress had been granted no authority to enforce the amendment against individuals who, without any claim of state authority, discriminated in offering accommodations

[1] 4 Wall 2.
[2] *See:* 8 Wall 603; 12 Wall 529; 12 Wall 457.
[3] 16 Wall 36.
[4] 109 U.S. 3.

to whites and blacks. In the view of the dissenting Justice Harlan and his followers, this was essentially judicial nullification of the amendment. In later cases the Court sustained "Jim Crow" laws on the same basis.

The legal soundness of these opinions has been a matter of unending debate. But, in their favor it must be said that they aided greatly at the time to ameliorate racial conflicts and festering hatreds in the South, which radical reconstruction had so needlessly intensified. The judicial power to interpret the Fourteenth Amendment as it saw fit, however, soon led to a new conflict between the Supreme Court and the state legislative power. At first the Court seemed inclined to uphold a broad exercise of state police power, at least in the regulation of public utilities. In the landmark case of *Munn v. Illinois* the Court held that state legislative regulation of rates charged by a public utility could not be condemned as depriving the owners of their property "without due process of law." But before long the force of the Fourteenth Amendment was to be revived—for the protection, not of individual civil rights, but of the property rights of corporations!

First came a decision [5] that a corporation was a "person" entitled to invoke the protections of the amendment. Next came the ruling that compulsory railroad rates must be "reasonable," [6] in order to make their regulation "due process." This imposed a drastic, and novel, limitation upon the state police power. "Due process" was thus held to mean more than formal action with due notice and a fair hearing, which had been the time-honored definition. "Due process" was now held to mean that an official regulation must be "reasonable." This profound change in interpreting a constitutional restraint presents an extreme example of judge-made law. Under it the judgment of the legislative authority be-

[5] *Santa Clara County v. Southern Pacific Railroad*, 118 U.S. 394.
[6] *Chicago, Milwaukee & St. Paul Railroad v. Minnesota*, 134 U.S. 418.

came subject to reversal by a reviewing judicial authority. A new and enduring conflict between the two independent "but coordinate" branches of government was thus begun.

Of course the judiciary rested its claim on the "supreme law" of the Constitution; but more and more the Constitution was to become "what the judges say it is." Here was the dawn of a new era, or the "dawn of a new error"—as critics might waggishly describe it.

We need not plow through a host of Supreme Court opinions to prepare ourselves for an understanding of the rise of the "progressive movement" (1890–1920), which was led by such differing personalities as Bryan, LaFollette, Theodore Roosevelt and Woodrow Wilson. It was evident from the early decisions of the Supreme Court under Chief Justice Fuller, appointed by President Cleveland in 1888, that conservatism in protection of rights of property was in the judicial saddle.

The income tax law of 1894 was held unconstitutional, after the constitutionality of such a tax had been accepted for nearly 100 years on the basis of a decision rendered in 1796.[7]

The Sherman Antitrust Act was made practically innocuous in the Sugar Trust case.[8]

"Government by injunction" was given a judicial benediction in the Debs case.[9]

The power of the Interstate Commerce Commission to fix rates was denied,[10] by a very strict construction of the federal statute.

State laws regulating insurance rates were struck down, with the club of the Fourteenth Amendment.[11]

In presenting this summary of cases there is no implication

[7] *Pollock* v. *Farmers' Loan and Trust Co.*, 158 U.S. 601.
[8] *U.S.* v. *E. C. Knight Co.*, 156 U.S. 1.
[9] *In re Debs*, 158 U.S. 564.
[10] Maximum Freight Rate case, 167 U.S. 479.
[11] *Allgeyer* v. *Louisiana*, 165 U.S. 578.

that there were no more liberal decisions nor that the decisions listed were all wrong. The purpose is merely to point out the many restraints imposed by the Court on the exercise of legislative power by either the federal or state governments. That is why, before the turn of the century the tide of popular emotion was rising in a demand, not only for greater exercise of legislative power to protect and advance the general welfare, but also for curbs on the power of the federal judiciary to reverse the legislative judgment as to what laws should and could be enacted to safeguard or to promote public interests.

Bryan, pleading for the submerged farmers and industrial workers, and denouncing "imperialism" and "dollar diplomacy," was defeated twice by McKinley. But McKinley was assassinated early in his second term and Theodore Roosevelt became President. His first appointee to the Supreme Court was Oliver Wendell Holmes. In the rustle of his black robe a prophetic listener might have heard the faint stirring of dry leaves, whispering of storms of criticism that were rising throughout the land, which soon would find echoes in the Supreme Court itself.

CHAPTER XI

Peace and a New America
(A. B.)

WHEN THE WAR ENDED it seemed easy for the victorious North to appraise the result in political terms. The Southern states had claimed the constitutional right to withdraw from the Union in defense of their cherished institution and had fought a long, hard war to make it good. The decision of the court of final appeal had been rendered at Appomattox and the case appeared to be closed. On the face of it two political changes had been accomplished: the Union was something more than a compact, how much more was yet to be determined; and slavery, "except as a punishment for crime whereof the party shall have been duly convicted," was prohibited. To these should be added the fact that the congressional policy of reconstruction had disfranchised the Southern wing of the Democratic party and so far as the radical Republicans could arrange it had insured single-party control for an indefinite time to come. To the North, rebellion had been crushed and Union forever guaranteed. To some Southern observers when the "war between the states" ended, an empire had been erected on the ruins of the old democracy.

These conclusions were too facile and superficial. The forces that determine the character and functions of government are too profound and pervasive to permit easy identification and analysis. During the war there had been much argument in the North over the major purpose of the military action. Was it to save the Union or to free the slave? At the outset the mercurial and somewhat hysterical Horace Greeley had urged that we "let the erring sisters go in peace." A little more than a year later he addressed a "Prayer of Twenty Millions," written of course by himself, to the President urging the immediate abolition of slavery by executive decree. Lincoln replied with his often quoted statement: "If I could save the Union without freeing *any* slave, I would do it; and if I could do it by freeing *all* the slaves, I would do it; and if I could do it by freeing some and leaving others alone, I would also do that." In general this agreed with other statements of the President. His own first purpose was to save the Union. He had declared this at his first inaugural and repeated the substance of it many times in messages, speeches, and letters. Even the Emancipation Proclamation freeing the slaves in states in rebellion against the United States was an act, or rather a gesture, of war, and in no sense a declaration of purpose or policy.

Seen in perspective such arguments as these carried on in the midst of war were merely exercises in dialectics, argumentative shadowboxing. At such a time the visibility of the future is even lower than it is in more normal periods. In his chapter, "The Economic Revolution," in the second volume of *The Growth of the American Republic,* Henry Steele Commager quotes three lines from the concluding chorus of Euripides *Medea* written nearly twenty-five hundred years ago by a Greek tragedian possessed of rare understanding:

> And the end men looked for cometh not,
> And a path is there where no man thought;
> So hath it fallen here.

In nineteenth-century America as in ancient Greece, five centuries before the birth of Christ, the unforeseen and unintended results often outweigh the seen and the desired. They still do. The acid test of any government is its ability to meet these sudden and unexpected challenges. The first business of Clio in such a case is with the record. What then does the record show? Part of the answer is easy. Approximately half a million men, North and South, had died in battle or of disease in the service. In the South the whole economy was in ruins. The old plantations had rested on the backs of the slaves and the slaves were no longer there. How much did the Thirteenth Amendment cost the South? At prewar prices at least $2,000,000,000, probably more. Banking capital, perhaps $1,000,000,000 more, was gone. Confederate bonds and currency outstanding, whatever the total amount and no one seems to quite know, were written off, representing large investments of patriotic Southerners; at the time of its disappearance the Confederacy owed considerable sums in unpaid current accounts, chiefly to Confederate citizens. Cities, mills, railroads, highways, homes—all the means by which an economy survives and functions—were in ruins or so dilapidated as to require practically complete reconstruction.

Another serious war casualty of the South was the old political leadership. The planter class was ruined politically as well as financially and most of the important members were disfranchised under the congressional plan of reconstruction. In the carpetbag period their place was taken by a mixture of Northern fortune hunters, Southern "scalawags," and representatives of small farmers and tradesmen, "poor whites" in the planting days. In destroying the old political controls Congress had called into being a new Solid South, which still exists. Out of it have come men of ability and distinction but it has also produced a rank crop of political ignorance, shortsightedness, and dishonesty, a political liability to the South, to the country, and to both political parties.[1]

By contrast with the South, the North was intact and flourishing. To be sure there was a national debt of about $3,000,000,000, mostly for prosecution of the war, and the currency was in a not too healthy state, but there were large entries on the credit side. Not all of these can be attributed to the war, but the conflict had been a stimulus as well as a drain. While many men were dying, some men were making money. Military supplies had offered large profits to shrewd operators, even to honest ones. The dishonest took as much as the traffic would bear. Government bonds, issued at a discount and carrying 5 to 7 per cent interest in gold, had paid well. As the war wore to its close, American credit abroad began to pick up and capital, both foreign and home-grown, was available for promising, if still speculative, investments. A new national bank act, passed during the war, offered considerable opportunities for profit with minimum risk, sometimes as high as 17 per cent per annum in the early years. The high tariff rates imposed under the Morrill Act for the needed revenue in wartime were continued and increased after peace came for the further protection of American industry.

As happens in all major modern wars the needs of the armed forces had speeded up the productive capacity of the North. Plants had grown in size, war orders had brought into use new and larger machines, laborsaving devices multiplied, new sources of raw material had been opened up, and new materials brought into use. The process of change of method and increase in capacity engendered by war should be easily understood by anyone now old enough to have seen the response of the United States in two world wars. It was even more marked during the Civil War as a heavy underlining

---

[1] A discussion of the legal and constitutional aspects of reconstruction will be found in Chapter X.

of the arrival of the industrial revolution on this side of the Atlantic.

Consider the case of steel. This was an English and Continental monopoly before 1860. A few token tons had been produced in this country to show that it could be done, but as late as 1867 only 2,600 tons of steel ingots had been turned out in spite of the fact that an American, William Kelly, had discovered the secret of steelmaking at about the same time Bessemer had pointed the way to the British ironmasters. Slow as we were to change, the clamor of war tools for steel had been too loud to ignore and, when the rapidly growing American railroads joined the chorus, steel was inevitable. In 1875, 375,000 tons were made and, in 1879, the output had grown to 929,000. The great Mesabi field, a miniature mountain range of iron ore, first located in the Minnesota wilderness along the shores of Lake Vermilion in 1844, was opened and the industrial giant began to flex his muscles.

Oil was another newcomer. The first commercial wells were sunk in Pennsylvania the year before Lincoln was elected and by 1864 over 2,000,000 barrels were coming out and a wild speculative boom was on. Coal-Oil Johnny became the symbol of the gambling possibilities of the new industry. The organization of Standard Oil in 1870 was less spectacular but more significant. As the Indians were driven into reservations prospectors turned up new deposits of mineral wealth, gold and silver in Nevada, gold in Colorado, silver and copper in Montana. Meanwhile the opening of the fabulous copper ore body in the more accessible region of the northern peninsula of Michigan was pouring new wealth into Boston.

Old familiar local and household industries, the making of shoes and clothing, the grinding of wheat, the slaughtering of cattle and hogs, the making of agricultural machinery had taken on large dimensions and new importance. This change was already on the way in the fifties, but the need of troops for food and clothing had speeded it up immensely. Fortunes were won in years that in the earlier time could hardly have been accumulated in the same number of decades. Some of them were to last, as a few names indicate: Washburn and Pillsbury in flour; Swift, Armour, Morris in meat packing; McCormick and Deere in agricultural machinery; Pullman with his newfangled "palace-cars" dates from this time, as do Carnegie, Frick, and Rockefeller in steel and oil.

The dynamism that had marked the westward movement and the creation of new states and cities was moving in a new direction and with far greater intensity of purpose and result. America was making more and buying more and the process was changing the lives of the people. As the crude mills driven by water power and the slaughterhouses just outside the small towns had gone down under the competition of big machinery and big business, the consumers were drawn more and more into the complexities of highly organized systems of production and distribution. Farmers who grew the wheat and bred the cattle were forced to buy their flour from someone in Minneapolis and their meat from a packer in Chicago. Big industries meant big cities, and the proportion of city dwellers to rural grew steadily. In this single fact was a social change of the first magnitude which we were slow to recognize.

Revolutions, and this was a big one, have an annoying way of destroying old institutions and upsetting old controls and balances. Revolutions that culminate in violence as in France, and lately in Russia, are easily seen, though still difficult to understand. Revolutions without mobs or guillotines or purge trials have low visibility and frequently correspondingly large effects. The transformation of the United States from a rural-agrarian nation to an urban-industrial society was profound and hard to discern. The combined correlation and conflict of the agrarian with the industrial and capitalistic can be seen more dramatically in the building and development of the transcontinental railroads.

A railroad from the Mississippi to the Pacific had been much discussed before the war, but the question of slavery made agreement impossible. Should the new highway be an extension of a slave or a free labor economy? There was no answer in sight until the Civil War provided it. On July 1, 1862, the first Pacific Railway act became a law. Construction began from both ends in 1865 and the two sections met at Promontory Point, Utah, near Great Salt Lake in May, 1869. As an engineering and construction feat, the building of the road was worthy of all praise. Of the financing, especially of the machinations and corruptions of the slimy Credit Mobilier which purported to finance the Union Pacific end of the project and took three or four hundred per cent profit, not so much can be said. That loathsome tale has been told. For our purposes here the significant new thing is the appearance of the United States government in the role of promoter and backer of a great private enterprise. That must have been one bet that Hamilton collected from Jefferson in the Elysian Fields. If this was *laissez faire* it was a new kind.

The manner of the backing was simple. The government had land in abundance, much of it on the high plains then of doubtful value. The two Pacific Railway acts gave to the company a free right of way through the public lands and ten alternate sections per mile of track within the limits of ten miles on each side. In addition the Secretary of the Treasury was ordered to issue to the company $16,000 of six per cent government bonds per mile of completed section, the bonds to be a second mortgage on the railroad to be paid off out of the profits of operation of the line.[2] The total

[2] The Act of 1862 had provided for five sections per mile and a first mortgage to cover the bonds. The second Act, two years later, doubled the land grant and substituted a second mortgage for a first.

amount of land granted to the two sections of the road, the Union and the Central Pacific, was 45,000,000 acres; the bonds lent to the two roads added up to $60,000,000. To that extent, at least, Uncle Sam was in the railroad business, but for purposes of promotion, not control.

The Union Pacific was only the first. Other railroad builders were prompt on the trail that had been blazed. The Northern Pacific, the Southern Pacific, and the Santa Fe followed fast; states chimed in with large and small beneficence, notably the state of Illinois for the Illinois Central. Before the railroad land grants came to an end, roads, large and small, had received title to a domain approximately equal to the total area of Texas. In some cases, particularly that of the Northern Pacific, the railroad income from the land sales was equal to the original construction cost.

The building of the transcontinental lines ushered in a new era not only in railroading but in the relationship of the means of transportation to the producers, especially the growers of food. The 35,000 miles of rail in operation in 1865 were practically all east of the Mississippi. As settlers moved west from the seaboard to the great river they found themselves in country not seriously different from that which they had left. Except for the belts of prairie in Illinois where wood was lacking, wood and water were abundant. Human beings led the way, dragging crude highways behind them. Canals and then railroads followed in the rear. With wood, water, and land available in apparent abundance the new farmers followed the old patterns of crops and methods. The first need of each new family was to maintain itself. Such surplus as developed found markets near by. Mixed farming was the rule, with a growing emphasis on corn. Most of this was fed on the farm or in the county of its origin.

The opening of the farther, wilder West changed all this in ways that were not anticipated. The prime conscious purpose of the Union Pacific was to reach the Pacific Coast and provide a shorter, cheaper route for the goods of the Orient to the Eastern market. The high plains, still known and thought of as the Great American Desert, were in the way. Hence they were crossed, but only because they were there. Millions of buffalo still roamed the plains and most of the way soldiers guarded the construction gangs against possible Indian attack. The Homestead Act, passed in May, 1862, put a new face on the adventure. This act announced the abandonment of the government's long and varied attempt to sell the public lands. Now they were to be given away, 160 acres to any person, man or woman, twenty-one years of age and a citizen or an alien who had filed declaration of intent to become a citizen. The only conditions were five years' residence on, and cultivation of, the land and the payment of a nominal fee for the issuance of the final patent. The homesteaders appeared immediately after the bill became law and in spite of the war increased steadily. By 1870 Nebraska had more than quadrupled its population over 1860. When the Union Pacific trains began running, homesteaders were soon important passengers and special rates were offered. This was repeated as more transcontinental roads were opened. Excursion trains exclusively for "landlookers" were run. With government land grants to sell, the Union Pacific, the Northern Pacific, the Santa Fe, and the Burlington became real-estate operators on a large scale. Rails were leading the procession and setting the pace.

The new settlers soon learned that farming on the treeless plains of Kansas and Nebraska was not like farming in Ohio or New York. As they followed the railroads west trees faded out and rainfall diminished. Only the land remained, level and endless, without stones or hills; likewise with little water. William P. Webb, whose book *The Great Plains* is the classic of this stage in our history, uses a striking figure to describe the problem of the Western farmer. East of the ninety-eighth meridian, says Webb, the farmer sat on a three-legged stool, soil, wood, and water. West of the line where rainfall drops below the average of twenty inches a year, his stool had only one leg, soil. Crops must be fitted into this new climatic pattern and wheat was the obvious answer.

This completed the reversal in the relation of the grower to the rest of the world. Wheat is for the market; only a trifle, if that much, for the grower's own table. The demand for wheat is world-wide. World markets can be reached only by rail and ship. The road lies through elevators, freight cars, distant mills, and shippers, with brokers, commission men, and other intermediaries all along the way. The grower was inextricably tied into the vast machinery of transportation, processing, and distribution. Prices were fixed at distant points, chiefly Liverpool, and only a fraction, a sixth or a seventh, filtered back to the original producer. The stage was set for the long agrarian war which culminated in the bitter campaign of 1896.

The busy East was slow to recognize the plight of the farmer. Industry was growing fast; banks, insurance companies, savings banks, and other signs of financial expansion and change filled the visible horizon. These were near at hand; the West was far off, a rainbow vision of a land where generous hearted Uncle Sam would "give us all a farm." If you dislike the mines or the mills, go West, young man, and grow up with the country. The man on the soil was still the lucky man. So the legend ran.

In general those who bothered to give a thought to the political, social, or economic aspects of the scene found easy comfort in the *laissez-faire* doctrine. A cynic might have summed up the prevailing attitude in the homely phrase, "Every man for himself and the devil take the hindmost," implying perhaps divine approval of the successful foremost. But the unrestricted competition imposed by *laissez faire* was dangerous and costly. Price wars, fraud, misrepresentation of goods, special favors from railroads to big shippers, all the corrosive features of free-for-all competition, pointed clearly in the direction of a competition that was not quite so dangerously free. It was the big men at the top who felt this more keenly, since they had the most to lose. Trade agreements, pools, combinations of various kinds, embryonic trusts began to appear.

The trust form of organization was one of several expedients designed to hold the competitive process within bounds. Its great advantage was superior authority and corresponding efficiency. Basically the form of the trust, Standard Oil for example, was simple. Separate corporations, parties to the agreement, turned in the stock in their individual companies to the new organization, receiving stock or certificates of trust in exchange therefor, thus creating a new corporate body dominating an entire industry or a series of processes. The details of formation and operation varied in different industries. Some sought control of a single process going on over a wide area, as in the case of the railroad freight pools. Others sought control over the whole course of an industry from the extraction of the raw material through the transportation, processing, and distribution of the product, down to the ultimate consumer. Important collaterals, such as the building and operation of tank cars, might be brought in, thus making sure that the wall might not be scaled or broken through at any point.

Capital seeking investment was not slow to see the advantages of the trust form, with its highly centralized control. Risk of loss from cutthroat competition was greatly reduced. Larger operations demanded more laborsaving machinery and more efficient manufacturing processes, facilitating mass production to meet growing demand for goods. As the big units increased, the small, individually owned plants, less efficient and less able to demand a share of the market, tended to fall into disuse. More production with fewer producing units became increasingly the rule.

Competition did not disappear. The independents did not yield the field without a struggle, as a reading of Miss Tarbell's *History of Standard Oil* reveals. In many cases it became more bitter, as with oil, and later in steel and agricultural machinery, but it was no longer a war between equals. Once a David killed a Goliath, but it seldom works that way. As the big ones grew bigger their ability to fix the terms of conflict increased. The bigger the shipper the better the rate, and the greater ease with which price cuts can be met when competitors try to win favor with the consumer. Where jobs exist by the thousand, labor pools can be more easily created and maintained, thus building up a bulwark against demands for higher wages or shorter hours.

The hard times of the seventies, ushered in by the collapse and panic of 1873, intensified the tendency toward consolidation and centralization. The weaker units died and the larger, better organized and financed, weathered the storm and came through stronger than ever. National wealth was increasing and the Philadelphia Centennial in 1876 presented a flamboyant but impressive picture of material achievement with brilliant promise for the future. The consuming public, without organization or leadership, gave little thought to what was going on behind the scenes. More goods were available, new kinds were appearing, and prices, while high, were not prohibitive. Mass production was making it possible for the little man to buy articles formerly out of his reach.

While industry was pyramiding in size and range of influence in the twenty-five years after the war, politics was a stagnant and malodorous pool. Through much of the time the personalities at both ends of Pennsylvania Avenue in Washington were at the best mediocre and incompetent. Much of the time too many of them were also corrupt, especially during the eight years of Grant. This was the lowest period in our political history. Graft was common and attracted little attention unless its size made it spectacular, as in the Credit Mobilier and the operations of the Whisky Ring. Minor posts in the civil service provided adequate reward and comfortable resting places for broken-down party hacks and the major positions were bonanzas for the smart and the unscrupulous. Only the administrations of Hayes and Cleveland offer a pleasing relief.

In general the state governments reflected the same political war-weariness and indifference, and the cities were even worse. The rapid concentration of population in the larger centers and the multiplication of urban needs and problems found both voters and politicians unprepared and ignorant, except in ways of dishonesty. Tweed in New York was only a particularly outrageous specimen of the political monstrosities that the climate of the time brought forth.

The attitude of the national government toward the kaleidoscopic changes that were taking place in our economy was one of indifference. Contributions had been made through protective tariffs, the Pacific Railway acts, the contract labor law of 1864, and the National Bank acts. Troops had been called out to quell strike disorder and protect strikebreakers. What more could be asked? Little thought was given to the fact that the form of organization which made the centralized control of industry possible was a creature of the government. Corporations had existed early in our history and after the decision in the Dartmouth College case defining a charter issued by a state legislature as a contract and hence secure against impairment by its creator, they had grown in favor. The limitation of individual liability was an invitation to investors and the corporate form facilitated reorganization and combination. Few took time to examine the questions raised by the spread of this legal personality. The corporation had all property rights pertaining to personality, but where did personality end and citizenship begin? The Fourteenth Amendment had used both terms to the later confusion of legislatures and courts. Who had the final responsibility in a corporation? To the laborer, who was the boss and how could he be reached?

There were also ethico-legal questions. Sin and crime were familiar attributes of natural persons. They were individual things and punishment was visited on individuals. A corporation could commit acts that would be crimes if done by an individual, but how could it be punished? It might be fined or ordered to dissolve, but it could not be flogged or hanged or put in jail. Could officers or boards of directors be punished as individuals for the acts of the corporation? Was it possible for a corporation to sin? What was a sin in economic terms? These and similar questions were not of obvious political form and color, but they had political implications. If there was no answer, it might be that government had imitated Frankenstein and created a monster that threatened to be more powerful than government itself.

The first influence that was to push us into political experiment with elementary controls of the burgeoning economy was the growing sense of oppression and inferiority on the part of the farmers. The end of the war had brought little change in the widespread assumption that ours was primarily a rural and an agrarian society. This was still the America that it had been, except that the attempt to destroy the Union had failed. Eighty years earlier the fathers of the Constitution had fixed December as the month for the annual assembling of the Congress as that was the time when the farmer members could most conveniently take time off from their farming, and it was taken for granted that most of the members would represent the farming interest. Now farms were spreading from the Atlantic Ocean to the Rocky Mountains, but the farmer's voice seemed to be heard less often and less powerfully in Washington than before. What had happened?

The first effort to do something for the farmer grew out of a trip made by a clerk in the Bureau of Agriculture, Oliver

H. Kelley, who had been sent by Andrew Johnson to make an inspection of Southern farming. His formal report, if he made one, is presumably buried in dust in a forgotten file somewhere in Washington. But the sordid poverty and isolation that Kelley saw among the small Southern farmers induced him to bring together other government clerks to form an organization with the pretentious title, Patrons of Husbandry. Thus was the Grange born in 1867. At the beginning the Grange was a social organization intended to lighten and diversify the dull, work-filled days of the man on the land. Ritual and formal ceremony were provided for the meetings of the local granges. Political discussions were barred and the evenings were to be devoted to music, declamations, small plays, and stimulating games.

At first there was little response from the farms, but toward the end of the first discouraging year a newly formed branch at Fredonia, N. Y., began to experiment with cooperative buying and selling. This was something the members could understand and the movement spread. By 1875 there were 20,000 locals with 800,000 members, mostly in the farming states of the West and South. The rule against political discussion was easily circumvented by declaring the formal meeting adjourned, permitting the members to proceed with what they called an "outside meeting." The farmer's political education of himself was beginning.

The direct political influence of the Grange was never large, but the feelings and ideas germinated in the outside meetings spread. State legislatures in the states where the farm vote was strongest began to experiment with laws for the control of those enterprises whose operations were of the first importance to the farmer, chiefly railroads and elevator companies. There were other sinners who were dipping a share out of the flood of farm products as it flowed from the field to the consumer, but railroads and elevators were near at hand and more easily reached. The interests affected fought back and, for a time, found a useful aid in the first section of the Fourteenth Amendment, "nor shall any State deprive any person of life, liberty, or property, without due process of law." [3]

In the course of the legislative and court battles over these so-called Granger laws, an important point in the relations of business and government was made in the case of *Munn* v. *Illinois*. The suit arose from an Illinois law fixing maximum rates for the storage of grain in Chicago. In handing down a decision upholding the law, Chief Justice Waite cited a decision made by Lord Chief Justice Hale in England more than two hundred years before that when private property is "effected with a public interest, it ceases to be *juris privati* only." This part of Chief Justice Waite's decision sets up an important milestone in our history:

> Property does become clothed with a public interest when used in a manner to make it of public consequence, and affect the community at large. When, therefore, one devotes his property to a use in which the public has an interest, he, in effect, grants to the public an interest in that use, and must submit to be controlled by the public for the common good, to the extent of the interest he has thus created.[4]

Effective as they were in the establishment of principles of law and a course of political action, the Granger laws had definite limitations. The differentiation between intrastate and interstate traffic set obvious bounds to state control and the vagueness of the boundary between what was intrastate and what was not made for confusion. Ten years after the decision in *Munn* v. *Illinois* another case came up to the Supreme Court involving the right of the state to the control of charges on the Illinois portion of a long haul terminating

---

[3] The cases arising under this clause and the decisions rendered are discussed in Chapter X.
[4] 94 U.S. 113.

at some point outside the state boundaries. This was the Wabash case, *Wabash, Pacific & St. Louis RR. Co., v. Illinois.* The Illinois Supreme Court had upheld the state law in prohibition of the long and short haul differential in connection with the rates from two Illinois points to New York. This was one of the farmer's important grievances. Justice Miller wrote the final decision and declared that the congressional power to regulate commerce between the states and with foreign nations denied to a state the power to control a part of such traffic passing through the state. The interstate commerce clause of the Constitution, said the Court, "would be a very feeble and almost useless provision, . . . if, at every stage of the transportation of goods and chattels through the country, the State within whose limits a part of this transportation must be done could impose regulations concerning the price, compensation, or taxation, or any other restrictive regulation interfering with and seriously embarrassing this commerce." [5]

The decisions in the two cases cited illustrate an important phase in the political quandary in which the farmers found themselves. It was easy to denounce the decision in the Wabash case as unfair interpretation of an artificial distinction, but the federated system was a reality sanctioned and confirmed by the Constitution. Interstate commerce crossing many states was also a reality and a growing one. The arena of political action was both state and national. The fact that the corporation was created by a state gave the creator no control over his creature except as stipulated in the charter. To the cooler heads among the farm leaders it was clear that interstate commerce was vital if farm products were to reach the wide markets that were demanded. If redress were to be had it must be sought in Washington as well as in the state capitals.

The first result of the realization of a need for national action was the original Interstate Commerce Act, which became law on February 4, 1887, a few months after the deci-

[5] 118 U.S. 557.

sion in the Wabash case. The government that had been the patron and the sponsor of railroad extension now turned its attention to control. The act was more declaration and warning than prohibition. It required that charges should be "reasonable and just," but offered no standard or definition by which those impressive terms could be applied. Rebates, discriminations, pooling of freight by different and competing roads were forbidden, but the commission created by the act had power only to examine and to censure. The power to compel lay with the courts. The law required full publicity of rates and forbade change without due notice, but again only the courts could make final decision.

The creation of the Interstate Commerce Commission served notice that the transportation of goods was a national interest as Chief Justice Waite had shown that circumstances could give a public character to private enterprise. The barrier of *laissez faire* had been bent but it was still far from broken. Three years later, July 2, 1890, the Sherman Antitrust Act served notice on industry that it too must recognize limitations of power and conduct. The act begins: "Every contract, combination, in the form of trust or otherwise, or conspiracy, in restraint of trade or commerce among the several states, or with foreign nations, is hereby declared to be illegal." It was a sweeping declaration, but laws and decisions do not enforce themselves and it was more than a decade before a President and an attorney general appeared to put the law into effect. Meanwhile the growth of trusts, combinations, and agreements went merrily on.

By this time the complexity and scope of the political scene had made it clear to the farm interests that the narrow, idealistic program of the Grange offered little real help. Political results could be secured only through political action, and the Grange was too vague in its political gestures to offer much help. In the late eighties organizations known as Farmers' Alliances appeared in different parts of the country, chiefly in the South and West. In the beginnings these organizations were responses to local or regional conditions and needs, but, as they spread and coalesced in the national alliance, their aims became increasingly political. Where the Grange had been vague and evasive the Alliance was forthright, positive, and sometimes radical. If transportation oppression could not be prevented in any other way, government ownership was proposed. The banking monopoly was to be destroyed by abolition of the national banks and the inflation of the currency to be achieved by increased coinage of silver or the issuance of greenbacks. Trading in futures was to be prohibited and government warehouses were to be established which should loan legal-tender money to farmers based on the value of nonperishable crops deposited in them. The Alliance program was largely political but it stopped short of proposing a distinct farm party; the ends sought were to be gained by pressure on one or both of the existing parties.

In most sections the Alliance attempted to carry on the social and economic features of the Grange, cooperative buying and selling, meetings and picnics with games and entertainments designed to relieve the tedium of farm life, but the major emphasis was increasingly political. The capitalistic and industrial East was imposing a form of slavery on the helpless West, and the sanctions and the means by which this tyranny was accomplished rested on the control of government by the East. While the Alliance did not attempt political organization it did lay down the lines that the Populist party platforms followed in the decade of the nineties.

Close to the center of their grievances were railroad and other charges incident to transportation. The railroad was the life line of the Western farmer. It brought him and his necessary goods into the country, in many cases it sold him his land, it carried his crops to market, all of them, and it decided what share he should receive of the final price. That that share should be as low as a seventh was in itself a gross injustice to the primary producer without whose efforts there would have been no traffic. The Interstate Commerce Act had made a gesture in the direction of control, but it was too easily ignored. The Commission could censure and warn, but the final power lay with the courts, and the judges listened too closely to the arguments of counsel for capital. Such terms as "reasonable and just" return, "what the traffic would bear," and "due process of law" had an ominous sound to the farmer.

Closely allied to the control of rates was the control of currency and credit. Here again the power lay entirely in the East, with the big banks and the directors and heads of corporations. The interest of the farmer lay in the existence of an adequate amount of circulating medium to prevent price manipulation. Gold was the money of the rich and the powerful; hence a medium not so easily subject to control, silver or paper or both, was the people's money. With silver or paper in general use the ruinous price fluctuations could be prevented. A favorite form of the farmer's dilemma was the simple statement that when the farmer borrowed money, a thousand dollars, he received the equivalent of a thousand bushels of wheat, but when he paid off the loan he was forced to deliver the equivalent of two thousand bushels. Prices of farm products had trended steadily downward through the seventies and eighties, giving a poignant realism to this process of simple rationalization. To the grower it was not so much that wheat was cheap as that gold was dear.

From currency to credit was an easy step in Western thinking. Land seemed cheap to the homesteader, five years of work and waiting, but it was not quite what it seemed. Agriculture was being mechanized along with industry. The level lands of the West made possible and, in fact, demanded the use of more and larger implements than the simple scale of the earlier day. McCormick binders were unqualified essentials for the large-scale production of wheat, and such machines were expensive. J. F. Glidden solved the problem of fencing on the treeless plains with his barbed wire, but barbed wire also tied the farmer more closely into the industrial and financial complex. When long-term loans were needed the chief sources of loanable capital, whether from banks or mortgage loan companies, were in the East. And here again the farmer's experience seemed to bind him inextricably in a tragic circle of railroad, land, wheat, capital, and ruin. The money necessary for the fencing of the land could be secured, but at the price of a mortgage on the land. When the interest of the manipulators of the currency sent the price of gold higher and the grower found himself unable to meet the debt charges out of the income from the land, it was the land he lost, and not the fence alone. The land was still there with the fence around it, but the farmer was gone.

This sinister sequence was too much of a reality to permit the wheat men to regard it as merely an unfortunate incident in the beneficent operation of *laissez faire*, especially after they became convinced that the corrective operation of free competition was more apparent than real. The Antitrust Act designed to prevent conspiracies in interstate commerce waited fourteen years for effective application. A final grievance was the inequity of taxation. Land and the equipment necessary for its use were easily seen and appraised. The landowner paid the tax or lost the land. Stocks and bonds were easily concealed and few capitalists were punished for tax evasion.

The farmer had organized for pressure on the older parties, but they were deaf both to the appeals of the Alliance and of kindred organizations. A Republican senator had introduced the Antitrust Act and a Democratic attorney general had announced his opinion that it was a bad law and no attempt would be made by the Department of Justice to enforce it. Finally a Democratic President forced the repeal of the Silver Purchase Act, placing gold firmly at the base of the currency.

West of the Mississippi, at least, it was clear that nothing could be expected from either party. The farmer's only hope was in a party of his own. The process of challenge and response was operating, but it was taking new and strange forms, fantastic and threatening to the East, necessary and legitimate to the West. The issues involved in this new political alignment were forged out of the material of the national experience chiefly since the Civil War. It was variously described as a People's Crusade, another Shay's Rebellion, a second Civil War, a fomenting of sectional discord. It may have been a part of a revolution. If so, it followed a familiar pattern. Terms of violent opprobrium were bandied about in both sections, concealing the fact that what was being demanded was not an overthrow of existing government but the turning of governmental attention to a new set of needs and conditions. After all, the desire of numbers of people for representatives of their own kind and choosing is hardly to be characterized as radical.

Another question of greater importance was inherent in the political change. What the farmers sought cannot be justified in explicit terms anywhere in the Constitution, except perhaps in the Preamble. Was the farmer's plight a part of the "General Welfare"? The farmers believed it was. If they were right, then the functions of government, both state and national, went far beyond the negative, neutral attitude previously ascribed to it by such authorities as William Graham Sumner and John W. Burgess. This raised a large and perplexing question. If government was to enter upon a program of positive participation in the promotion of the general welfare, outside the realm of the policeman and the judge, where if anywhere were the limitations? We are still looking for the answer.

CHAPTER XII

The New Nationalism and Social Responsibility
(A. B.)

THE AMERICA of the closing decade of the nineteenth century seems difficult to characterize in a word or an epigram. Thomas Beer called it "The Mauve Decade" and wrote an interesting but unconvincing book to prove it. To the ultraconservative, viewing Oscar Wilde and the vagaries of *The Yellow Book*, it was decadent. To those born too late to have known it, it was a quaint survival of an earlier day, with faint premonitions of modernism. There is documentation for these and other verdicts, but each requires the exclusion of a mass of more pertinent evidence.

For those who lived through it and were old enough to understand, at least in part, it was a time of discontent and discord, of want and uncertainty, of blind striving for a sure road where no road was sure. In industry profits were high and markets were growing broader. Wealth was increasing at a bewildering rate and new combinations were appearing with large and promising opportunities for capital. It was also a time of doubt and questioning. In the previous decade two books had appeared to call attention to a tendency previously noted by Henry George in his *Progress and Poverty*. George had stated his thesis in a simple phrase, "The rich are getting richer and the poor are getting poorer." To many of his readers this was a complete summary of their own experience and observation.

The two books that shocked the complacency of all but the most secure and satisfied were Edward Bellamy's *Looking Backward* and Henry Demarest Lloyd's *Wealth Against Commonwealth*. *Looking Backward* was a utopian romance purporting to describe America in the year 2000 as a socialistic paradise in which all were equal and equally secure. The only seriously disturbing feature of the book was its assumption that this heaven on earth was the logical result of centralization and consolidation of industry which had finally organized and consolidated itself into a complete and all-inclusive form of society. Of socialistic or communistic theory there was no trace.

Wealth Against Commonwealth was more immediately disturbing. Here was the first direct presentation of evidence that industry and capital were in possession of power that threatened to dethrone government. In fact, Lloyd argued, we were living under two governments, one, the political, indifferent, mediocre, powerless; the other, organized capital, powerful, growing, and already the master of government. His documentation was extensive and damning. Much of it was from official reports of hearings and court proceedings.

In 1890 Charles B. Spahr published his study, *The Distribution of Wealth in the United States*. Here was presented a bewildering array of statistical evidence, all pointing in the same direction as George's oversimplified formula. One per cent of the population had more wealth than the combined totals of the other ninety-nine, said Spahr. Seven eighths of the families in the United States had less than eighteen per cent of the wealth. These and similar statistics were widely quoted, amplified, disputed, argued over. The difficulties in the collection of reliable information on such a condition with so many vague variables were obvious, but it was clear to an increasing number of people that the rapid increase in the concentration of wealth held menacing possibilities. Too many families, eighty per cent some critics said, were living on or near the margin of subsistence. The classical doctrine of *laissez faire* had been firm on the substantial justice of the distribution of the fruits of industry in a regime of free competition. Was the doctrine wrong as a basic concept? Or, perhaps, this was not free competition. These were disturbing thoughts.

Few of the doubts were expressed by those who sat in high places, financial or political. Just rewards were being gathered by those who had earned them. To doubt this was to doubt the foundations of society. New and more powerful combinations appeared as the decade wore on, American Sugar, Amalgamated Copper, American Smelting and Refining, Consolidated Tobacco (1901), a new Standard Oil. The closing years of the decade saw the rapid growth of combinations in iron and steel, culminating in 1901 in the appearance of United States Steel, the biggest yet, with a capitalization of $1,402,847,000. There was talk of world conquest for markets and materials, an industrial empire operating from within a political democracy.

It was a time of titans, Morgan, Rockefeller, Carnegie, with a host of lesser giants. In the railroad world the names of individuals supplanted the familiar names of roads. In place of New York Central, Erie, Great Northern, Southern Pacific, Rock Island, men spoke of Vanderbilt, Morgan, Gould, Rockefeller, Harriman. Banks were Morgan or Rockefeller banks.

That was one side of the shield. The other side was not so pleasing. Wages were low and labor was restless. In the great strike in the Carnegie works in Homestead, Pennsylvania, in 1892, strikers fought a pitched battle with armed guards. Strikers won the battle but lost the strike. In 1894 a strike in the Pullman works, south of Chicago, spread to the railroads entering Chicago and traffic was at a standstill. In spite of Governor Altgeld's insistence that there was no problem of order beyond the ability of the local police and the militia to deal with it, President Cleveland took the ground that the passage of the mails was being interfered with and sent Federal troops to Chicago. This was followed by a sweeping injunction denying the right to strike and the strikers gave up. Eugene Debs, the head of the American Railway Union which had sponsored the strike, was sentenced to prison for a year.

This was not the first time that Federal troops had been used to suppress strike disorder as both Baltimore and Pittsburgh had witnessed such a step in the railroad strikes of the seventies, but the citing of the Sherman Antitrust Act as the government's authority for the procedure followed in the issuance of the injunction, contempt of which was the ground for Debs' conviction, offered a new and unexplored extension of governmental power. The decision of Judge Woods, of the Federal Circuit Court for the Northern District of Illinois, contained an admission that the original design of the act was to suppress trusts and monopolies, but justified the ruling against Debs for the reason that the Congress had failed to add a clause to the law specifically exempting labor unions from its control and found a loophole in the words "or otherwise" in the description of the combinations prohibited. It may or may not have been good law, but the immediate result was to provide labor advocates with proof for the growing belief that government was an agency in behalf of organized capital.

Tempers were already high because of the wide unemployment caused by the depression of 1893. The same year had seen the repeal of the Silver Purchase Act, spelling disaster in the minds of the farmers who were demanding inflation rather than restriction of the currency. A run on the Treasury stock of gold had forced the administration to float an issue of bonds through the banking firm of J. P. Morgan & Co. without competitive bidding. President Cleveland defended his action on the ground of urgent and immediate need to relieve the Treasury. An income tax measure adopted in 1894 was speedily held unconstitutional by the Supreme Court.

This array of evidence that neither farmer nor laborer need hope for help or understanding from Washington destroyed what little confidence might still remain of help from the existing parties. If political action was to be taken it must be through a new party. The Populist party was the farmers' answer. The Populists opened their campaign in the congressional elections of 1890, when, without a formal national organization, they were able to take over the Democratic party in a few Southern states and to attract serious Democratic attention in the West. The year 1892 saw them in the field with a presidential candidate in the person of James B. Weaver of Iowa, a respectable but unimpressive figure in agrarian reform. In spite of an unexciting campaign Weaver received more than a million votes and twenty-two electors. The preamble of the Populist platform that year was a passionate denunciation of those whom they held responsible for the widespread depression, destitution, and corruption.

> The newspapers are largely subsidized or muzzled, public opinion silenced, business prostrated, homes covered with mortgages, labor impoverished, and the land concentrating in the hands of capitalists. The urban workmen are denied the right to organize for self-protection, imported pauperized labor beats down their wages, a hireling standing army, unrecognized by our laws, is established to shoot them down, and they are rapidly degenerating into European conditions. The fruits of the toil of millions are boldly stolen to build up colossal fortunes for a few, unprecedented in the history of mankind; and the possessors of these, in turn, despise the Republic and endanger

liberty. From the same prolific womb of governmental injustice we breed the two great classes—tramps and millionaires.

Readers unfamiliar with the emotional heat generated in American political campaigns might well have viewed this as a prelude to a demand for the violent overthrow of the government which produced nothing but millionaires and tramps, but the specific demands which followed were tame by contrast: first, of course, the free and unlimited coinage of silver and gold at the ratio of sixteen to one. The amount of money in circulation should be increased to a minimum of fifty dollars per capita. (It had previously been declared to be something less than half of that amount.) Other planks in the platform were: a graduated income tax; government ownership and operation of railroads, telegraphs, and telephones; ownership of land to be restricted to actual settlers, aliens being barred; a subtreasury plan for the issuance of money to take the place of the privately owned national banks, the adoption of the initiative and referendum; single term for President and Vice-President; direct election of United States senators; no subsidy or other forms of aid to any private corporation for any purpose.

The specific demands of the Populists dealt mostly with matters that were legitimate political concerns, the currency, taxation, land, banks, the relation of government to corporations. Laws concerning such subjects were already on the statute books, both state and federal, and more had been proposed. The only weapon urged by the Populists for gaining control of the government was the ballot. The nearest thing to revolution planned in the platform was the overthrow of the old parties who were charged with ignoring or betraying the interests of farmers and laborers. Legitimate as were both demands and methods, the conservative East took fright and shrieked of mob violence and anarchy. The language of some of the Populist leaders in the years from 1892 to 1896 increased the alarm. Mary Ellen Lease, in Kansas, called on the farmers to raise less corn and more hell, at least a form of crop restriction. Governor Waite of Colorado announced that it was better for the farmers to "ride through blood to their bridle bits" than to lose their fundamental liberties. Then there were "Sockless" Jerry Simpson and "Pitchfork" Ben Tillman, whose nicknames are indicative of a new tenor in American politics.

It was a period of new names as well as of wild and often unrestrained declamation. Ignatius Donnelly, of Minnesota, poet, philosopher, literary adventurer, discoverer of the lost Atlantis, Baconian enthusiast, reformer and dreamer; Tom Watson of Georgia, writer of history and philosophical idealist, whose life of Napoleon is far from being the worst that was ever written; "Coin" Harvey, author of *Coin's Financial School,* probably the greatest piece of political propaganda ever published in the United States—these were only a few of the names that were supposed to be on the proscribed lists of the plutocratic despots of the East.

The campaign of 1896, "the" free-silver campaign, was the top level performance of this political melodrama that was being played with such strident seriousness in the nineties. What made it notable was the figure and the eloquence of one man, William Jennings Bryan, of Nebraska, "the boy orator of the Platte." The fireworks were set off by the Democratic convention of that summer. In the congressional elections of 1894, Populist gains had been made largely at the cost of Democratic losses. As 1896 approached, the Democrats found themselves facing a party split. The free-silver adherents insisted that they and they alone held the formula for the salvation of the Democratic party. The Republican leaders were jubilant at the prospect and in their convention nominated William McKinley of Ohio, author of the McKinley tariff, an old soldier, and a protégé of Mark Hanna, Ohio industrialist and a new and powerful figure on the Republican side. Under Hanna's ruthless control the platform declared unequivocally for protection, "as the bulwark of American industrial independence and the foundation of American development and prosperity." On the currency question they played it as safe as they dared, opposing the free coinage of silver "except by international agreement with the leading commercial nations of the earth, which agreement we pledge ourselves to promote." Western delegates refused to be satisfied with this political double talk, and Senator Teller of Colorado, lifelong Republican, walked out of the convention followed by twenty-two other delegates.

Three weeks later the Democrats met in Chicago. Their problem was more difficult than that of the Republicans and they were without powerful and acceptable leadership. Bryan and "Silver Dick" Bland of Missouri had been able to prevent a wholesale switch of dissatisfied Westerners to the Populists, but there was wide disagreement on the choice of a candidate. The big moment came in a disorderly discussion of the currency plank of the platform. Hill of New York and Russell of Massachusetts were determined to fight to the last for at least a modification of the "free and equal" plank which the silver bloc demanded. The convention was in an uproar. Tempers were high and heat and weariness combined to make a deadlock likely when Bryan took the speaker's stand. What followed was the famous "Cross of Gold" speech, hailed by his followers as a clarion call to victory and by the opposition as sacrilegious drivel. Most of the criticism, as well as much of the praise, centered on the peroration: "You shall not press down upon the brow of labor this crown of thorns; you shall not crucify mankind upon a cross of gold."

Bryan had been a college orator at Illinois College and his phrases were in the pattern of the college oratory of that time. The general content of his speech was material that was familiar to political leaders large and small, the plight of the farmer and his helplessness in the grasp of the powerful interests. "Upon which side will the Democratic party fight; upon the side of the 'idle holders of idle capital' or upon the side of the struggling masses." His nomination followed almost as a matter of course. The issues of the campaign were set.

The Populist convention which also nominated Bryan was an anticlimax by contrast, although a slight variety was offered by the nomination of Watson of Georgia for Vice-President instead of Sewell, a Maine shipbuilder, whom the Democrats had chosen for the second place. Bryan had sought in his famous speech and throughtout his campaign to enlist the support of labor on the Democratic side, but with indifferent success. The basic issue was agrarian versus industrial, debtor versus creditor, the West (and South) versus the East. The old East-West conflict had appeared again.

As the convention had been Bryan's in the outcome, so was the campaign. Democratic party funds were low and speakers were largely unskilled amateurs, with here and there an unimportant exception. The speeches that counted were Bryan's, sometimes ten or twelve a day. With amazing vitality and persistence he stormed from end to end of the country, holding his supporters spellbound and compelling even hostile crowds to at least listen to him. In the final count he had 6,467,946 popular votes to McKinley's 7,035,638, and 176 electors to 271. The eastern half of the country heaved a sigh of relief. The great heresy had been crushed, the country was safe again. In reality the campaign of 1896 was a beginning, not an end.

Two years after the free-silver campaign the front-page news that held the attention of the American people was the war with Spain. As a military performance it was neither important nor glorious, in spite of much fervid oratory and waving of banners. Our discussions with Spain over the sinking of the battleship *Maine* in Havana harbor had approached the point of peaceful settlement. Spain had agreed in substance to our terms, to the great disappointment of the newly powerful and highly vocal "yellow" press, when President McKinley, suddenly and without adequate explanation, asked the Congress for a declaration of war. The fighting lasted less than three months, but the end of it found the United States in an entirely new and unexpected relationship with the rest of the world and facing governmental problems for which we were without preparation or understanding. Throughout our history we had proceeded on the tacit assumption that our natural territorial expansion was within the continental and hence contiguous area. Just after the Civil War there had been abortive attempts to acquire certain West Indian islands which had failed to arouse perceptible political interest at home. The overwhelming, if implicit, opinion was that the last paragraph in the chronicle of our territorial growth had been written with the Oregon and the Guadalupe Hidalgo treaties in Polk's administration. To be sure we had bought Alaska from Russia in 1867, but that was Seward's "folly," and Seward had also annexed Midway Island.

The ending of the war with Spain found us holding Cuba and Puerto Rico in the Caribbean and the Philippines in the Asiatic waters of the Pacific. The summer of 1898 also found Hawaii in our hands, although not as a result of war. In the midst of wild talk about "manifest destiny," "cosmic law," "the white man's burden," "world power," "imperialism," and the like, one clear, cold question demanded an answer. What were these new possessions? In the case of Hawaii this was easy. Call it a territory and let it go at that, and in due course this was done, to the satisfaction of the American commercial interests there. In the case of Cuba we had made our purpose clear from the outset, it was to effect the liberation of the island from Spanish misrule and to aid in the establishment of independent government there. Guam, five thousand miles from the Pacific Coast, became a naval base, another hint of our longer vision.

But what about the Philippines and Puerto Rico? Apparently neither the Cuban nor the Hawaiian expedients applied here. Our problem in the Philippines was further complicated by our belated discovery that in paying Spain $20,000,000 for her shadowy hold on the islands we had also bought the Spanish end of a rebellion led by Emilio Aguinaldo. The suppression of this movement lasted until 1902 and cost about as much as the war with Spain and when it was accomplished we still had the Philippines, and the question of the disposition of the islands was still unanswered. After wearying and unsatisfactory experiments with military government, followed by fair to good civil governments, promises of "ultimate independence," made, postponed, sometimes broken, the Hawes-Cutting Act in 1933 made a definite assurance of independence after a probationary period of ten years. The last act, as of this writing, was the granting of "complete" independence after the defeat of Japan in World War II. Responsibilities and problems, however, are not so easily disposed of.

Now how about Puerto Rico? We had no provision for colonies in our laws or our history. Territorial status was promptly rejected as unworkable, at the least, and leading toward the embarrassing question of ultimate statehood. It was easy to coin a phrase, "insular possession," but what did that mean? A negative answer was given by the Supreme Court in the case of *Downes* v. *Bidwell* in 1901. In the majority opinion in that case, Associate Justice Brown held that "the Island of Puerto Rico is a territory appurtenant and belonging to the United States, but not a part of the United States within the revenue clauses of the Constitution." At least we knew what Puerto Rico was not, it was not within the tariff wall which sheltered the rest of the United States. Peter Dunne summed it up caustically in Mr. Dooley's comment to his perennial customer and stooge Hennessy, "the Constitootion follys the flag, but the Soopreme Court follys the eliction returns." Evidently "World Power" sounded impressive in Congress, but it was much easier to say it than to be it.

The campaign of 1896 had demonstrated one important fact which the American people had been in danger of forgetting in the period of political mediocrity, obliquity, and iniquity which followed the Civil War: campaigns need not be dull sham battles. The silver war had been lively, at least, and it had been serious. The choice of free silver as the words to be inscribed on the banner of the crusaders was a queer one to the academic economists for whom the nature and function of money was a highly technical and complex subject that only economists and bankers could understand. But the followers of Bryan made it a symbol of righteousness and justice, whose luster was not dimmed by the frequently mentioned fact that free silver was also to the interest of owners of silver mines. The function of money was spelled out for them in simple terms in the pages of *Coin's Financial School*, and hundreds of thousands of copies were circulated during the campaign. Every zealot was both learner and teacher and any streetcorner or crossroads debate was bound to produce at least one expert.

The farmers were not so foolish as the Easterners thought. They knew whose ox was gored and they knew the disproportion in bushels of wheat between the dollars they borrowed and those they repaid to the bankers. When they counted the money remaining in their pockets at the end of the year they were painfully aware that not enough money had circulated in their direction. The conclusion was obvious: more money and of a kind that was not so easily controlled by somebody else in his own interest. That spelled silver. They fell short of victory but no near adult who lived through those hot, hectic months of the summer of 1896 could ever again think that a campaign was an exercise in shadowboxing with an obligato of rhetoric or that government didn't matter. That year threw a long shadow which fell on the future, not the past.

The same candidates appeared in 1900, but the war, the discovery of gold in Alaska, and a rise in farm prices dulled the arguments. McKinley increased his popular majority to nearly a million. This time it was the Vice-Presidency that was important, as the immediate future was to prove. Theodore Roosevelt had been colonel of the Rough Riders, a picturesque volunteer cavalry regiment made up of frontier sheriffs, exdeputy United States marshals, college athletes, soldiers of fortunes, big game hunters—picked men all of them. They could all ride and shoot, they craved action, and they hated drill. Their day of glory was at the battle of San Juan Hill outside Santiago, Cuba, where they performed creditably, although the hill up which they charged was not San Juan. Roosevelt had attracted attention as a police commissioner in New York City. He was the son of a well-to-do New York businessman, graduate of Harvard, for a short time a cattle rancher in North Dakota, and a restless, ambitious, and active political aspirant. As Assistant Secretary of the Navy when war was declared he had cabled the orders to Dewey, commander of our tiny Pacific squadron, to cut loose from Hong Kong and steam for Manila. Immediately after, Roosevelt resigned from his Washington post and set about the business of his Rough Riders.

After the end of the war he was elected governor of New York, and proceeded to make life so uncomfortable for the Republican bosses at Albany that they welcomed his nomination for the Vice-Presidency in 1900 as a nomination to obscurity. A lunatic with a revolver changed the course of events at Buffalo, New York, in September, 1901, when he fatally wounded the recently re-elected President. "That damned cowboy" was now President. Cowboy he might have been; he was also a man of means and family, an American aristocrat, in that respect a throwback to the days of Washington and Jefferson.

What kind of President would he be? His first message to Congress, December 3, 1901, began to give the answer. Early in the message he declared: "The old laws, and the old customs which had almost the binding force of law, were once quite sufficient to regulate the accumulation and distribution of wealth. Since the industrial changes which have so enormously increased the productive power of mankind, they are no longer sufficient." What was to be done about it? Much of the body of the message was devoted to an examination of the problem. At the center of it were the great corporations; care must be taken in dealing with them, but it was clear that the obligation of finding a way lay upon government.

> It is no limitation upon property rights or freedom of contract to require that when men receive from government the privilege of doing business under corporate form, which frees them from individual responsibility, and enables them to call into their enterprises the capital of the public, they shall do so upon absolutely truthful representations as to the value of the property in which the capital is to be invested. Corporations engaged in interstate commerce should be regulated if they are found to exercise a license working to the public injury. It should be as much the aim of those who seek for social betterment to rid the business world of crimes of cunning as to rid the entire body politic of crimes of violence. Great corporations exist only because they are created and safeguarded by our institutions; and it is therefore our right and our duty to see that they work in harmony with these institutions.

Here was cause for thought. Writers of wild books and impractical college professors could be ignored or laughed into obscurity, but this was the President speaking to Congress and asking that something be done about the concentration of wealth and the control of interstate commerce. No new philosophy of government was offered, and no amendment or new construction of the Constitution was suggested. Implicit in the message was the assumption that the President and Congress were competent to do whatever was needed in the protection and furtherance of the public interest. It was clear that the new man in the White House intended to make the executive a positive force in government and to seek from Congress whatever was needed in the way of additional statutory warrant.

It is not easy to appraise the exact meaning and worth of the seven-and-a-half-year regime of this first Roosevelt. To his contemporaries he was many things, hero, traitor, peerless leader, crusader for anarchy, savior of the country, enemy of the republic. Young idealists applauded him and flocked to his support. Industrial leaders and financial tycoons hated him and old guard Republicans charged him with the betrayal of the Grand Old Party. In reality he was neither complex in his purposes nor subtle in his techniques. One observer and chronicler called him the "Apostle of the Obvious." At bottom he saw himself as a moral leader calling his people to righteousness. The necessary steps were simple and forthright, easily stated and requiring only courage and determination for the taking. His interests were broad as the country and his friendships many and diverse. He was a party man and a firm Republican. He hated Democrats as much as old guard Republicans hated him. He was an emotional nationalist, given to waving the flag on appropriate occasions, superficial and dogmatic in his thinking, impulsive in his manner, but generally cautious in his acts. Two terms which cannot be applied to him with any justification are "radical" and "thoughtful," although he read widely and talked much with many men. His administration can best be understood as a series of assertions of executive power. In that respect his nearest peacetime model in the White House was Andrew Jackson. Lincoln's acts had reflected the warrant and justification of war. Since that time only Cleveland had made of the presidency anything more than an aloof and neutral force. Even here "T.R." was more guarded and cautious than his critics were willing to admit.

His first large assertion of power was in demanding that the anthracite coal miners and the mineowners bring an end to a long and vexing strike in 1902 by submitting their cases to a board of arbitrators. This the head of the miners' union, John Mitchell, promptly agreed to do. George F. Baer, president of the Philadelphia & Reading R.R., one of the big mineowners, solemnly declared that these great interests should be left in the hands of those to whom God in His wisdom had consigned them. This was *laissez faire* with a blessing attached but, on J. P. Morgan's "advice," the mineowners agreed to arbitrate and the strike was settled, without further political or theological discussion.

As police commissioner in New York, T.R. had refused to acknowledge any distinction between good and bad laws. If a law was on the statute books it was to be enforced. The Antitrust Act had been on the books more than ten years when he became President, with no attempt at enforcement. If corporations were exercising "a license working to the public injury," here was the rod for their chastisement. A prominent victim presented itself in 1901 in the case of the Northern Securities Company. This was a holding company combination of competing railroads commonly known as Hill-Morgan and Harriman lines, the Great Northern, Northern Pacific, Southern Pacific, and Burlington. Suit was brought and, in 1904, a decision was handed down ordering the company dissolved. Encouraged by this success the Department of Justice brought suit against a number of similar combinations, including the American Tobacco Company, the meat packers and a combination of fertilizer manufacturers. In most cases a decision favorable to the government was secured, but the results seemed curiously disappointing. Reorganization produced little change in the economic landscape and the control of the machinery of production remained in the same hands as before.[1]

Perhaps the Sherman Act had oversimplified the legal problem. Certainly additional legislation was needed if railroad rates were to be under any kind of governmental control. The practice of rebating to favored shippers had spread widely since the early days of Standard Oil, and the railroads themselves were beginning to groan under the burden of it. In 1903 the Elkins Act, prohibiting variations from the published rates, was passed and, in 1906, the Hepburn Act gave the Interstate Commerce Commission power to establish maximum rates. Protesting roads had the right of appeal to the federal courts, but the burden of proof lay on them and not on the Commission. Four years later this was extended to telegraph and telephone lines and to various activities associated with interstate commerce, such as express and sleeping-car companies, pipe lines, and storage warehouses and other terminal facilities.

It was at least a change in the form of political action from outright prohibition and dissolution to continuing regulation. Government was beginning to tell business how far it could go and to some extent in what manner. Another expression of this was in the passage of the first pure food and drugs act in 1906. The poisoned food scandals of Spanish-American War times had caused an outcry against the meat packers, highlighted by Upton Sinclair's *The Jungle,* a sensational novel portraying conditions in the packing houses and in the homes of the employees in the "packing house district" of Chicago. The use of food adulterants and preservatives was quite general, according to Dr. Wiley, chief chemist of the Department of Agriculture. A series of articles by Samuel Hopkins Adams in *Collier's Weekly* had exposed the use

[1] Readers will find a more detailed discussion of some of these and other cases in Chapter XIII.

of dangerous drugs in patent medicines and the making of misleading and fraudulent claims on labels and in advertising. Later legislation was necessary to give the 1906 law full force and effect, but the right of federal inspection and prohibition had been established.

The most lasting mark made by T.R. was in the conservation of our national resources. The need was great. Forests were being cut away at a suicidal rate, soil was being eroded, the national domain set aside for forests or parks had been invaded by cattle and mining interests. State action had been limited and generally ineffective. The problem, while basically Western, was broader than the boundaries of any state. The President had the advantage of a wider acquaintance with the West than had been possessed by any previous President. He proceeded promptly under a law passed in 1891 to set aside some 150,000,000 acres of government land as a forest reserve and withdrew more than half as much more from public entry for detailed survey and study. An inland waterways commission was established for thorough study of river, forest, and soil problems with particular reference to the development of water power. The high spot of his campaigning for the conservation of our national wealth was the conservation conference of governors, members of the cabinet, judges, and prominent citizens, at the White House. The immediate effect was to call wide attention and give high prestige to the whole movement. Twenty years earlier a President would have sent a message of welcome and best wishes to such a gathering. This President called the meeting and sat in on the discussions.

In this brief treatment of the "Age of Roosevelt" I can do little more than touch a few instances by way of illustration. Much must be omitted when the purpose is to indicate the particular thread that is beginning to appear in the national tapestry. For example, a new cabinet post was created in 1903, that of Commerce and Labor. Not much was heard from it for several years but the name was symptomatic of a new purpose and point of view in government. It must not be assumed that the national government stood alone in this search for new ways and results. Ferment was stirring in states and cities as well, and it was in some of these rather than in the White House that a new attitude toward government appeared and was given a name. That was "Progressivism."

Progress was not a new idea in American thinking. We had taken it for granted from the beginning of our national history, but it was regarded as automatic, inherent in our character, our geographical position, and our resources. Providence had selected this land and people for a new and higher civilization, a model and a beacon light for the rest of the world. Serious doubts had appeared as to the automatic operation of progress. It was still possible, but it was not inevitable. Human beings must do something to bring it about. As Herbert Croly put it in his *Promise of American Life*, the full realization of our potentiality required the substitution of national purpose for national promise. To accomplish this, more was needed than a call from the White House to "hit the line hard." Righteousness was not enough. Yankee traders had proved long before that extreme piety and exorbitant profits could go hand in hand.

To define and understand Progressivism it is necessary to examine the record again. True to their traditions, the American people were more concerned with things than with theories. The growth of industry and of cities had brought a by-product of inefficiency and corruption in city and state governments, much more marked than in Washington. Old political machinery and techniques were inadequate for the needed work, the cleaning up or out of slums, the cleaning of streets, the improvement of school facilities, the control and eradication of the conditions that breed disease and degeneration. Such public improvements as had been attempted in the past were regarded quite as often as opportunities for private profit as for public benefit.

In cities and states, cliques and bosses held control. Charges were made that the machinery of nominations and elections was too cumbersome and antiquated to be of effective use in turning the rascals out. The rascals controlled the machine by which they could be overthrown and democracy was breaking down at its most vital point, the ballot. Party conventions had ceased to be more than the announcing of a "slate" previously prepared, and the act of voting was merely a choice between rascals. Popular illustration was the manner of electing United States senators. State legislators were more easily "controlled" than the voting mass. As a result the Senate had become known as a rich men's club, and senators represented the predominant business interests of their states rather than the general interest. In widely separated states— Wisconsin, Oregon, Iowa, California, Michigan, North Carolina, Ohio—leaders appeared to demand that the voters reassert their sovereignty and that laws and methods be changed to permit a freer channeling of the popular will to legislative and administrative bodies. Their names belong in the list of founders of Progressivism, LaFollette in Wisconsin, Cummins in Iowa, Hiram Johnson in California, Golden Rule Jones and Tom Johnson in Ohio, Hazen Pingree in Michigan, Folk in Missouri. These are only a few.

Methods and targets varied with the states. Robert LaFollette made of Wisconsin a political and social laboratory, with a state railroad commission, a sweeping reform of an old and inequitable tax system, and a state industrial commission. An alumnus of the state university he demanded that it place itself more closely and effectively at the service of the state as a center and testing ground for social and political study and experiment. In California, Hiram Johnson centered his fire on the Southern Pacific Railroad empire. Folk in Missouri and Cummins in Iowa demanded the emancipation of the state government from corporate domination.

On the political side the proposed reforms began to fall into definite patterns, direct primaries for the nomination of candidates, a constitutional amendment to permit the direct election of United States senators, and the right of initiative, referendum, and recall. These changes had a common purpose, to make the popular will more immediately and effectively felt. Adoption of these proposals was uneven in time and degree. Direct primaries spread through the states and are now standard procedure, with rather unsatisfactory results due to the lack of wide participation by the voters. The amendment for the direct election of senators was ratified finally, in May, 1913. Initiative, referendum, and recall have been adopted, in whole or part, by many states. These also have disappointed the hopes of their supporters. The right of initiative, which has been the one most widely used, has been too often the means of clogging the ballot with unimportant, obscure, or selfish proposals, confusing and annoying the voters out of all proportion to the positive aid afforded. The referendum has been less used and therefore less subject to criticism as to the type of question offered. The recall has found little actual use or support, except for occasional employment against local and city officers.

Municipal reform followed somewhat different roads. City governments were outmoded in form and unable to deal with the results of congestion of population and multiplication of necessary services, transportation, sanitation, lighting, water supply, housing, paving, police. Milwaukee, Toledo, and Cleveland set about cleaning house and making government more adequate to its problems, but it was a hurricane that produced the most drastic results. In 1900, Galveston, Texas, was devastated by a tropical storm with appalling loss of life and property. To deal with the chaos that followed the storm, a commission of prominent, energetic citizens took charge in such an effective manner that, when the emergency passed, Galveston asked the commission to continue as the city government.

Other cities noted the good effects in Galveston and followed the example, sometimes with excellent results. A shining instance was Cincinnati, Ohio, which, under the old boss-ridden mayor and city council system, had been one of the worst, now became one of the best. Graft disappeared, streets became clean, bridges, schools, and other public buildings that were worth what they cost appeared. The secret lay in a combination of expert direction of city activities—police, public health, education, construction—with centralization of power and responsibility under a commission elected on a nonpartisan basis, with a city manager as coordinating center.

The plan lacked the familiar democratic look of councilmen elected by wards or districts, an elected mayor, and local department heads, but it was streamlined—and it worked. The expert had arrived in government to stay, and the dust of Andrew Jackson stirred uneasily in Tennessee earth. Most large cities still cling to modern versions of city council and elected mayor with varying success, but the city-manager plan has become almost standard practice in smaller towns, even in communities of five or six thousand. It is at least a way of handling the highly complicated activities of a modern municipality requiring expert knowledge and training that is vastly superior to the old method of rewarding party service at the expense of the community, but if it is democracy it is the democracy of business rather than of politics. Whatever it is, pragmatic Americans like it and city government has improved.

The clearest index of a change in social and political thinking was the appearance of humanitarian ideas in legislative action and in judicial decisions. Human betterment had not been ignored by Americans in the past for all their material aims and growth. The period from 1820 to 1850 had been productive of many organizations and formulas for improving the lives of individuals, including the socialistic, communistic, religious, cooperative, vaguely idealistic, and those seeking to withdraw from society rather than to change it except by example. None of them had set landmarks by which a course might be found later. After the Civil War the ideas of Herbert Spencer and Charles Darwin, as interpreted by William Graham Sumner, had strengthened the native tendency to individualism of thought and action. Poverty was the natural proper result of indolence and incompetence, an incidental item in the bill of costs that progress demanded. Sumner's famous essay, *The Forgotten Man,* was widely read and highly approved, especially by those who had profited in the struggle. The man who was in danger of being forgotten, said Professor Sumner, was the taxpayer who was being asked to reward the poor and lazy for their lack of thrift.

Andrew Carnegie, keenly aware of the growing criticism of the inequality in the distribution of wealth, had come forward with his doctrine of the stewardship of wealth. "He who dies rich dies disgraced" was a good newspaper headline, difficult to interpret to a worker in the steel mills, particularly at Homestead. It was observed, too, that his great gifts to a bewildering variety of causes failed to benefit the millions who felt themselves overworked, underpaid, and badly housed, and that for all his giving he remained a wealthy man. To be sure it was an acknowledgment of social responsibility, but individual and isolated, failing to reach the underprivileged and distressed. The responsibility that the new humanitarianism stressed was of society itself to those of its members who were unable to help themselves.

Led by Jacob Riis, whose book *How the Other Half Lives* had attracted wide attention to city slums, interest and criticism spread. Such settlement workers as Jane Addams, head of Chicago's Hull House, and workers in charity organizations added proof of the dangers inherent in congested living quarters; disease, crime, degeneracy, delinquency were the evil fruits of such conditions. Since society must pay the ultimate costs of crime, disease, and deterioration, why not alter the conditions? Theodore Roosevelt, as governor of New York, appointed a tenement-house commission to investigate and make recommendations for action. The result was the model tenement law of 1901 which compelled radical changes in construction and led to the clearing away of rookeries that were impossible to change. A state had accepted responsibility for the conditions under which human beings are compelled to live.

A clearer invasion of this new domain was the passage of state laws limiting the hours or other conditions of labor in particular industries. As early as 1898 a case reached the Supreme Court involving a law passed by the legislature of Utah limiting the hours of work in mines and smelters. The defense had appealed to the Fourteenth Amendment and had also argued that the law interfered with the worker's right of free contract. In his decision Associate Justice Brown made significant assertion of the right of the state to protect the worker against himself.[2]

This decision was far from settling the question of the limitations of the police power of the state in the regulation of hours and conditions of work. In 1905 the Court decided another case, *Lochner* v. *New York*.[3] The case dealt with the right of the state to limit the hours of work in bakeries to sixty per week or ten per day. In the prevailing decision Associate Justice Peckham held against the law as a violation of "the right of the individual to liberty of person and freedom of contract."

Still another case involving hours of labor, this time from Oregon, reached the Supreme Court in 1908. The Oregon law had prohibited the employment of women in factory or

[2] *Holden* v. *Hardy*, 169 U.S. 366.
[3] *Lochner* v. *New York*, 198 U.S. 45.

laundry for more than ten hours a day. In arguing the case counsel for the plaintiff, alleging error in the trial court, had appealed to the decision in *Lochner* v. *New York* as a determining precedent. The Supreme Court rejected this plea and sustained the law on the ground of structural and functional differences between the sexes. The right of the state to enact laws for the protection of women was defined by Associate Justice Brewer in the majority decision: "Differentiated by these matters from the other sex, she is properly placed in a class by herself, and legislation designed for her protection may be sustained even when like legislation is not necessary for men, and could not be sustained." [4]

There were other signs and portents of a change in the attitude of government toward the general welfare, indicating a doubt of the old faith in the automatic spread of prosperity and progress as inevitable by-products of material growth. Social workers called attention to the increase of juvenile delinquency and traced it to the slum quarters in which families were living. Under English common law little or no distinction had been made between children and adults in their responsibility for crime. As late as 1894 the penal code of New York declared that children over seven were capable of crime and over fourteen were fully responsible under the law. They were tried in the same courts as adults and confined in the same jails.

Illinois made a beginning in 1899 by setting up a special children's court. Judge Ben Lindsey of the juvenile court in Denver, established soon after, attracted wide attention by his articles and books on the problem of juvenile delinquents. State legislatures, under increasing pressure, raised minimum work ages in spite of opposition which argued that such action destroyed the authority of the family and denied to youth the early opportunity to acquire habits of industry and thrift. The fact that this legislation cut off a considerable

[4] *Muller* v. *Oregon*, 208 U.S. 412.

supply of low-cost labor in certain industries, notably the textile, was not stressed by the opposition. During the Taft administration, Congress authorized the establishment of a federal Children's Bureau. Miss Julia Lathrop, long associated with Jane Addams at Hull House, was the first head.

A small but devoted group of women had been agitating for woman suffrage and equality of legal rights with men from the time of the Seneca Falls Declaration in 1848 and had gained considerable support in spite of a steady barrage of abuse and occasional violence. Women had played a prominent part in the social-reform movements and state action had improved woman's status by removing many of the civil liabilities, as well as giving her more protection in industry. Her right to an equal educational opportunity with men was generally recognized, although this was done unevenly and grudgingly in the professional fields. Women as doctors or lawyers were still regarded as unusual if not eccentric phenomena. State universities admitted her on equal terms with men and coeducation was a commonplace in colleges, especially outside of the Atlantic seaboard. Full equality was still in the future, but the leaven was working.

The political emancipation of the sex began in the newer states, particularly in those where women were taking an active part in public affairs. Wyoming, Idaho, Utah, and Colorado had given women the vote before the turn of the century and by 1912 nine states, all west of the Mississippi, had adopted woman suffrage amendments. Until the adoption of the Nineteenth Amendment in 1920 these states illustrated one of the curious paradoxes of our system, the exercise by state authorization of a share in national affairs by a large portion of the population implicitly denied the suffrage by the national government. The inability of the founders to agree on the qualifications for voting in 1787 spelled opportunity for women a hundred and twenty-five years later. Democracy was making another experiment. The laboratory was still working.

The administration of President Taft has an unhappy and at least partly undeserved reputation in many minds. Handpicked by T.R. as his successor, a highly useful governor-general of the Philippines, an able member of the Cabinet, he was highly rated as a judicial-minded administrator, and much was expected of him as President. Two events marred his record, his support of the Payne-Aldrich tariff bill increasing duties when reductions had been promised, and a disgraceful squabble between Gifford Pinchot, head of the Forestry Bureau, and R. A. Ballinger, Secretary of Interior. The President permitted it to grow to the proportions of a national scandal before he ended it by the dismissal of Pinchot and the alienation of Roosevelt and his followers.

On the other hand, a good case can be made for the claim made on behalf of Taft that he had faithfully carried on the Progressivism of his predecessor. The Sixteenth Amendment permitting an income tax was ratified, the Department of Commerce and Labor was divided, parcel post and postal savings banks were created, publicity for individual campaign expenditures was required by law, and second- and third-class postmasters were transferred to the merit class, prohibiting removal for political reasons. How much the President was responsible for these improvements is uncertain, but his signature was on the bills.

President Taft's prime fault was a lack of political skill and understanding. Admirably suited to the prescribed tasks of an administrative or judicial post, as he abundantly demonstrated, he was ill at ease in the give and take of politics. His failure illustrates a widely held fallacy, the belief that the function of a President is that of an administrator, as that term is understood in the business world. The business of governing is political business. The end products are good will and human welfare, not profits. Lincoln's phrase, "of the people, by the people, for the people," cannot be forgotten with safety.

The campaign of 1912 was exciting, with a rump convention nominating T.R. as the candidate of the Progressive (Bull Moose) party. The inevitable result was the election of the Democratic nominee, Woodrow Wilson, former president of Princeton and lately governor of New Jersey, by a plurality of 2,160,000 over Roosevelt, who had a lead over Taft of more than 600,000. The next act in the progressive drama had begun, but the family quarrel in the Republican party had given the star parts to the Democrats.

It can be said of the new President that he came nearer to stating a philosophy of Progressivism than anyone else in responsible position has yet done. He was admirably adapted for this task. Intellectually superior to any President before or since except Jefferson, he had spent his previous active years in the study and teaching of political history and theory. The titles of his books, *History of the American People, The State, Congressional Government,* and *Constitutional Government in the United States,* are indicative of his interests. It was known of him that he inclined to the Hamiltonian concept of government and, like Hamilton, was an admirer of the English parliamentary system. As governor of New Jersey he had been a liberal and had fought the corporate-political alliance. His birth and background were Southern and Bryan's support in the convention that nominated him put him under obligation to the Bryan wing of the party. What did this add up to, if anything? Part of the answer was in his cabinet appointments—Bryan as Secretary of State and Josephus Daniels, a newspaper editor in Raleigh, North Carolina, as Secretary of the Navy—but beyond a willingness to recognize political obligations they revealed little.

In his inaugural address President Wilson declared that the purpose for which the nation sought to use the Democratic party was to "interpret a change in its own plans and point of view. Some old things with which we had grown familiar . . . have dropped their disguises and shown themselves alien and sinister. Some new things . . . have come to assume the aspect of things long believed in and familiar, stuff of our own convictions." He listed the items which were to be altered: tariff which had made the government "a facile instrument in the hands of private interests"; a banking and currency system "perfectly adapted to concentrating cash and credit"; an industrial system "which holds capital in leading strings, restricts the liberties and limits the opportunities of labor" and exploits our natural resources. He called attention to the neglect of agricultural interests both technically and financially, and charged the nation as a whole with failure to study the true cost or economy of production "as we should either as organizers of industry, as statesmen, or as individuals." The recurrent theme in the address and in other addresses later was the need of positive action by government to restore the freedom of opportunity and of action that we had lost sight of in the hurry and confusion of our stupendous growth. This he presented, not as a philosophical concept, but as a guide to political action. It was illuminative of his intentions and to that extent a philosophy of his Progressivism.

Only a year and five months of his eight years in the presidency can be searched for evidence in the purely domestic scene, but they were busy and fruitful years. The Underwood tariff did revise the tariff downward and increase the free list. It was not free trade, but it was freer. The Federal Reserve Act, passed in December, 1913, did provide a more elastic currency and establish federal control by a board made up of the Secretary of the Treasury and the Comptroller of the Currency and six other presidential appointees. Results have shown the wisdom of this act. The Federal Trade Commission was created to prevent improper trade and competitive practices, rather than to punish them afterward. The Clayton

Antitrust Act dealt in detail with monopolistic tendencies and prohibited interlocking directorates, a practice which had occupied much of the time of the Pujo Committee in 1912. Corporation officers were made personally responsible for violations, but this broke down when attempts were made to enforce it. In general the Clayton Act was the least effective of the major measures enacted in this brief period.

The implementation of the Wilsonian version of Progressivism was interrupted by European events. In June, 1914, an obscure Serbian student assassinated a superfluous Austrian grand duke and, on August 1, the stable, peaceful world that we thought we lived in fell apart. We do not yet know all the ways that war has changed us or the extent, but when we sought to return to the old ways of domestic interest after it was over we learned to our later sorrow that the world we thought we had helped to save was still at our elbow. The dreams of world power that had tickled our vanity after the Spanish-American episode had been supplanted by a grim and anything but pleasing reality.

Certain facts and implications emerge in a retrospective summary of the period from 1890 to 1914. The opening years are marked by a focusing of political attention on economic and social issues, of a sort previously unseen in political campaigns and action. The temper and change of the time were revolutionary, the proposals and platforms were in strict accordance with traditional American practice. It is worth noting that in one way and another the most important demands of the Populists were complied with, most of them before 1914. Only two constitutional amendments were required, the Sixteenth, Income Tax, and Seventeenth, Direct Election of Senators, and both of them were ratified in 1913, the closing year of the period.

The doctrine of *laissez faire* as the guiding star of governmental action had been dealt with roughly and a new concept had been advanced by Woodrow Wilson. This can be stated as a belief that in an industrialized and urbanized state political action is needed to make and keep men free. As a corollary to this the helplessness of the individual city dweller had been brought to light and his needs made a lever to bring about sweeping renovations and change in city governments. Social workers had cast grave doubts on the theories of Herbert Spencer, and the practice of twisting the evolutionary hypotheses of Charles Darwin for economic and social purposes had fallen into disrepute.

Outside of the cities the structure of the government was unchanged. Theodore Roosevelt had shown that a powerful President will exercise more power than a weak one, hardly a new discovery to those familiar with the administrations of Jefferson, Jackson, Polk, and Lincoln. Our foreign relations were unchanged in form, although we had found ourselves the somewhat embarrassed possessors of overseas areas for which we had no traditional name or place in our system. We had dug the Panama Canal, we had shaken the big stick at our neighbors to the South, and we had called for the Open Door in China. In spite of these outward glances, our interest was in ourselves, and our future, good or bad, lay within our unchanged continental boundaries. Our relations with Europe were friendly but wary. We were growing in wealth, power, and population and the restless millions of Asia were far away; we were willing to trade with them and to send missionaries and teachers to them, in times of flood or famine to contribute to their relief, but that was all. Our foreign policy could still be stated in the words of Jefferson at his first inaugural: "peace, commerce, and honest friendship with all nations, entangling alliances with none." We had no thought that a prolonged change was on the threshold.

CHAPTER XIII

New Wine in Old Legal Bottles
(D. R.)

THE DEVELOPMENT of new demands upon government to remedy economic ills and to rectify economic injustice produced a large crop of state and federal laws in the quarter century following the enactment of the Sherman Antitrust Act of 1890. The federal judges, custodians of the old bottles of constitutional law, were confronted with the difficult problem of determining what amount and variety of the new wine could be safely tolerated in the old containers and what must be rejected, else (in Biblical language) "the bottles break, and the wine runneth out, and the bottles perish."

Statutes enacted for the protection of manual workers raised profound issues of constitutional law. How far could a state go, in the exercise of its conceded "police power," to limit hours of labor or to prevent discrimination against unionized employees? Did such laws unduly limit the constitutional "liberty of contract" of both employers and employees? How far could the national government enforce such protections under its power to regulate interstate commerce?

The five to four decision in the famous Lochner case [1]

[1] *Lochner* v. *New York*, 198 U.S. 45.

laid down most clearly the pattern of thinking of the conservative and liberal judges. The majority opinion, by Justice Peckham rejected the contention that a limitation of hours of labor for bakers was a "health law." Their occupation, he wrote, "was not an unhealthy one to that degree which would authorize the legislature to interfere with the right to labor, and with the right of free contract on the part of the individual, either as employer or employee."

In the dissenting opinion of Justice Harlan (concurred in by Justices White and Day), and in the separate dissent of Justice Holmes, the error of a judicial reversal of a legislative judgment which was not unreasonable was vigorously asserted. Both opinions insisted that it was not for the Court to decide upon the soundness of any economic theory adopted by the lawmakers. As Justice Holmes put it: "I strongly believe that my agreement or disagreement has nothing to do with the right of a majority to embody their opinions in law."

Against the argument that under the Fourteenth Amendment the restriction upon hours of labor was a deprivation of liberty (of contract) "without due process of law," Holmes succinctly observed: "The Fourteenth Amendment does not enact Mr. Herbert Spencer's Social Statics." He continued:

> I think that the word "liberty" in the Fourteenth Amendment is perverted when it is held to prevent the natural outcome of a dominant opinion, unless it can be said, that a rational and fair man necessarily would admit that the statute proposed would infringe fundamental principles as they have been understood by the traditions of our people and our law. It does not need research to show that no such sweeping condemnation can be passed upon the statute before us.

This same division of opinion resulted in the judicial nullification of a federal law,[2] and then a state law,[3] both prohib-

[2] *Adair* v. *United States*, 208 U.S. 161
[3] *Coppage* v. *Kansas*, 236 U.S. 1.

iting discrimination by a railroad employer against union employees.

Many liberal commentators have expressed surprise that Justice Harlan, the forceful dissenter in the Lochner case should have written the "reactionary" opinion in the Adair case. This quality seems evident in his assertion that "employer and employee have equality of right," the one to hire and the other to quit work without let or hindrance. This is something like the "equal right" (made famous by Anatole France) of both rich and poor to sleep under bridges.

But, it is also plain that legal restraint upon either party's freedom to make, or refuse to make, a contract of employment is a far more serious curtailment of liberty than a mere regulation of working conditions. A farseeing judge might well envision the time when the exercise of unlimited legislative power would not only destroy private management control of private business, but also substitute political regulation of working conditions for collective bargaining by labor unions. It would be a grave decision, and perhaps, as Justice Harlan felt, a very bad decision, to sustain the power of government "to *compel* any person in the course of his business and *against his will* to accept or retain the personal services of another, or to *compel* any person, *against his will*, to perform personal services for another." [Italics ours.]

It provides an interesting footnote to the Adair case to report that, forty-one years afterward, the "reactionary" opinion of Justice Harlan was the main reliance of attorneys for the American Federation of Labor and the C.I.O. in seeking to have the Supreme Court declare state anti-closed-shop laws to be unconstitutional! In the interval, however, the Supreme Court (to quote its own language) "beginning at least as early as 1934" ... had "steadily rejected the due process philosophy enunciated in the Adair-Coppage line of cases." [4]

[4] *Lincoln Federal Labor Union* v. *Northwestern Iron & Metal Co.*, 335 U.S. 525.

In the Coppage case the Court had held that there could not be "one rule of liberty for the labor organization and its members and a different and more restrictive rule for employers." This doctrine did not disturb organized labor and its liberal friends so long as practically all "labor laws" were enacted to restrict the freedom of the employer and to enlarge the liberties of the employees. To our fathers it was, as to our sons it will be, "liberal" to approve of using political power to accomplish what we regard as "good" ends, and "reactionary" to oppose the granting or sanctioning of extreme political powers because of the likelihood (indeed almost the certainty) that they will be abused.

From the beginning of the controversy over judicial restriction of legislative power it should have been made plain that the difference between a strict construction of the Constitution and a broad construction was not a difference of conservative or liberal thought. Chief Justice Marshall, a Hamiltonian conservative, was a "broad" constructionist in sustaining large powers for the federal government, and a "strict" constructionist in restricting the powers of a state to modify a contract. Chief Justice Taney, a Jacksonian liberal, was a "strict" constructionist in limiting the powers of the federal government over slavery, and a "broad" constructionist in sustaining the powers of a state to modify property rights.

As the nation grew and economic controls by government were sought more and more by increasingly powerful segments of society, the "broad" constructionists tended to sanction wider and wider exercises of legislative power. They held that these were authorized by general grants, or by inherent or implied powers. Against these pressures the "strict" constructionists tended to insist stubbornly upon the absence of a *specific grant* of power to the federal government, or upon an *express denial* of federal power, or upon the limits of the legislative powers of either federal or state governments which were fixed by constitutional amendments forbidding either government to deprive a person of "life, liberty or property without due process of law."

The judicial transformation of this requirement of "due process of law" from a simple test as to whether the *procedure* in administering a law was arbitrary or traditionally fair, to a test as to whether the *substance* of a law was destructive of an essential liberty of contract or right of property, worked a gradual but profound change in the government of the United States. This change became apparent soon after the Fourteenth Amendment provided a basis for invalidating a regulatory state law on the ground that it deprived persons of property rights without "due process." Although in *Munn* v. *Illinois*[5] the majority opinion left property "devoted to public use" at the mercy of legislative destruction, the dissent of Justice Field expressed the oncoming doctrine that lawmakers were forbidden by the Constitution to deprive persons of the essential values of property just as they were likewise forbidden to deprive them of the essential values of life.

As this doctrine came to prevail, the authority of the judiciary to sustain or to nullify laws became a powerful factor in the operations and development of our government. When *Muller* v. *Oregon*,[6] sanctioning a state hours-of-labor law for women, was followed by *Bunting* v. *Oregon*[7] upholding a state hours-of-labor law for men, the Court appeared to have blessed the same exercise of state police power upon which it had frowned in the Lochner case. In the same period, federal laws were sustained as within the federal power to regulate commerce, in cases such as those involving the Pure Food Act, the White-Slave Traffic Act, Hours of Service Acts, Narcotics Acts and the Eight-Hour Day Act. Then came the stun-

---
[5] 94 U.S. 113 (1877).
[6] 208 U.S. 412.
[7] 243 U.S. 426.

ning decision in the famous Child Labor case [8] in which, despite the conceded power of Congress to regulate interstate commerce, the Court by five to four denied the power of Congress to forbid interstate transportation of the products of child labor.

Here was "strict" construction with a vengeance, because, since the act only forbade the transportation of child-labor products across state lines, it was a simple exercise of federal power to regulate what was plainly interstate commerce. The majority of the court was forced to base its decision on the "intent" and "effect" of the law, which was, in its view, to regulate by indirect coercion the working ages and hours of labor for children employed in "local" factories and mines. If the Congress could use its power to prevent interstate commerce in commodities unless they were produced under conditions approved by Congress, then, said the majority, "all freedom of commerce is at an end, and the power of the States over local matters may be eliminated, and thus our system of government be practically destroyed."

There were good grounds for the forebodings of the majority that the end of local government control of local business might follow the sustaining of an unlimited power of Congress to forbid interstate transportation of products, harmless in themselves, because of condemnable methods of production. Twenty-three years later when *Hammer* v. *Dagenhart* was formally overruled in the Darby case [9] the federal government was exercising the power to regulate practically all the terms and conditions of employment and the relations between employer and employee which it desired to regulate, in all the major trades and industries of the United States. State regulation of local business had shrunk from an independent power of local self-government to an almost com-

[8] *Hammer* v. *Dagenhart*, 247 U.S. 251.
[9] *U.S.* v. *Darby*, 312 U.S. 100.

plete subordination to federal regulation of all business, including agriculture.

The sharp dissent of four justices, voiced in the notable opinion of Justice Holmes in the Child Labor case is generally regarded as soundly based on a "broad" construction of the commerce clause in the Constitution. But this might also be regarded as a "strict" construction in that Justice Holmes relied on a specifically granted power, when he wrote that the Court had long "made it clear that the power to regulate commerce and other constitutional powers could not be cut down or qualified by the fact that it might interfere with the carrying out of the domestic policy of any State."

It was many years before the doctrine of the dissenting opinion became "the law of the land" and in the meantime not only were many federal laws nullified on the ground that they invaded the reserved powers of the states, but many state laws were nullified on the ground that they deprived persons of liberty of contract and rights of property "without due process of law." The period from 1910 to 1937 may well be regarded as the primary era of "judicial supremacy" in which every critical question regarding what laws could be enacted and enforced by federal or state governments waited upon a final decision by a majority of the justices of the Supreme Court of the United States.

On the answer to these questions, controls of commerce by government or by private monopolies, the protection of civil liberties, the rights and obligations of employers and employees, and other desperately important issues hung in the balance. The Constitution not only created a structure of government, but also imposed limitations on the governing power, primarily to protect individual freedom of action and to prevent oppressive uses of government force; and, secondarily, to avoid concentrations and centralizations of political power which would destroy the safeguards against tyranny which lay in the citizens' ability to watch and to control a localized government. But, in the primary era of "judicial supremacy" it became more and more evident that the Constitution was (in the language of Justice Hughes) "what the judges say it is." It also became clearer every year that more and more people disagreed with what a majority of the judges were saying.

The learned justices who voted to annul state and federal laws were conscientiously fearful of pouring so much new wine in old legal bottles. They feared the destruction of the containers. Justice McReynolds expressed this view in one of his somewhat emotional dissents, as early as 1919:

> Until now I had supposed that a man's liberty and property —with their essential incidents—were under the protection of our charter and not subordinate to whims or caprices or fanciful ideas of those who happen for the day to constitute the legislative majority. The contrary doctrine is revolutionary and leads straight toward destruction of our well-tried and successful system of government.

But Justice McReynolds was not among the persistent dissenters in the long line of cases in which federal and state laws were held unconstitutional during the period from 1920 to 1937. During this period the "strict" constructionists were definitely in the saddle. In Professor Bates' compilation [10] he enumerates nineteen federal laws nullified in the decade 1920–1930, which may be compared with two prior to the Civil War; thirteen from 1860–1880; ten from 1880–1900; and sixteen from 1900–1920.

In addition to these direct restraints of federal power mention should be made of the indirect restraints imposed by the constriction of federal powers which the Congress sought to exercise in various federal statutes.

After the Court had written the qualification of "reasonable" into the sweeping prohibition of any "restraint of

[10] *The Story of the Supreme Court* (1936).

trade," enacted in the Sherman Law,[11] the opinion in the case involving the United States Steel Corporation [12] largely subordinated executive enforcement of the antitrust laws to the economic views of the Court. The Congress then enacted the Clayton Antitrust Act in 1914 to provide for administrative regulation of "unfair competition" by the Federal Trade Commission, and also to exempt labor and farm organizations from prosecutions as monopolies, when pursuing their legitimate objects by lawful means. But, in a series of cases, the effectiveness of the Federal Trade Commission was so seriously impaired and the protections designed for labor unions so diluted, as to nullify to a considerable extent the intentions of the federal legislators.

Perhaps the outstanding example of the retrogressive views of the Court in this era, was given in the case [13] in which a majority held that the District of Columbia minimum-wage law for women was unconstitutional. In essence, the majority opinion reversed the Bunting case, of 1917, and revived the supposedly dead doctrine of the Lochner case, of 1905, over the amazed dissents of Chief Justice Taft and Justices Sanford and Holmes (Justice Brandeis not sitting, but obviously also in dissent). The Taft dissenting opinion and the biting criticisms of Holmes could not shake the majority of the Court, but they voiced a public opinion which was slowly gathering a force that would eventually compel the express overruling of the Adkins case by the Court (in 1937) as a measure of self-preservation,[14] as will be hereinafter explained.

But fourteen years must elapse before the political-economic predilections of the Supreme Court would cease to operate as a veto power upon the political-economic decisions of the Congress and state legislatures. In the meantime, the country was plunged into the worst depression of our his-

---

[11] *U.S.* v. *Standard Oil Co.,* 221 U.S. 1.
[12] *U.S.* v. *U.S. Steel Corporation,* 251 U.S. 417.
[13] *Adkins* v. *Childrens' Hospital,* 261 U.S. 525.
[14] *West Coast Hotel Co.* v. *Parrish,* 300 U.S. 379.

tory. As a result the popular demand that the government "do something" to relieve widespread privation and unemployment was rising to revolutionary intensity. The masses of citizens were no longer deeply concerned with the preservation of their constitutional freedom from government coercion. Individual rights to be free from "socialistic controls" became less important to unemployed workers and bankrupt farmers than their need for some concerted action to reorganize and regulate our economy so that all able and willing workers in the cities and on the farms might find it possible to earn a living, and so that the temporary victims of economic disasters might be relieved of intolerable distress.

The doctrines of *laisez faire,* of "rugged individualism," the arguments against government "paternalism," had little appeal to men and women struggling helplessly against forces beyond their control or understanding. What was government for if it could not protect its citizens against such a disorganization of an economic system upon which their ability to support themselves depended? Thus arose a political demand, essentially new in American thinking, that the national government must assume a responsibility for developing, as well as maintaining, an economic system under which all the people could enjoy "economic security."

It was obvious that the states separately could not meet this demand. They might offer local relief from localized misfortune. But they could not reorganize or develop a national economy. They could not separately establish a zone of "economic security" any more than one state bordering on the Mississippi could alone make itself secure from a devastating flood. The arteries and great veins of the nation carried interstate commerce, which must be a healthy, life-maintaining flow or the entire body would be diseased. Only the national government could regulate interstate commerce.

Thus the temper of the nation called upon the federal government to expand its operations, regardless of historic limitations upon its powers, and the inaugural demand of President Roosevelt for "action" was like a trumpet call announcing the arrival of an army of liberation at the gates of a besieged and starving city.

In the Supreme Court the black-robed guardians of the Constitution for a time sat apparently in intellectual and almost physical isolation from the masses of people in the cities and on the farms who were struggling with the daily problem of obtaining the means of tolerable existence. It is no discredit to the intelligence, integrity, or humanity of these judges that they persisted in a determination to restrain the legislative and executive officers of government within the limits of their constitutionally granted powers. If the people had amended the Constitution, their will would have become the law. The people had adopted the national prohibition amendment in 1919, and the Supreme Court had enforced it and the laws passed under its authority, despite the obvious fact that millions (probably a majority) were unwilling to obey the laws they had authorized. Indeed, the Court had sustained laws which even the prohibition amendment hardly justified, such as the confiscation of an automobile used by a nonowner to transport liquor illegally.[15]

There is no doubt that a constitutional amendment granting enlarged powers to the federal government over the national economy would have been enforced by the Supreme Court. But it was not in the mood of the people, or their representatives, to delay for the slow process of amendment. The emergency demanded "action." The Court speaking through Chief Justice Hughes, said: "Emergency does not create power." In one sense that is true; but it is also true that, as the same Chief Justice said: "Emergency may furnish the occasion for the exercise of power." And, with only a slight modification of this reasoning, it can be held that emergency conditions may justify extensions of an existing power

[15] *U.S. v. One Ford Coupe*, 272 U.S. 321.

which would not be justified under normal conditions. For instance, to embargo freight without good reason would be an arbitrary exercise of the power to regulate commerce; but to embargo freight because congestion of traffic or a strike made its transportation or delivery impossible would be clearly justified.

Probably the Supreme Court could have taken a broader view of federal power, while insisting on fundamental limitations, and thus sustained as temporary "emergency" measures laws that it would not have sustained as permanent legislation. This would have permitted the people, when deliberate action became possible, to decide whether or not it was permanently necessary to enlarge federal powers by a constitutional amendment. But, the stubborn insistence of the Court on denying "emergency" powers made the Court apparently a barrier to the "will of the people" and made the issue, not whether the Constitution should be remade but whether the Court should be remade.

The unfortunate result of this neglect of the real issue was that the American people became indoctrinated with the idea that the Constitution should be revised by the Congress assuming power to pass any laws having popular support and the submission of the Supreme Court to the judgment of the Congress as to how far the federal power should be extended. As the result of this popular acceptance of "legislative supremacy" there has been a profound change in the government of the United States which began in 1937. We have embarked on a new experiment in government.

Exactly how much vitality is left in the old constitutional limitations upon the powers of the national government is for the time uncertain. Apparently the present Supreme Court regards the protections of civil liberty, written particularly into the Bill of Rights, as beyond the legislative power of destruction or even substantial modification. But, many other constitutional limitations on federal power, long established by judicial construction, have been practically nullified by recent judicial constructions.

The federal power to regulate all commerce, both interstate *and intrastate* has been sustained. The federal power to tax in any manner, to any extent and for any purpose seems to be held subject to no substantial limitation. There are indications that perhaps the newly expanded "treaty power" can be so exercised with the acquiescence of the Court as to give the President and two thirds of a quorum of the Senate a far-reaching and unprecedented power to make laws which, regardless of conflicting state and federal laws, will become a part of the "supreme law of the land."

Just how this abdication of "judicial supremacy" and devitalization of the Constitution came about is a long story, fairly well known to students and vaguely understood by a minority of the American people. It should be at least summarized here.

After a series of decisions by the Supreme Court which nullified various New Deal laws such as the Railroad Retirement Act,[16] the National Industrial Recovery Act,[17] the Farm Mortgage Act,[18] the Agricultural Adjustment Act,[19] and the Guffey Coal Act,[20] came the presidential election of 1936 in which President Roosevelt was elected by the overwhelming electoral vote of all the states except Maine and Vermont. Apparently he had a "mandate," if ever a President had, to extend federal power, either by a constitutional amendment or by breaking down in some way the Supreme Court barrier to extended exercises of federal power.

As before explained, the issue popularly made was "change the Supreme Court"—and not "change the Constitution." The great political debate, which had been developing for

[16] 295 U.S. 330.
[17] 295 U.S. 495.
[18] 295 U.S. 555.
[19] 297 U.S. 1.
[20] 298 U.S. 238.

years, had been not over the wisdom of, and limitations imposed by, the Supreme Court. If it was the Court that was in fault, why change the Constitution? A master of politics, which Roosevelt was, naturally undertook to change the Court. He chose the rather rough method of asking Congress to pass a law authorizing the President to appoint more judges. Theoretically this law would permit the President to "rejuvenate" the Court, by adding "younger" judges, if the "old men" refused to retire, increasing the number of justices, if necessary, to as many as fifteen. Practically, it was intended to give the New Deal administration the support of a New Deal Court.

The reaction of the Congress and the people as a whole was surprising, particularly to the President. Almost overnight the independence of the Court became a great popular issue. The appointment of justices who were in political sympathy with the appointing President had been a practice from the earliest days. But frequently these appointees had disappointed the expectations of the appointer. Jefferson's appointees succumbed to John Marshall's persuasiveness. The anger of Theodore Roosevelt over Justice Holmes' dissent in the Northern Securities case was well known. The Coolidge appointment of Justice Stone had added a liberal whose opinions hardly reflected the conservatism of the appointing President.

It was evidently a common assumption that justices of the Supreme Court would never regard themselves as political agents to decide cases in accordance with presidential desires. It could be argued that President Roosevelt was seeking only a sympathetic and not a subservient court. But, the obvious intent to reverse the opinions of an antagonistic majority by replacing it with a friendly majority could not be disguised. In fact, it was practically proclaimed; and this was too offensive to the ideal of judicial impartiality to be acceptable to a host of people who would have applauded a partisan appointment, but revolted at the idea of a deliberately created partisan court.

Possibly the so-called "court packing" plan would have succeeded except for the change wrought by Chief Justice Hughes in the prevailing majority of the Court itself. To the amazement and confusion of the critics of the Court, while the legislative battle was still raging, the Chief Justice himself wrote the majority opinions, first in the West Coast Hotel case (300 U.S. 379) definitely overruling the Adkins case, and then in the Jones & Laughlin case [21] sustaining the constitutionality of the Wagner Act. Both decisions were against the dissent of the four irreconcilables of the former majority, Justices McReynolds, Van Devanter, Sutherland, and Butler. It was necessary for the Chief Justice in the Jones & Laughlin case to reverse practically all his arguments (without of course overruling his decision) in the NRA case decided only two years before. But he did this manfully and in a masterful fashion—and saved the Court from a possible legislative reorganization.

The Congress and the people generally breathed a sigh of relief. It was no longer necessary to remake the Court. It was not necessary to revise the Constitution. The Court, under its new and broad construction of the Constitution, would no longer nullify any extensions of the power of the national government to regulate all industry. The implications of the opinions were far-reaching and were borne out in the succeeding opinions of the Court, and in the procession of resignations of the older judges until all were gone and a court composed entirely of New Deal appointees was established. As President Roosevelt put it: "We lost a battle, but we won the war."

A far-reaching change in the character and operations of the American government was now well under way. New wine had been poured into old legal bottles. The provisions of the Constitution had been stretched into a new shape and

[21] 301 U.S. 1.

a capacity to contain federal powers that would have astonished—as well as frightened—those who made the old containers. There is perhaps one advantage for the American people in this method of remodelling their government. If the Constitution had been deliberately amended in this revolutionary era, we might have written into it amendments as unwise and harmful as the prohibition amendment, and it might have taken much longer than fourteen years to get rid of them.

The Congress and the Supreme Court, having collaborated for many years in stretching the Constitution, until its limitations on the centralization of power in the federal government have practically disappeared, may, in due time and under popular pressures, collaborate to reverse this program and to restore some of the individual liberties and powers of local self-government which the Constitution was written to preserve. The constitutional requirement that three fourths of the states approve any amendment of the Constitution having been avoided, no such three-fourths majority will be needed if a restoration of the original Constitution should be desired by a lesser but substantial majority of our citizens. The experiment of the American people with self-government will continue to be their great experiment—a seeking for good and competent ways to govern ourselves—so long as we are a free people.

CHAPTER XIV

World War and Halfhearted Internationalism
(A. B.)

WAR TALK had been endemic in Europe for at least twenty years before the reality came in 1914. The delicately balanced concert of powers which had kept an uneasy peace since 1815 was beginning to totter. The German states had finally achieved political unity under the leadership of Bismarck after the defeat of France in 1871. The industrial development of the Ruhr, particularly in the heavy-goods industries, had made of the new Germany the dominant economic power of the Continent. Austria-Hungary, like her emperor, was old and feeble. Russia was still the sleeping giant, but stirring uneasily. France was resentful, tormented with internal discord and desire for revenge for Sedan. Only her North African colonies gave signs of her returning strength. England was the old lion, glutted with success, complacent but with moments of apprehension, with a small army but a powerful navy to guard her shores.

Americans, busy with their own growth, had given little heed to the shifts and changes on the Continent. We had no desire to join in the race for colonies and trade outlets and the new and growing German merchant marine was no threat to us. The Kaiser's massive army maneuvers and his frequent saber-rattling added to the high comedy of international relations in a world with which we were only remotely connected, although German gestures in Morocco and at Agadir had lacked familiar comic aspects. In any event we had little need of Europe and could afford to look on from the sidelines while the tension mounted.

The sequence of the final days from June 28 to August 1, 1914, was swift and deadly. The killing of the Archduke Franz Ferdinand by a Serbian student, member of a revolutionary group, was hardly front-page news west of New York, but it was the spark that touched off the explosion. Austria, weary of the perennial unrest in the Balkans, and more especially in Serbia, made demands that amounted to a loss of Serb independence. Russia, conscious of her Slavic destiny, mobilized her army when Austria attacked Serbia, and Germany came in on the side of the Dual Empire. Having little respect for Russian arms, the Germans moved swiftly against France, bound by treaty to come to Russia's aid. The short road to Paris lay across Belgium and there the German legions marched, trampling underfoot the solemn promise of Germany to respect and maintain the independence and integrity of the little kingdom. Outraged by this callous treaty breaking and conscious of the near approach of danger, Britain declared war. The world had changed in a fateful month.

The first reaction in America was one of incredulity and horror. It couldn't happen, but it had. So we found what comfort we could in the thought that it would be, *must* be, a short war. Jean deBloch, in his book *Is War Now Impossible?* that had attracted the attention even of the Czar, had proved conclusively that modern war would bankrupt any nation engaging in it. We need only wait until the funds ran out. Meanwhile the President offered our good offices, which were promptly rejected by all the parties to the quarrel, and we proclaimed our complete neutrality.

Our standards of neutrality were high, based on the concepts of 1799 when England and France had been at death grips. We asserted our right to trade with all the belligerent nations and called on them to observe the freedom of the seas. Meanwhile we would refrain from giving aid and comfort to either side, within the reasonable limits of our neutral rights. The President's words in his message to the Senate on August 19 seem weirdly unrealistic when read across the years that intervene.

> The United States must be neutral in fact as well as in name during these days that are to try men's souls. We must be impartial in thought as well as in action, must put a curb upon our sentiments as well as upon every transaction that might be construed as a preference of one party to the struggle before another.

Of course such impartiality was beyond the power of any but the most strong-willed angels. With exceptions and qualifications the general feeling of the country inclined toward the side of the Allies. In spite of anti-British talk by special groups and sections, our ties of blood, interest, and tradition held us close to England, and there was a deep emotional affection for France. The ruthless violation of Belgium and the reports of "atrocities" that soon began to circulate with high Allied backing accentuated this partiality. But it was by no means universal. Our citizens of German origin were numerous, particularly in the Middle West, and their reputation for thrift and good citizenship was high. Hatred of England was part of the duty of every self-respecting Irishman, most of them extremely articulate. Add a large admixture of citizens who traced their descent from all the countries of Europe and the complexity of our position can be understood.

Through all this medley of opinions, voices, and prophecies, one thought was clear, we were well out of it and we must stay out. Many of our young men slipped across the border to Canada or made their way to France and enlisted with the British or the French, but these were individual and isolated cases.

It was the extent and the nature of the war, the weapons and the points of attack that first made us disagreeably aware of our relation to the conflict. When the first German rush had been stopped and held at the Marne, the land fighting went underground. The front lines were hidden in deep trenches and large-scale action became less frequent except as one side or the other was able to mount a major attack. The British navy held the sea and the German fleet was shut up in the great base at Kiel. The only dangerous sea weapon of the Germans was the submarine, not yet thoroughly tested in combat.

Feeling themselves in desperate straits, the British set themselves to the exploitation of their sea control. A blockade was declared of all German ports which was soon extended to the ports of neutral nations contiguous to the Central Powers and affording easy access into Germany. The doctrine of continuous voyage was extended to cover all goods ultimately reaching the enemy in any form, and contraband was defined as including almost anything of which the Central Powers stood in need. American vessels bound for ports that had been declared within the blockade zone were stopped on the high seas and, if desired, taken into British ports and held pending adjudication in British courts. The net result was the virtual prohibition of all American trade with Europe except through the Allies. American reliance on the rules of international law was deprived of all force and before the end of the first year of fighting our foreign trade activities outside our own hemisphere were inextricably interwoven with the operations of the Allies, particularly those of the British.

A corollary to this was the sale of munitions to the Allies and the setting up of the necessary credits. In August, 1914, our State Department warned American bankers that loans to any warring nations were not consistent with our neutrality. This was altered in September to permit something euphemistically called "credit loans," and by September, 1915, the sale of British bonds in this country was permitted. Secretary Bryan protested vainly and resigned, to be succeeded by Robert Lansing. Before we went in, in April, 1917, $1,500,000,000 of private funds had been loaned to the Allies, against $27,000,000 to the Central Powers.

The British trade restrictions and blockade were annoying in their disregard of neutral rights that the Americans had at least asserted for more than a hundred years, but the submarine warfare waged by the Germans was more dangerous. The generally accepted rule among civilized nations required that when unarmed ships, whether neutral or belligerent, were taken at sea passengers and crew should be removed safely and transported to a neutral port when possible. Confederate privateers and cruisers during the Civil War had destroyed many Northern ships, but without the loss of a single noncombatant life. This could not be duplicated by the Germans with submarines as their only ships of war able to keep the seas. Available space and oxygen allowance were overcrowded without additional occupants and the vulnerability of the submarine to gunfire of any kind made it dangerous to approach even an ostensibly unarmed vessel. The only alternative to sinking was to let the cargo carrier go free, to carry her needed contents to the Allies. On February 4, 1915, the German government gave warning that the waters around the British Isles were a war zone in which all commerce bound for neutral ports would be destroyed. The sinking of American ships and the loss of American lives began, culminating with the sinking of the Cunarder *Lusitania* off the Irish coast on May 7, 1915, with a loss of more than eleven hundred lives, including a hundred and twenty-eight Americans.

Stupid as this act was from a tactical point of view, it brought the hard realities of total modern war home to Americans as nothing else could have done. For the first time there was public demand that we enter the war on the Allied side. Unsure of general public support and under the pacifistic influence of Bryan, the administration sent a sharp note to Germany asserting the rights of neturals and "the rights of humanity." The tone, if not the language, was that of an ultimatum and after several exchanges of notes and the loss of other American lives on the British liner *Arabic,* Germany disavowed the acts of her submarine commanders and promised to refrain from the sinking of liners without arranging for the safety of noncombatants. This lasted until February, 1916, when Germany gave warning of resumption of attack on armed merchantmen and soon after sank the *Sussex* with further loss of life. This time the United States threatened the breaking of diplomatic relations, unless a promise to refrain from the sinking of further merchant vessels was given. Germany agreed on condition that the British also be held to "strict accountability," whatever that meant.

This abridged account of the steps by which we approached war illustrates the growth of the unavoidable conflict between old ideals and concepts of international rights and the new reality of modern war. It was a hard school in which we had suddenly found ourselves and we had no textbooks or precedents by which we could be guided. The election of 1916 came in the midst of this tangle of pressing problems. In spite of the political risks of election year a beginning had been made in preparing for war. The National Defense Act provided for increasing the Army, but only to 175,000; the Naval appropriations were more generous, making provision for a large number of additional vessels, and the newly created U.S. Shipping Board was authorized to spend $50,000,000 for merchant ships.

The campaign revolved chiefly around an absurd oversimplification of an issue which was far from simple. The supporters of Wilson declared that he had kept us out of war, the opposition charged him with trying to force us into it. Neither statement was true nor had anything to do with the question confronting us. In their relations with both Germany and England the administration had displayed remarkable patience and forbearance, as great as that shown by John Adams when we were caught between the millstones of the Napoleonic war. There were two relevant questions which both parties dodged: How *could* we stay out? If we came in what would we take with us? In the final count Wilson was re-elected by an electoral margin of twenty-three votes. California went for him by a plurality of only 3,806; his over-all popular lead was nearly 600,000.

Events moved fast in the early months of 1917. In late January the Germans announced unrestricted submarine war on all vessels, armed or unarmed, in the waters around the British Isles or the Mediterranean. We retaliated by arming merchant vessels. Before that had happened the incident of the Zimmermann note had destroyed the last hope of those who still worked for peace. The highly efficient British intelligence had "picked up" a communication from an undersecretary in the German foreign office to the German Ambassador in Mexico proposing a German-Mexican alliance, with Texas as the reward for Mexican aid along the Rio Grande. This was the high point in a long list of German bunglings in diplomacy and propaganda. On April 6, 1917, war was declared.

In his war message the President reviewed briefly the stages by which we had approached the decision and our attempts to avoid such an outcome. He indicated some of the things that must now be done, recognized the existence of a new force in the world against which we had been unable to maintain our traditional position, and declared that his own purposes remained unchanged:

> ... to vindicate the principles of peace and justice in the life of the world as against selfish and autocratic power and to set up amongst the really free and self-governed peoples of the world such a concert of purpose and of action as will henceforth insure the observance of those principles. Neutrality is no longer feasible or desirable where the peace of the world is involved and the freedom of its peoples, and the menace to that peace and freedom lies in the existence of autocratic governments backed by organized force which is controlled wholly by their will, not by the will of their people. . . . We are at the beginning of an age in which it will be insisted that the same standards of conduct and of responsibility for wrong done shall be observed among nations and their governments that are observed among the individual citizens of civilized states.

Little attention was given at the time to that part of the message declaring the impossibility and undesirability of neutrality in a war involving the peace of the world and the necessity of higher standards of conduct and responsibility among nations similar to those required of individuals in a civilized state. The old concept of a limited-liability war, the operations and effects of which could be confined within a narrow area, was still too strongly fixed in our minds for us to realize that the scope and impact of war had been altered with the increased power of the machines of war. That lesson is still imperfectly learned despite later experience, but in the passages quoted lies much of the essence of the "new internationalism."

Once in the war we moved swiftly to make our presence felt. The Emergency Fleet Corporation was organized and, before the war ended, submarine losses in merchant shipping were being replaced at a better rate than two for one. Industrial resources were mobilized rapidly under the direction of Bernard Baruch at the head of the War Industries Board, railroad transportation was unified under government control, and the making of a great army undertaken. Selective service put four million men in uniform, of whom about half saw service in France. In the Argonne fighting in the summer of 1918, American soldiers tilted the balance for the Allies and, on November 11, Germany asked for an armistice.

The Great Adventure was over. What did it add up to? After the first burst of thankfulness and celebration the reaction was a desire to get the soldiers home and out of uniform as quickly as possible. Europe was far away and our mission there had been accomplished. Now we could go back to the accustomed ways of peace—business as usual. War production stopped almost overnight. The ships of the new merchant fleet that had been conjured up to offset the wastage of the submarines were laid up, except for a few which sought peaceful cargoes to justify their existence. The speed and completeness of our demobilization were proof that we had only begun to serve our apprenticeship as a world power. Great wars do not end overnight, as the fighting may. The peace was still to be made, and the debts were still to be paid.

During the war the United States had advanced more than seven billion dollars to her allies, mostly in guarantees for goods bought in this country. After the armistice, nearly four billion more were advanced for reconstruction and rehabilitation purposes. How and when were these sums to be paid, with interest first at five per cent, later reduced to four and a half? The matter was complicated by the rather fantastic hopes of German reparations. These were primarily a European concern, but it was difficult to see how England and France could pay the bill to us without the aid of reparation payments from Germany. After long discussion, frequent revisions, and the generation of much ill will, the financial collapse in Austria in 1931, which spread through Europe, brought the argument to a close. By that time the Allies had paid us something more than two and a half billions, Germany had paid slightly less than five billions of which more than half had been borrowed in the United States. At the diplomatic level, the discussions, though sometimes pointed, had been carried on in polite language, but the popular opinion on the two continents had been more uncomplimentary. The common term in this country for our late allies was the "Welcher Nations"; England and France responded with "Uncle Shylock." The whole experience has become a fading but unpleasant memory that can well be forgotten entirely. At that time it made a deep impression on the American mind, deepening the growing determination to have as little as possible to do with Europe. "Let them stew in their own juice" was the common phrase.

What about the peace? Here the President had laid the groundwork for his proposal in a speech delivered in January, 1918, when German strength appeared to be still at the maximum. Here he declared for a "peace without victory" and without punitive conditions. Among the terms suggested were freedom of the seas, reduction of armament, governments chosen by the peoples concerned, and a league to enforce the peace. Here was the germ and the substance of the famous Covenant of the League. Our allies had been bled too deeply to consider a peace without victory. Better defeat than such a humiliating settlement.

The meeting at Versailles which began January 18, 1919, was attended by the heads of the four major powers, Lloyd George for England, Clemenceau for France, Orlando for Italy, and President Wilson for the United States. Wilson was much criticized for taking upon himself the chief burden of representing the United States and particularly for not asking prominent Republicans to join the delegation. The name of Henry Cabot Lodge was foremost among these mentioned. He had been a critic of American foreign policy frequently in the past and had been among the organizers of a league to enforce peace that had attracted some attention in the early months of the war. Wilson ignored these demands and took with him Secretary of State Lansing, Henry White, also in the State Department, General Tasker H. Bliss, and Colonel House, who had held no official position in the United States.

Probably no man has ever stood higher in popular esteem than did Wilson among the people of England and France in those first hopeful days. A hard-bitten British correspondent said of that time, "It was as though he held in his hand the hope of humanity." The glory soon dimmed. Of his three colleagues, Lloyd George was a glib, skilful politician with a touch of the demagogue. He had already assured the English people that Germany would pay the entire cost of the war to the Allies. Clemenceau for France was an old, disillusioned man, who had but one purpose, the protection of France. In his lifetime he had twice seen German armies on French soil. The idealism of Wilson was only empty words to his cynical ears. Orlando for Italy saw the conference chiefly as an opportunity for his country to pay off a long-standing grudge against Austria, and incidentally to wipe out some of the bitter memories of the Caporetto rout. To these hard realists Wilson was a bungling, well-meaning amateur.

In spite of the opposition and indifference of the other powers to his proposals, Wilson persisted and finally won grudging approval of the Covenant of the League and its incorporation in the treaty. The body of the treaty was less stringent than the extremists had demanded, but was still impossibly drastic. Germany lost her colonies, also Alsace-Lorraine and some additional territory to the west, agreed to the payment of an indemnity of $5,000,000,000, with later

and much heavier payments to be determined; $60,000,000,-
000, was mentioned as a possibility. She was disarmed and
stripped of the remnants of her navy and was forced to accept
foreign control of her coal mines in the Saar. War guilt was
admitted and when the Germans signed the treaty, June 28,
1919, it was as representatives of a defeated and helpless
nation. Later events gave ample demonstration of its futility
as a guarantee of French security or of the peace of Europe.

The Covenant of the League makes melancholy reading
these days but it has its importance as evidence of the first
large-scale American attempt to influence world policy. In
substance it embodied fourteen points as stated by the President in his speech of January of the previous year and repeated at the time of the armistice as a basis for the negotiations. The main points were:

> Open covenants openly arrived at.
> Complete freedom of the seas.
> Equality of trade conditions.
> Reduction of armaments.
> Self-determination, especially for the peoples of Austria-Hungary and the Balkan States.
> Independence of Poland.
> The formation of a League of Nations.

It was the fourteenth point, the formation of the League, around which most of the controversy centered. As stated by the President in his January speech: "A general association of nations must be formed under specific covenants for the purpose of affording mutual guarantees of political independence and territorial integrity to great and small states alike." The idea was enticing, but how would the guarantees be made good? And who would decide when independence or integrity was in danger? It was clear that the power to decide lay with the League but where would the League get the armed force necessary to make the guarantee good? Manifestly from the member nations. This was tantamount to usurpation of the Congressional right to declare war.

When the treaty, including the Covenant of the League, reached the Senate called in special session, the battle began. At one extreme were the men who favored ratification as it stood, which was the President's position. Many, perhaps most of the senators, favored some modification to protect our rights and interests. Then there was the bloc unalterably opposed to ratification at all, led by such members as Lodge, Borah, LaFollette, and Hiram Johnson. Undoubtedly some of them were moved by personal hostility to the President, some were sincerely confident that our duties and responsibilities lay within our own borders and not overseas and that our traditions of isolation were sound and practicable. Whatever the motives, the treaty was defeated in the first vote in November, 1919. Reconsideration failed in the next session and, in August, 1921, we made a separate treaty with Germany and the war was officially ended.

The lessons of the war were confused and conflicting. We knew that we had put more than two million men in France and that our weight had counted heavily in the fighting from early July to the armistice, a fact that we were not reluctant to emphasize. Now we were back home. As a lesson in international friendship for the men in the ranks it had been a failure. Doughboys seeing Europe for the first time took a dim view of the Old World. Many declared that we had gone in on the wrong side. As for the future, they had experienced enough.

The Senate had refused to ratify the treaty, but failure to act does not always solve the problems demanding action. While we had stayed out of the League we did not utterly turn our face away from it. In 1922 we began sending "unofficial observers" to League conferences on the narcotics and white-slave trade and later we were more officially represented at conferences on the trade in arms. We expressed our interest and possible membership in the World Court and we finally became a part of the International Labor Organization. In 1922 a conference of the Pacific powers was held in Washington on invitation from the United States, and members agreed to a program for the limitation of naval armaments and fortifications in the Pacific, with a fixed ratio of naval construction of the participating powers after a ten-year suspension in the building of capital ships. Our attitude was a curious mixture of approval of the basic purposes and most of the activities of the League and refusal to commit ourselves wholeheartedly to the League itself.

The belief that the treaty, meaning the League, was beaten by the votes and influence of a small group of stubborn, selfish senators will hardly stand close analysis. Claims that the Republican victory and the election of Warren G. Harding as President in 1920 amounted to a popular rejection of the League are even harder to prove, except by rather tenuous inference. The congressional elections of 1918 had gone against the Democrats even in the midst of the war, indicating a widespread doubt of the administration. The tragic collapse of President Wilson during a speaking tour in behalf of the League in the fall of 1919 had left the Democratic party leaderless and disorganized. The nomination of a comparatively unknown figure, Cox of Ohio, did nothing to correct this.

The clearest reading of the election returns showed a widespread disillusionment and disgust with our overseas adventure. "Make the world safe for democracy" was a phrase of bitter irony on the American tongue and "Our gallant allies" a term of derision and reproach. Why didn't they pay us what they owed us? To that extent, and that only, the vote was a rejection of the idea of collective action to guarantee the peace of the world of which the League was to be the central instrument. "Return to normalcy" was an oblique statement of a general desire to stay at home and mind our business.

Two amendments to the Constitution, the Eighteenth and Nineteenth, ratified respectively in January, 1919, and August, 1920, shared public attention with the League and to many seemed more important than the peace of the world. The first of these establishing prohibition was an impressive demonstration of what can be accomplished by moral fervor capably organized and well financed. There was no evidence of a special urgent need for such a step at the time. Prohibition was already a fact in many Western states and all the Southern, and by comparison with European and our own earlier practices we were a temperate people. By the time the "noble experiment" was repealed in December, 1933, household bars and home drinking had become disturbingly prevalent; rumrunners, bootleggers, hijackers, and organized gangsters had made the crimes of bribery and murder a commonplace on the front page of most newspapers, even in states that had been dry long before the adoption of the amendment. Evidently there is a limit to the control of personal conduct by law, even with the most moral of motives. It is a lesson worth remembering.

Woman suffrage which had been much discussed with a great deal of rather foolish argument on both sides came finally almost as a matter of course with the adoption of the Nineteenth Amendment. There had been minor demonstrations in Washington, parades with banners in the marching lines and shouts of ridicule from the sidewalks. A fervent suffragette or two chained herself to the iron fence in front of the White House, only to be later unchained without casualty. The result is easily assessed. The great improvement in social legislation and the raising of the levels and standards of legislative behavior so freely prophesied by the supporters is not evident, but polling places are cleaner and more orderly. Manners have improved around the ballot box and the noisy, contentious voter is a rarity. The total potential vote has been doubled and the sense of injustice and inferiority felt by many intelligent women has been removed, both desirable ends. Women's organizations, especially the League of Women Voters, have applied themselves to the political education of their members, setting an example that men might well follow. Probably the proportion of informed intelligence that speaks on election day is higher than before, but the votes of women have not yet brought peace to the world. Comparatively few women have appeared in Congress or in state legislatures, but of those few it can be said that they compare favorably with the male average. The "experiment" of woman suffrage which began with an act passed by the Wyoming territorial legislature in 1869 is now an accepted and important part of our political system.

The most important result of World War I was the shift in the balance of economic and financial world power. Germany had gambled for world leadership and lost her stake—merchant marine, colonies, navy; her heavy industries were held in pawn and her prestige was nil. France and England had lost heavily in manpower and the war had been fought chiefly in the area of France's greatest industrial resources. English soil was untouched, but her reserves of credit and investments overseas had been depleted. Revolution had thrown Russia into the turmoil of civil war from which she emerged as the U.S.S.R., communist and a pariah among nations, especially in the United States. So great was American fear of this new government that we abandoned our traditional *de facto* rule and withheld recognition for fifteen years. Austria-Hungary was dismembered and helpless.

Only the United States emerged unscathed and more powerful and prosperous to all appearances than ever before. During the war we had been both the arsenal and the banker for the Allies, and we now held their notes for a disputed number of millions. The old prestige as the bankers and merchants of the world that had rested so long with the British was shifting across the Atlantic. We were slow to recognize both the fact and the meaning of our change from debtor to creditor, and we are not yet fully aware of its profound significance. As late as 1934, Congress passed the Johnson Act prohibiting the sale in this country of the securities of a nation that had "defaulted" on its debt to us. Our absorption in our home market and consequent indifference to export except of agricultural products had denied us the education in international relations that the British had enjoyed for so long. Our easy contemporary attitude was in close accord with the report of the Nye committee purporting to prove that it was the munitions makers and international bankers who had pushed us into the war for their own profit. "Merchants of Death" was the phrase, and to be an "internationalist" was to be a combination of traitor and communist. A corollary to this was the belief that our diplomats were ignorant blunderers helpless in the deft hands of the Europeans and especially the British. Our long record of successful dealing with the British Foreign Office was ignored or rewritten to our disadvantage.

Politically speaking the years from 1920 to 1930 were confused and futile. We demanded payments from our allies and passed two tariff bills, the Smoot-Hawley and Fordney-McCumber, raising the tariff walls higher than ever, thus making it impossible for our debtors to pay our claims in the only way possible for them. During the war it had been our boast that America could feed the world. Under the stimulus of overseas need, prices of farm products skyrocketed, followed closely by the price of farm land. Marginal lands were put under the plow, swamps were drained and diked, and the way cleared for the dust-bowl years that were to come. With the ending of the war, European demand dropped with unexpected abruptness because of the quick revival of European wheat with bumper crops. Prices dropped as fast as they had risen and before the middle of the decade the American farmer found himself caught between high-cost land and low-price crops. Foreclosures mounted and unemployment appeared and grew.

Then a strange and contradictory phenomenon became manifest. In the midst of much talk, some of it from the White House, about a "new economic level," "two cars in every garage," "permanent abolition of poverty," the stock market started its long upward swing. This was the curious setting for the long carnival of paper prosperity that was to end in the collapse of the market in the fall of 1929. The process was self-promoting and self-destroying but there were almost no voices raised in warning. The writer of this chapter happened to be in a position to observe both the farming decline and the stock market boom and asked a New York banker friend to explain the paradox of agricultural depression and the mushrooming of stock-market wealth. The answer was "No paradox at all. All it means is that the farmer is no longer of any importance." Perhaps that explains the confused state of mind in that hectic time. Certainly there is no rational justification for a belief that a basic industry can go bankrupt without injury to the rest of the country.

In one phase of our political change the decade was sterile. For twenty years and more a sense of social responsibility had spread steadily through our structure of thought and practice. From 1890 to 1914 our chief aim had been to correct the inequities and remove the injustices that had appeared in our society. Legislative and executive acts and declarations had marked our course, culminating in the "New Freedom" announced by Woodrow Wilson. The war had cut squarely across this current and it failed to resume its flow after peace came. On the contrary all three of the succeeding presidents, Harding, Coolidge, and Hoover, were at some pains to make it clear that no resumption was contemplated. Shortly before his election in 1928 Mr. Hoover delivered his famous "rugged individualism" speech, outlining his fundamental theory of government and administration.

> When the war closed, the most vital of all issues both in our own country and throughout the world was whether governments should continue their wartime ownership and operation of many instrumentalities of production and distribution. We were challenged with a peace-time choice between the American system of rugged individualism and a European philosophy of diametrically opposed doctrines—doctrines of paternalism and state socialism. The acceptance of these ideas would have meant the destruction of self-government through centralization of government. It would have meant the undermining of the individual initiative and enterprise through which our people have grown to unparallelled greatness.
>
> The Republican Party from the beginning resolutely turned its face away from these ideas and these war practices. . . . When the Republican Party came into full power it went at once resolutely back to our fundamental conception of the state and the rights and responsibilities of the individual. Thereby it restored confidence and hope in the American people, it freed and stimulated enterprise, it restored the government to its position as an umpire instead of a player in the economic game.

Had we then turned the clock back to 1890? A year later almost to a day, the collapse of the New York stock market gave notice of the opening of another new era, that of the Great Depression, and that, to steal a phrase from Kipling, is another story.

CHAPTER XV

The New Treaty Power
(D. R.)

Before we march through the economic and political experimentation and the international entanglements which played their parts in the so-called Roosevelt Revolution, we should pause to examine briefly a new power of national lawmaking which developed rapidly during and after World War I.

The power of the President "to make treaties, provided two-thirds of the Senators present concur," is, of course, as old as the original Constitution. It was expressly granted in Article II. But, until the twentieth century there was no apparent prospect that the treaty power would be deliberately used to curtail local self-government in the states and to centralize the legal regulation of our economy, our moralities, and our civic and social relations in the national government.

Increasing intimacy and concern with the affairs of other nations inevitably developed out of our participation in two world wars, with a world-wide depression in between. It is curious and amusing to note that in December, 1916, when Great Britain was deep in the first World War and the United States was teetering on the edge of it, a treaty between the two nations was proclaimed—to protect migratory birds flying through the United States and Canada! And, *it was this treaty* which brought from the Supreme Court of the United States the portentous revelation of what vast authority had been lying dormant in the treaty-making power.

It had been understood from the earliest days of the republic that treaties were—as expressly provided in Article VI—a part of "the supreme law of the land" and that "the Judges in every State shall be bound thereby, anything in the Constitution or Laws of any State to the contrary notwithstanding." Accordingly, when the United States made a treaty with another nation giving rights in the United States to aliens, no state law could deny the enforcement of such rights. Thus aliens might obtain or hold land or other property in a state, notwithstanding prohibitory state laws, if such rights were granted to these aliens by a treaty.

But it had never been suggested, prior to 1900, that, by making a treaty, for example, with France, providing that both countries should adopt a uniform marriage and divorce code, the United States government could then compel the enforcement of that code in all the states of the Union. It had never been suggested that, by making a treaty, for example, with Russia, providing that in both countries the managers of all industrial enterprises must be chosen by vote of their employees, the national government could then enforce that law in every state regardless of its property and corporation laws. It had never been suggested that by making a treaty with another nation agreeing to abolish slavery, or to establish the right of women to vote, the national government could enforce these desirable reforms without first obtaining the authority specifically granted in the Thirteenth and Nineteenth amendments. Such uses of the treaty power were not merely unheard of, but apparently unthought of, prior to about 1940, or perhaps 1945.

In fact, as late as 1890, the Supreme Court had held [1] that the treaty power was subject to "restraints which are found in that instrument [the Constitution] against the action of the government or of its departments, and those arising from the nature of the government itself and of that of the States." The opinion of the Court further stated: "It would not be contended that it extends so far as to authorize what the Constitution forbids, or a change in the character of the government or in that of one of the States."

Thirty years after this opinion the Supreme Court, in 1920, sustained a federal law enforcing the Migratory Birds Treaty of 1916 against the State of Missouri and asserted: "No doubt the great body of private relations usually fall within the control of the State, but a treaty may override its power." [2]

It did not appear at the time that any revolutionary change in our form of government was presaged by merely sustaining national authority to prevent the killing of migratory birds, which, as the Court pointed out, were no person's property and only transiently within the state borders. But the sweeping language of the opinion disturbed legal scholars, especially when the opinion of the Court cavalierly brushed aside contentions that under the Tenth Amendment all "powers not delegated to the United States by the Constitution, nor prohibited by it to the States, are reserved to the States respectively, or to the people." The opinion answered the question as to whether the migratory birds law was "forbidden by some invisible radiation from the general terms of the Tenth Amendment," by the startling statement: "We must consider what this country has become in deciding what that Amendment has reserved."

That cryptic observation apparently meant that, since we had become a great nation, the powers of local self-government once reserved to the states could not be regarded as any

[1] *Geofroy v. Riggs*, 135 U.S. 258.
[2] *Missouri v. Holland*, 252 U.S. 416.

longer reserved to the states! In this manner a judicial amendment of the Constitution was born, to be quietly nourished in the Court and then brought to full maturity in an opinion delivered sixteen years later, in 1936. In that opinion,[3] speaking for the Court, Justice Sutherland developed the novel argument that the treaty power, although expressly granted, did not depend on the constitutional grant, because the power was "inherent" in any national government, one of the "necessary concomitants of nationality."

The opinion asserted that the treaty power was not carved (in 1787) out of the "legislative powers *then possessed by the States,*" because the separate states "never possessed international powers." This is historically inaccurate because the separate states claimed separate sovereignties (as in the Declaration of Independence) which they later agreed to yield, in external affairs, to the federal government. But, by distorting history and creating, judicially, for the federal government an "inherent," unlimited power in place of a delegated, limited power, the Supreme Court opened a wide door to a combined national-international control of all local government in the several states.

Through this door zealous advocates of international federations or "unions" have been seeking a way to escape from the difficulties of remodelling our constitutional government by amendments to the Constitution which, under the Constitution, must be proposed by two thirds of the representatives of the people and then approved by three fourths.

In an exercise of the treaty power the Charter of the United Nations was adopted as a part of the "supreme law of the land." In that charter it was provided, by Chapter IX, Article 55, that "The United Nations shall promote universal respect for, and observance of human rights and fundamental freedoms for all without distinction as to race, sex, language or religion." Article 56 then provided that "All members pledge

[3] *U.S.* v. *Curtiss-Wright Export Corporation,* 299 U.S. 304.

themselves to take joint and separate action in cooperation with the organization for the achievement of the purposes set forth in Article 55."

In pursuit of the objectives thus stated, the General Assembly of the United Nations adopted in 1948 a "Universal Declaration of Human Rights" proclaiming among other things that, "Everyone is entitled to all the rights and freedoms set forth in this Declaration, without distinction of any kind, such as race, color, sex, language, political or other opinion, national or social origin, property, birth or other status," and that "Everyone has the right to own property alone as well as in association with others." In this manner international lawmaking advanced aggressively to substitute laws made by an international assembly for the laws made by state legislatures to govern the internal affairs and relations of inhabitants of our several states.

Even prior to this declaration the Supreme Court of California, when it nullified a California statute of long standing and overruled prior decisions against mixed marriages, made specific reference to the United Nations Charter.[4] Then in April 1950 the District Court of Appeal of California held [5] that the United Nations Charter itself overrode and nullified a California statute (upheld by previous decisions) which disabled aliens from owning land. Prior to this decision state and federal courts (including the United States Supreme Court) had, without exception, sustained the validity of state alien land laws—although it was frequently indicated that they might be nullified by a treaty.

There has been a vigorous disagreement among able lawyers as to whether a treaty is, or can be made, self-executing (as the California court held) or whether it must be implemented by laws enacted by the Congress. But there is little question that the Supreme Court, unless it qualifies some of

[4] *Perez* v. *Lippold,* 198 P. (2nd) 17.
[5] *Fujii* v. *State,* 217 P. (2nd) 781.

its recent broad assertions, will uphold as a general rule federal laws enacted to carry out a treaty obligation, against conflicting laws written in state constitutions or statutes. It has been apparently well established law that a treaty and treaty laws could not be sustained if they violated an express prohibition of the national Constitution; if, for example, they required and imposed a tax on exports, contrary to Article 1, Section 9. But even express prohibitions of the Constitution have been threatened with evasion by constructions urged by advocates of many new international laws.

These broad, "free wheeling" constructionists have pointed out that the Congress is given plenary power "to define and punish . . . offenses against the Law of Nations." Hence, they have argued that new crimes can be defined by treaty as "offenses against the law of nations." Then provision can be made for their punishment by domestic *or international* courts, and thus the constitutional protection of trial "by jury in the State where said crimes shall have been committed" [6] can be denied. Thus, it is claimed, the constitutional right in all federal courts of trial "by an impartial jury of the State and district wherein the crime shall have been committed" [7] can be denied *in a court established by the federal government!*

It has been contended that the right to trial by jury, now universally protected by state constitutions, should not be sustained against its abrogation by a treaty law, merely because of what one of the more zealous internationalists has described as "some tenuous concept of constitutional law labeled 'traditional domestic jurisdiction of our States.'"

In a dispassionate review of impending changes in our form and methods of government through the use of the treaty power it would be out of place to argue whether such proposals as the Human Rights Covenant or the Genocide

---

[6] U.S. Constitution, Article III.
[7] Sixth Amendment, U.S. Constitution.

Convention should or should not be supported by American delegates or approved by the Congress. But it is necessary to call attention to the unprecedented changes in our domestic law that have been approved by the Supreme Court and are being made effective by such judicial decisions as those cited in California. It is also necessary to point out that advocates of expanded federal power have been diligently engaged in urging the use of the treaty power by the national government to lift itself "by the bootstraps" into powers which the Supreme Court for decades held had not been granted by the Constitution, and in some instances had been clearly denied.

On the other hand it should be reported that presidents and notable leaders of the American Bar have repeatedly expressed the opinion, probably approved by a great majority of American lawyers, that the rapidly expanding use of the treaty power "may easily result in treaty law superseding and destroying large segments of domestic law and even changing many fundamental features of our form of government." [8]

Mr. Frank E. Holman, the president of the American Bar Association, who was just quoted, has called attention to the warning of Chief Justice Hughes in 1929 when, according to Mr. Holman, the Chief Justice, and former Secretary of State, pointed out that "when any attempt is made to use the treaty-making power to deal with matters which do not pertain to our external relations and to control matters normally and appropriately within the local jurisdiction of a state, it must be resisted and grounds found for effectively limiting the treaty-making power to matters relating to foreign affairs and not allow its use to make laws for the people of the United States in their internal concerns."

Brief mention should also be made here of the ruling of the Supreme Court [9] that "executive agreements" made by the President with a foreign government have a "similar dig-

---

[8] *American Bar Association Journal,* Vol. 36, p. 790.
[9] *United States* v. *Pink,* 315 U.S. 203.

nity" with treaties, although not made with the constitutional "consent of the Senate." Thereby the President alone is empowered to nullify state laws and to make his solitary decision the "supreme law of the land." This is a power of executive lawmaking that the framers of the Constitution undoubtedly thought they had denied to the President when they wrote the first words of Article I: "All legislative powers herein granted shall be vested in the Congress of the United States, which shall consist of a Senate and House of Representatives."

Because the development and use of treaty-power lawmaking is a current phenomenon, anyone reviewing today the growth and change of government in the United States must endeavor to report not only what has occurred but also the trend of current political experimentation. In what direction are reformist forces moving? What are the factors that are likely to advance or check or divert them?

We know that, in political movements, action and reaction are as assured concomitants as they are in physical dynamics. The trend of the last fifty years has been toward a steady increase and centralization of authority in the federal government, for the purpose of providing more securities for our people. This trend may be reversed in coming years by a reaction in favor of reducing and decentralizing the powers of the federal government for the purpose of preserving more of the liberties of our people. Such a reaction would follow the thought of Woodrow Wilson who wrote: "Liberty has never come from the government. Liberty has always come from the subjects of it. The history of liberty is a history of limitations of governmental power, not the increase of it."

Among the generous-minded, essentially moral people of the United States every moral crusade has always had a wide appeal. There is always a great urge among such a self-governing people to write their moral convictions into laws. The denial of what are called "human rights" and the persecution of racial or religious minorities create a strong emotional demand and a pressure upon public representatives to do anything within their power to prevent such denials and persecutions—not only in the United States but in any other country. No congressman, confronted with the necessity of voting for or against an international "Covenant on Human Rights," or a "Convention on the Prevention and Punishment of the Crime of Genocide," will wish to be recorded as opposed to "human rights" or in favor of "genocide."

There is, however, nothing to prevent the Congress, without the aid of a treaty, from enacting laws for the United States protecting in our land "human rights" and punishing "genocide"—if the Constitution has granted to the Congress the power to enact such laws. But if that power is not granted by the Constitution, whereby the Congress is authorized to enact laws supplanting and nullifying the powers of local self-government within the states, which are reserved to the states and not delegated to the federal government, how can congressmen, who are sworn to support the Constitution, approve and enforce an agreement made with other nations that the federal government will exercise powers which the Constitution has denied to it?

If the treaty power should be wrongfully exercised, the failure to fulfill treaty promises would seem to be the fault of those who made the promises, not the fault of those who refuse to follow the argument that two wrongs will make a right. And, finally, who should expect or rely upon the Supreme Court, which is sworn to uphold the Constitution, to enforce laws written in violation of the Constitution?

The American people are being urged and exhorted to supplant domestic lawmaking by international lawmaking, to have the laws under which they must live and work written by an international assembly of representatives of many nations where people live under physical and mental conditions profoundly different from ours, instead of by the Congress of their own representatives, who at least may understand their hopes, their needs, and their possibilities. If the American people yield to this persuasion they will make or acquiesce in a greater change in the government of the United States than they have made or permitted in all the years since the adoption of the Constitution. It is their privilege to do this if they wish; but no prognosticator should assume that they will do it, if they understand what they are doing.

When the Constitution has been deliberately amended self-government by trial and error has been at work. The American people adopted and repealed prohibition; they adopted and retained federal income taxation. They indirectly extended federal power over industry and agriculture, partly by pressures upon their legislators, partly by opposing rigid judicial restraints upon federal power, and partly by approving judicial relaxation of former restraints. In all these developments of federal power, the force of a fairly well-informed public opinion has been effective to maintain a government of and by, as well as for, the people.

The great issue which has grown out of two world wars—and the impending shadow of a third—may be defined as internationalism. What should we do for the rest of the world? What will the rest of the world do to us? In a world where other peoples throughout the world are pre-eminently national in their interests and outlook—including the nations espousing "international communism"—it has become essential to self-preservation, as well as to the general welfare that we keep ever clearly in mind our national interests and responsibilities, as well as those which may be international.

More than ever before the American people now see the need for a powerful national government. Also more than ever before they are being shown how individual liberty is reduced and individual ambition confined as the community in which they live grows larger and the community government enlarges its control over their lives. They must give to their national government the powers essential to cooperate with other nations so that we may, if possible, live in peace or, if that is impossible, we may be able to resist aggression. But, whether it is necessary or wise to give to our national government the power in its dealings with other nations to subject our daily lives and work to international controls, or to impose international moralities upon our conduct in our homes and workshops are questions not to be answered lightly. These are the questions presented by the development of the new treaty power.

The Supreme Court, as the ultimate guardian and preserver of our Constitution, might check hurried and ill-considered expansions of federal power and extensions of international control over our internal affairs. It might well set up barriers to amending the Constitution by a mere congressional majority, which would compel the submission of amendments for approval by three fourths of the states, thus insuring careful consideration of such amendments by all the people. But if, because of the prevailing philosophy of what is called the "new Supreme Court" (which will be explained in a later chapter) the Court sets up no barriers—and even issues no warnings to alert public opinion—it is still likely that the popular debate between nationalists and internationalists will become more and more acute in the years ahead. The choice of representatives in Congress may be more frequently determined in the future than in the past by their opinions, programs or convictions as to how the powers of the government of the United States should be developed, how and where extended, and how and where restricted. It is a new posing of the old problem: How can our government be made strong enough to meet its responsibilities for protecting and promoting the welfare of our people in a world of certain enemies and uncertain friends, and yet not strong enough to fasten a tyrannical control of their lives on a people who for four hundred years have been ready to sacrifice, if necessary, their lives and their fortunes in order to remain free men and women?

CHAPTER XVI

The Roosevelt Revolution
(A. B.)

THE ERA that was ushered in by the first inauguration of Franklin Delano Roosevelt in March, 1933, has been the subject of such bitter controversy that it will be impossible to reach anything like a balanced conclusion for another generation, if then. Northern and Southern students still disagree over the soundness and pertinence of Calhoun's theory of the Constitution, although the bitter anger engendered by the reconstruction period has largely disappeared. Perhaps that is the most that can be hoped for, for the time and the events with which this chapter must deal.

Fortunately a sober discussion of the ways in which our government changes with changing times does not involve the sort of moral issues which cause anger and sometimes war. The ways in which a people organized in a state deal with the matters that confront them may be wise and bold, or stupid and fumbling; the political scene may be a forum of justice ably administered, or an arena of conflict where harsh ambition seizes and wields brutal power. Our time has seen both kinds, and others. The things done may be unjust and cruel and to that extent unethical, but political acts are not in their essence exercises in ethics. An analysis of the New Deal as a series of political changes and improvisations is difficult enough without the addition of moral premises and conclusions.

Both logically and in point of time the New Deal was the product of a destructive war and a decade of mingled effort to reconstruct a badly shaken world structure and, on this side of the Atlantic, to escape out of that crumbling world. We had experienced our great adventure and we wanted no more of of it. Our national debt in 1919 was just under twenty-five and a half billion dollars, three times the debt at the end of the Civil War. There were offsets. Our late allies owed us a large, undetermined amount, and our overseas investments had increased from three billion in 1914 to approximately fourteen billion in 1932. On balance, our national situation was excellent. There had been a brief recession early in the twenties dismissed generally as an incident to the liquidation of our wartime activities. Liquidation had not yet acquired the sinister implications that Messieurs Hitler, Mussolini, and Stalin were later to give it.

Financially we had a heavier stake in a stable world than we had ever dreamed or wished to have; politically and in general opinion we were chiefly concerned to withdraw from all participation in world affairs. The Fordney-McCumber Tariff Act in 1922 and the Smoot-Hawley Tariff Act of 1930 made successive raises in the protective wall around our infant industries to the highest point in our history and made foreign trade all but impossible. Within two years after the passage of the Smoot-Hawley bill, twenty-five countries had adopted retaliatory tariffs and the dream of the economic rehabilitation of the world was growing very dim.

In domestic affairs, as in foreign, the action of the government seemed contradictory and confused. While protective barriers were being strengthened and industrial prosperity seemed to be increasing steadily, the plight of the farmer was steadily growing worse. By 1932 the prices of farm products were only a third of those in 1920 and the wartime boom in farm lands had been liquidated in proportion. Foreclosures were increasing, and the proportion of tenant farmers to owners was growing ominously. During the war, farmers had responded enthusiastically to the reassuring slogan "Food Will Win the War." Painful as it is to close down surplus industries, it is even more painful to take out of cultivation farms that are no longer needed. In 1927 Congress passed the McNary-Haugen bill in an effort to cope with the mounting surplus in basic food products and give the farmer an equivalent to the protection that was being granted to industry. This bill provided for a somewhat complicated structure of export debentures in the form of an equalization fee to be spread over the total farm price level. In his message vetoing this bill on February 25, 1927, President Coolidge declared:

> It runs counter to the well-considered principle that a healthy economic condition is best maintained through a free play of competition than by undertaking to permit a legalized restraint of trade in these commodities and establish a species of monopoly under Government protection. . . . For many generations such practices have been denounced by law as repugnant to the public welfare.

The language of this sententious generalization was familiar American doctrine, but the embattled farmer could hardly be blamed for wondering why it was not applied with equal literalness to other forms of enterprise, some of them of less importance than farming. Meanwhile he remained caught in the fatal coil of circumstance. If he planted all his land, the market could not absorb the product, and the price dropped still further; if he let part lie fallow, he lost immediate and essential income. It was failure either way; the only difference was in speed of approach.

A variation of the dilemma was presented in the fate of

Senator Norris's bill for the government operation of the Muscle Shoals fertilizer plant and the production of electric power for the Tennessee Valley. In his veto message of March 3, 1931, President Hoover restated the case for individual enterprise versus government aid:

> The real development of the resources and the industries of the Tennessee Valley can only be accomplished by the people in that valley themselves. Muscle Shoals can only be administered by the people upon the ground, responsible to their own communities, directing them solely for the benefit of their own communities and not for purposes of pursuit of social theories or national politics. Any other course deprives them of liberty.

Here were presented the same antagonisms that had been implicit in the discussions of governmental philosophy for a generation. Would free competition and unrestricted enterprise automatically establish and maintain a state of freedom and equity? Or were some sort of controls necessary to prevent more people from becoming less free? Other questions pressed increasingly for answer: How free was a bankrupt farmer? Or an unemployed worker? Was it a prime function of government to demonstrate a concept of social action or inaction? The realities of the time were increasingly impatient of the debating of abstractions. Unemployment was growing and the reports of business failures were not reassuring.

The fatal day was October 24, 1929. That was the day when the stock market that had been showing steady and impressive gains for months turned down into the abyss. Twelve million shares were traded in on the New York exchange in four hours, and paper fortunes melted in the avalanche of selling. The descent slowed after a few days but, in spite of assurances that "Business is fundamentally sound," and "Revival is just around the corner," there was no upward trend. Two years later stock prices were only a fourth or a fifth of those that prevailed before the 1929 collapse, and unemployment was beginning to be a visible menace, twelve to fifteen million by the beginning of 1933. A political result was the election of a Democratic House of Representatives in 1930 and the old familiar discord between the House and the President.

By the time the party conventions were held in the early summer of 1932, the hope that the swing of the pendulum would bring back at least a semblance of the "prosperity" of 1928 had become dim. The Republicans nominated Hoover, but without enthusiasm. The Democrats chose Franklin D. Roosevelt, then serving his second term as governor of New York. The platform was sweeping in its denunciation of Republican policies and performance, and guarded in its promises. The tariff was to be put on a "competitive" basis, holding companies were to be controlled, federal aid to states for the relief of unemployment was recommended, general concern for the improvement of the farmer's condition was expressed but, beyond the establishment of special credit facilities, details were lacking. Strong emphasis was laid on the necessity of reducing government expenses and balancing the budget. (The national debt had increased twelve billion dollars in the budget year ending June 30, 1933.)

The campaign was remarkable chiefly for its studied avoidance of the economic realities of the time, especially unemployment and rapidly increasing bank failures. Roosevelt was elected by a popular majority of slightly over seven million votes. The new President was inaugurated in an atmosphere of gloom and foreboding. Bank failures had become epidemic, spreading from such industrial centers as Detroit and Toledo and threatening to engulf the whole country. There were few banks which felt themselves strong enough to withstand the drain of rapidly growing withdrawals by depositors and a general banking collapse seemed imminent.

The inaugural address by the new President, in which he

laid down the broad and rather vague lines of his policy, was in substance a call to action in a time of crisis; "the only thing we have to fear is fear itself, nameless, unreasoning, unjustified terror which paralyzes needed efforts to convert retreat into advance." He declared that the primary task was to put people to work, "treating the task as we would treat the emergency of war." He called attention to the need of a redistribution of population in the crowded industrial centers where the need of relief was greatest, thereby making possible a more effective use of the land. The purchasing power of the farmer must be increased by "definite efforts to raise the values of agricultural products." The foreclosure of farms and small homes must be prevented and relief efforts should be unified. The cost of governments, federal, state, and local, must be reduced.

> Finally, in our progress toward a resumption of work we require two safeguards against a return of the evils of the old order; there must be a strict supervision of all banking and credits and investments; there must be an end to speculation with other people's money, and there must be provision for an adequate but sound currency.

Roosevelt's first official act, the declaring of a national bank holiday, has been called a decree, and that is what it was. To the strict constructionists it should have been a fighting challenge. The fact that the constitutionality of the presidential order was not seriously raised by even the severest critics of the administration is a measure of the feeling of helplessness of the time. A major emergency had been met in a prompt and forthright manner and the effect was surprisingly reassuring. The widespread inconvenience was regarded as an incident, almost an amusing one, and the predominant feeling was that a menacing reality had been dealt with realistically. Five days later the Emergency Banking Act gave the color of strict legality to the decree by providing for the early ending of the holiday and the reopening of the sound banks under careful regulation and control. By the middle of April the hoarding of gold had been prohibited, again by presidential order, and the country had formally gone off the gold standard. On June 5 a joint resolution of Congress formally cut the Gordian knot of legal tender, that had been such a legal tangle after the Civil War, by cancelling the gold clause in all government and private contracts. The power of Congress to take such action was challenged and, in 1935, five cases involving this question reached the Supreme Court. In one of these, *John N. Perry* v. *U.S.*, the right of a holder of a gold bond issued by the government, "payable in United States gold coin of the present standard of value," to recover an amount of currency sufficient to compensate for the reduced value of the dollar due to the abandonment of the gold standard, the right of Congress to override an obligation of the government was vigorously denied but the plaintiff's claim for a larger amount of currency was denied on the ground that he had not proved damages.

A layman might summarize the decision as a warning that Congress had set foot on a road that held dangers but that the facts of the case at least did not justify the claim that injury had been done. The dilemma of the emergency was clearly implied. Congress had done an improper thing, but they had a right to do it. This perhaps was the essence of many controversies over the deeds and misdeeds of the New Deal. The chapter was rounded out in January, 1934, when the President asked and received authority from Congress to devalue the dollar to 59.06 cents, "to make possible the payment of public and private debts at more nearly the price level at which they had been incurred," thus meeting in part the old complaint of the farmer that he borrowed at one level and repaid at another, and less favorable, rate.

These banking and currency steps had dealt with only one

aspect of the emergency, that presented by the collapse of the banks. This was only the most immediately pressing need, a prelude to what was to follow. Congress was immediately called in special session and unwillingly passed a bill authorizing the President to cut salaries of federal employees and reduce veterans' benefits, in line with promises made during the campaign. It was only an empty gesture, a feeble fist shaken in the teeth of a hurricane. The next hundred days were to see the foundations laid for expenditure that would make this economy look like petty cash. It was clear that something much more drastic was needed if the government was attempting seriously to get the nation's economy out of the ditch.

The task of analyzing and interpreting the New Deal in terms of political philosophy and significance is not yet possible of accomplishment with any assurance, but there is reason for classifying the various acts in two categories: those aimed at setting the nation on the road to recovery; and those directed toward preventing a recurrence of the crisis. The terms recovery and reform have been often used as distinguishing these classifications and will serve as well as any for purposes of rough separation, although several measures fall under both headings. Neither the President nor his advisers offered anything more satisfactory by way of label or concept, and none has appeared since.

Considering recovery as the first necessity, next in line with the banking crisis were unemployment in industry and the farm collapse. Estimates of the numbers out of work differed widely, but agreed that it was excessive and was increasing. A common guess of twelve to fifteen millions out of jobs was only part of the story. Many were working part time and part-time work is also part-time unemployment. Wages had fallen out of proportion to the cost of living. Any figure of the total of jobless must be multiplied by three or four to indicate the number directly affected. The farmer was still at work, but to less purpose. His cash income had fallen from seven billion dollars in 1929 to two billions in 1932, a drop of seventy per cent in three years. Unemployment and farming collapse combined to produce an appalling breach in the nation's buying power. It was a vicious spiral leading downward, and there seemed little hope of reversing its movement.

It was farming that received the earliest "shot in the arm" in the form of the first Agricultural Adjustment Administration. The bête noire of agriculture was the huge surplus of staple products which was steadily mounting as each crop was harvested. The proposal of the first A.A.A. was the limitation of acreage and the compensation of the farmer, for the land thus left fallow, from the proceeds of a processing tax on farm products. Prices rose, but not as rapidly or as far as had been hoped. On January 6, 1936, the Supreme Court threw the act out as an improper use of the power to tax and an encroachment on the rights of states. Little attention was paid to the deeper significance of the bill as an attempt to bring about a reconstruction of the farming economy on the basis of self-sufficiency. This was a long look away from the old assumption that America was the breadbasket of the world. Two years after the Supreme Court had killed the A.A.A., it was revived with the objectionable tax feature omitted, and a standard set for prices of farm staples in the form of parity payments with authority to the Secretary of Agriculture to fix acreage, aimed at the establishment of an "ever normal granary." For the present this marks the termination of the "farmers' war" which had been in progress since the end of the Civil War.

The most sensational and controversial of the New Deal acts in that turbulent hundred days was the National Recovery Administration, the famous N.R.A. Here the administration reversed the procedure that it had followed in the case of farming. Instead of asserting a new policy and authority as in the A.A.A., the N.R.A. was an attempt to assist industry to effect its own recovery. Means were provided by which each industry could establish and administer codes under which it should agree to operate. Fair competition was to be defined and the opportunity offered for the elimination of price cutting as a competitive weapon. The clause around which the greatest controversy raged was the famous 7a, assuring to labor the right to organize and to bargain collectively with employers. A common criticism of the law was that it favored the large enterprises and was in effect a suspension of the Antitrust Act. It was charged also that the benefits to labor under 7a were illusory since company unions could easily be fitted into the framework of the law. The whole experiment enjoyed the doubtful advantage of being headed by General Hugh Johnson whose words and acts were usually of headline caliber. This, too, came to an early end at the hands of the Supreme Court on the double ground that Congress had made improper delegation of power to an administrative agency and had undertaken the control of intrastate commerce.

To the supporters of the New Deal the striking down of the N.R.A. was the high spot in the struggle between the administration and the Supreme Court and an extreme assertion of the right of the Court to sit in judgment on the wisdom and necessity of legislation beyond the widest implications of the Constitution, but it was only one of several. In addition to the N.R.A. and the A.A.A., the Court had invalidated the Guffey Coal Act, the Municipal Bankruptcy Act, the Railroad Retirement Act, and an act to prevent foreclosure of farm mortgages. In reaching these decisions the Court had invoked the old interpretation of the Fourteenth Amendment and in the coal and railroad cases had implied the existence of a no man's land in which neither state nor federal government could take effective action. The situation suggested that which had provoked Justice Holmes' famous comment on the power to legislate Herbert Spencer's *Social*

Statics. Whatever the merits of the conflict or of the individual cases, here was a clear issue involving the respective rights of the coordinate branches of the government. Until it was settled, the power of the administration to deal with wide and pressing social and economic problems was severely restricted. It is unfortunate that it was finally adjusted by resignations from the bench under the threat of the "court-packing" bill.[1]

The recovery project which aroused as much attention as any other of the New Deal experiments was the Works Progress Administration, W.P.A. in popular parlance. This was not in itself one of the recovery acts of the first hundred days, but was an outgrowth or a projection of the Public Works Administration of 1933 and the Civil Works Administration which was a child of the P.W.A. The W.P.A. was an attempt to relieve unemployment without too much risk of the corrosive effects of a direct dole, the obvious alternative. The plan involved the coordination of local, state, and federal governments. The work was limited to projects which could be classified as public with the local authorities proposing the specific enterprise and furnishing tools and materials and the federal government paying the wage bill. Workers as far as possible were taken from the relief rolls of the community concerned. The number of days and hours per week or month that each individual could work was limited to avoid the appearance of competition with private industry for workers. W.P.A. workers were a favorite theme for ironic comment, but the record of accomplishment was impressive. In the first two years of its existence, the years of greatest need, the record showed 1,634 school buildings, 1,497 water works, 883 sewage plants, 105 landing fields, 36,000 miles of new or improved rural roads, 263 hospitals, 166 bridges, 70 power plants, chiefly in small communities, and a bewildering array of

[1] This whole question and the cases concerned with it are discussed in detail in Chapter XVII, The Old and the New Supreme Court.

accomplishments in the provision of school hot lunches, medical and dental clinics, visiting nurse activities, and street and highway improvements.

There was boondoggling of course, not all of it of the leaf-raking variety. Lists of projects submitted by local governments revealed an embarrassing poverty of imagination in defining and applying the term "socially useful and necessary." Municipal stadiums and auditoriums in communities unable to make effective use of such structures were showy but expensive and of doubtful value. The so-called white-collar projects, especially the art, writers', and theater experiments came under a barrage of criticism and ridicule that was largely undeserved. The theater projects particularly were the means of taking some of the classics of the stage to thousands of people who had never seen a good play professionally produced. Congress seized an early opportunity to assert its superior virtue and save a few thousand dollars at the same time by cutting the theater allowance out of the appropriation. Before the writers' and art programs were discontinued, many useful state guides and local histories had been produced and the dull gray walls of many large and small post offices had been adorned by murals that were at the worst a welcome change from expanses of kalsomine in need of cleaning.

The total cost of relief in the three years of 1934, 1935, and 1936, the period of greatest need and relief activity, was something in excess of eight billion dollars. No attempt has been made to strike a balance between total cost and value of accomplishment, no such balance is possible. Whatever the worth of the roads and buildings and other improvements there remains the large imponderable item of the saving in human spirit and self-respect. Viewed as a labor force, a W.P.A. work crew contained naturally a large number of people to be classed as marginal even in normal times. In addition many were set at tasks for which they had little training or fitness. Their work efficiency has been set as low as fifty per cent of normal. Whatever it may have been, there remains the question of what would have happened to these human beings on a cash dole. An English study of the effect of the dole, published under the title, *Men Out of Work,* indicated that two years of continuous and complete worklessness went far toward destroying the will and the ability to work.

In the event of a recurrence of the conditions of 1933, it is highly probable that we shall see a return to the W.P.A. type of relief. In the political realm it is hard to see any new lesson learned except as a demonstration of the necessary responsiveness of government to widespread human need. England had made grudging admission of this fact as far back as the reign of Queen Elizabeth. We had learned, too, that the limiting of relief to local, state, and private agencies was a traditional assumption that lost its validity in the face of a national emergency. If a governmental philosophy is needed it can be found in Alexander Hamilton's assertion that government must have the powers that are necessary to enable it to govern. The charge that men on relief work were being pampered and would be unwilling to shift to full-time, full-pay jobs when opportunity offered has no weight in the light of actual experience when the demand for man power went into high gear.

The most dramatic and impressive of the New Deal measures was the oft-debated T.V.A., the Tennessee Valley Authority. A government nitrate plant at Muscle Shoals, Tennessee, built in the first World War too late to reach the production stage presented the opportunity. Attempts had been made to sell it to private capital, and Senator Norris of Nebraska had proposed its utilization for power production under government operation. Both proposals had fallen by the wayside, Senator Norris's meeting a presidential veto. During the presidential campaign of 1932 the Democratic candidate had served notice of an intention to work for the construction of government owned and operated power plants on the Columbia, St. Lawrence, Tennessee, and Colorado rivers.

The constitutional warrant for the act passed by Congress in May, 1933, was in the federal control over navigable rivers, but the authority given to the T.V.A. went far beyond flood control or dredging. The T.V.A. had power to produce electric power, to manufacture and sell nitrogen fertilizers, to promote reforestation and to withdraw marginal lands from cultivation to prevent erosion, and generally to "provide for the general welfare of the citizens of said areas." The "said areas" comprised some forty thousand square miles in seven states—Kentucky, Tennessee, Mississippi, Alabama, Georgia, North Carolina, and Virginia. Here was something new in government activity, nothing less than the rehabilitation of the whole region. Government was going into business, competing with private industry in the manufacture and sale of power and fertilizer on a large scale.

Naturally it was attacked as unconstitutional and hence invalid. In 1936 the constitutionality of the act was challenged in the Supreme Court in a suit brought by holders of preferred stock in the Alabama Power Company opposing the sale of certain properties of the company to T.V.A.[2] The decision handed down by Chief Justice Hughes held that the right of Congress to erect the original plant under the act of 1916 for purposes of national defense was clearly established and held further that the continuance and extension of the enterprise contemplated in the creation of the T.V.A. "constitute national defense assets." On the direct issue of the case before the court, the right to manufacture and sell power, the Chief Justice declared:

> The Government acquired full title to the dam site, with all riparian rights. The power of falling water was an inevitable

[2] *Ashwander et al.* v. *Tennessee Valley Authority*, 297 U.S. 288.

incident of the construction of the dam. That water power came into the exclusive control of the Federal Government. The mechanical energy was convertible into electric energy, and the water power, the right to convert it into electric energy, and the electric energy thus produced, constitute property belonging to the United States.

The T.V.A. experiment is still in the realm of the debatable and the controversial, a country in which the historian is ill at ease. The official reports are highly favorable, but these probably should not be taken at their face value. Too often such statements are overly optimistic. President Eisenhower has called it "creeping socialism," a characterization with which a Fabian socialist might cheerfully agree. Among the sober criticisms of the operation of the plan as an illustration of production at lower rates than with private enterprise it is necessary to note the tax-free aspect of T.V.A., thus throwing doubt on the statements of cost and largely invalidating the "yard-stick" use for comparison with private company rates. There is also serious question of the provision of adequate reserves for the replacement of plant. These are matters that no private company dares ignore. The Authority sedulously denies these charges and defends its accounting methods. Another claim made by the Authority in its own behalf is that private production in the region affected has increased rapidly and standards of living have risen steadily.

When so many experts of varying grades differ so sharply, the wise historian declines the role of judge. For the present T.V.A. remains as a historical fact of major dimensions and a visible reminder of the sweeping character of New Deal changes. It is also an example of government participation in a field previously held exclusively by private enterprise, perhaps an important dating point.

The terms recovery and reform have been used as offering a rough and ready classification of New Deal measures. It is a mistake to attempt to apply them literally and generally. In the main the steps taken in the first few months, especially the first hundred days, fall in the first category, and the reform, or preventive, measures came later. But many acts had elements of both, the ill-starred N.R.A., for example. W.P.A. which came later was entirely recovery, while measures that were primarily financial in purpose and character can be classed as reform or preventive. This was strikingly true of the Glass-Steagall Banking Act, signed by the President on June 16, 1933. This provided for the separation of investment from deposit banking and was aimed to prevent the imperiling of necessary banking functions by such speculative waves as had developed in 1929. This was followed by Federal Deposit Insurance, completely described in the title of the agency in charge, and in 1934 by the Securities Exchange Commission, the S.E.C.

The S.E.C. was entirely preventive in form and purpose. While the Glass-Steagall Act took the handling of investments away from banks of deposit, a step which had been taken by England nearly fifty years earlier, the S.E.C. set controls on the issuance of securities, gave the Federal Reserve Board the power to control margin trading and required the licensing of stock exchanges. At the time of its passage many financial leaders approved it as a type of reform that might well have been instituted by the governing bodies of exchanges in their own interest. The use of pools and options for the manipulation of stock prices was prohibited. A permanent securities commission was established and subsequent legislation has extended and strengthened its authority. The essence of the act was the protection of the investor against unnecessary and unfair risks of loss.

Allied in purpose to the S.E.C. was the Public Utility Holding Company Act designed to prevent the use of the holding company device by which a small number of men were able to control a large segment of the industry with a minimum of actual investment. The collapse of the Insull "Empire" gave special prominence to this proposal, but Insull was by no means alone. Congressional hearings had revealed that, in 1932, thirteen of the largest holding companies controlled seventy-five per cent of the public utilities industry. In many cases four or five individual companies separated the financial control, at the apex of the pyramid, from the operating companies, at the base, with which the consumer dealt. In its original form the bill gave the holding companies five years in which to prove that they performed useful functions, the alternative being dissolution. This was the famous "death sentence" clause. As finally passed in August, 1935, two levels of holding companies above the operating company were permitted. This, together with the control exercised by the S.E.C. over the issuance of securities and the financial practices of the companies, was accepted by the President as adequate for the purpose.

It is unnecessary to list and discuss all or even a majority of the multitudinous New Deal steps taken for purposes of recovery or reform or both. The Federal Farm Credit Corporation, the Home Owners' Loan Corporation, the Rural Electrification Administration, and a host of others are adequately characterized by their titles, and there is no need to multiply illustration and instance. Much of the legislation was ill-conceived and hastily drawn; many new authorities served a useful purpose but in an unnecessarily censorious and dictatorial manner.

The most valid criticism aimed at the whole body of New Deal legislation was that Congress was seeking to make general delegation of legislative and judicial powers as well as administrative, although in all cases recourse to the courts was possible. The charge of undue delegation raises a large question which is not likely to be answered by the courts, except temporarily and in specific cases. The nub of the problem is the increasingly technical and specialized character of relations and functions in a highly industrialized society. A hundred years earlier Jackson's claim that any man could fill any governmental post acceptably held a measure of truth, but it is true no longer. If an illustration is sought, a casual survey of the routine activities of any department, say the Department of Agriculture, will provide it. As the tapestry of American life becomes more involved and overlapping the acts and responsibilities of government are drawn into the weaving. In concluding his *History of the Constitution of the United States,* Andrew Jackson McLaughlin recorded his conclusion that we were inevitably shifting from a government that does as little as possible to one that does as much as is necessary.

In the beginning years of the New Deal, organized labor complained that its interests were being ignored although its stake was large. The N.R.A. in section 7a had recognized the right to organize, but to labor this was more than offset by the door that other sections opened for the formation of company unions. The invalidation of the N.R.A. by the Supreme Court in May, 1935, threw 7a into the scrap heap and added to labor's bitterness. In July of that year the Wagner-Connery Act came to their rescue. This act, officially styled National Labor Relations Act, was described in its official title as "An Act to diminish the causes of labor disputes burdening or obstructing interstate or foreign commerce, to create a National Labor Relations Board, and for other purposes." Section I prohibits employers from denying to employees the right to organize and to bargain collectively through representatives of their own choosing. The board created by the act consisted of three persons and had wide authority "from time to time to make, amend, and rescind such rules and regulations as may be necessary to carry out the provision of this Act." Provision was made in section 9 for the free choice by employees of the representatives that were to act, and section 10 prohibited unfair labor practices by employers, particularly interference "with the formation or administration of any labor organization," or discrimination against union members. The board also had the power to hold and supervise elections for the determination of the union to be formed where two or more unions were seeking to organize. The board had power to conduct investigations and to issue subpoenas to compel the attendance of witnesses or the presentation of documentary evidence. Section 13 guaranteed to labor the "right to strike." Appeal to the courts by any aggrieved person or group was specifically assured.

The Board was bitterly attacked as autocratic and unduly favorable to labor, especially to C.I.O. which had been recently organized. The constitutionality of the act came in question in the case of *N.L.R.B.* v. *Jones & Laughlin Steel Corporation* which was decided by the Supreme Court in 1937. The decision, written by Chief Justice Hughes, denied the claim that the acts of the board were an attempt to control labor relations rather than commerce and that the defendant was not in effect engaged in interstate commerce. The defendant's allegation that the activities of the company were in reality production within a single state and as such not subject to congressional control, whether direct or delegated to a body created by act of Congress, was rejected on the ground that the business concerned was an interdependent enterprise involving action in many states and that the labor practice complained of had direct effect on interstate commerce. Justices McReynolds, Van Devanter, Sutherland, and Butler dissented.

The Wagner Act was amended by the Taft-Hartley Act, passed by Congress, June 23, 1947, over President Truman's veto. In spite of strenuous efforts to force the repeal of Taft-Hartley, Congress stood pat and the act is still the law of the land. This is a long and complicated measure and not always easy to understand, but the basic provisions are clear. One of the more important is the declaration that the employer shall have equal right with the employee to appeal to the board on the ground of unfair union practices. Employers are given full freedom for the expression of their views of unions, short of threats of reprisal and promise of benefits. They are also permitted to ask for the election of bargaining units. The closed shop is banned and restrictions are placed on union shops. Unions are required to give sixty days' notice of the termination or modification of contracts and can be sued for breach of contract. Union heads are also required to make affidavit that they are not members of the Communist party.

The most complicated provision of the act is that dealing with "national emergency strikes." After a report from a board of inquiry appointed by the President, the attorney general may apply for an injunction restraining all strike activity for sixty days. If no settlement is reached in that period, the injunction may be extended for twenty days to permit a secret ballot among employees to discover their willingness to accept the terms offered by the employer. If no settlement is effected by these procedures, the act provides that the President shall make a full report to Congress "with such recommendations as he may see fit to make for consideration and appropriate action."

The Taft-Hartley Act was heatedly debated in Congress and throughout the country. Senator Taft said of it, "This bill simply reduces special privileges granted to labor union leaders." Labor denounced it as a "slave labor act," but offered no substitute or compromise. The demand made for outright repeal was denied and the bill was put in operation.

Foster Rhea Dulles, in the discussion of Taft-Hartley in his *Labor in America,* sums up the present status and significance of the act, saying:

> . . . it primarily marked a still further assumption of governmental responsibility in what had always proved to be the immensely difficult task of maintaining a reasonable balance be-

tween labor and industry. It was a further expression, for better or for worse, of the popular feeling that labor relations should be subject to the sovereign power of the people and controlled in the interests of the public welfare.[3]

Labor had an especial interest in the Social Security Act passed in August, 1935. This was a multi-barrel affair comprising ten particular acts, or "titles," providing aid for the aged, the unemployed, dependent children (children under sixteen deprived of parents' support) mothers and children "especially in rural areas and in areas suffering from severe economic distress," for public health services, and for the blind. By the provisions of this act the operation was a joint responsibility of the federal and state governments. Federal payments were made to the states for the uses named and the administration was under state control but subject to federal approval and supervision. No appropriations were to be made to states failing to make adequate financial contributions. In the case of the unemployed, funds were to be provided by payroll taxes paid by employer and employee.

The act has been criticized because of the systems of records and accounts used. It is charged also that the estimates of the total numbers eligible in the various categories are much too low. There is serious question of the ability of the government to maintain the large reserves necessary for prompt action.

The provision for old-age pensions emphasized the changing character of our population. Life expectancy has increased bewilderingly in recent years and, in consequence, our total age averages the country over have risen, although this is partially offset by the increased birth rate in recent years. To put the general tendency bluntly more of us are living longer and each year finds more of us still lingering around beyond the normal working age. An unexpected corol-

[3] Foster Rhea Dulles, *Labor in America* (Thomas Y. Crowell Company, 1950).

lary is the extent to which pension and retirement plans in private industry are being added to the government stipend provided.

If the principle of government responsibility for the aid of the aged, the unemployed, the needy, and the helpless is accepted, the only political aspect to be noted is the coordination of federal and state governments in financing and administering. This is not a new development but it does help to point up the tendency of states to become more and more administrative agencies rather than guardians of reserved and sovereign rights. Here again the pattern of change is in the direction suggested by Alexander Hamilton. We praise Jefferson, but we follow Hamilton.

When did the New Deal end, if ever? What are the marked differences between the first and second terms? These are favorite themes for argument with the great advantage that a final answer is impossible, and unimportant even if possible. One thing is certain: the election of 1936 gave overwhelming approval to results to that date. The Republican candidate was Alfred M. Landon, formerly governor of Kansas. He was a political unknown outside his own state when he was nominated and only slightly less unknown when the campaign ended. Only Maine and Vermont stayed in the Republican column, eliciting the rueful comment that the other forty-six states had withdrawn from the Union.

By the time the President was inaugurated the second time, Europe was obscured by the clouds of war and thick overcast was reducing visibility over Asia. In the fall of 1937 the President suggested the desirability of quarantining aggressor nations, obviously Germany, Italy, and Japan, and, although the general opinion of the country failed to support him, it was growing increasingly clear that the overseas menace was real and growing. The events that followed rapidly after the beginning of European war in the fall of 1939 are generally known, but their essential meaning is still unsure. For purposes of political appraisal the New Deal faded as the war drew nearer. The major lessons that it contains are to be found largely in the first four or five years, and any attempt to trace its influence and meaning into the future, near or remote, belongs under another heading. The Roosevelt Revolution, if that is what it was, belongs to the first term.

To what does it add up? In spite of the hectic discussions of alleged unconstitutionality and frequent charges of violation, the venerable document seems to have come through with no perceptible impairment. Certainly no parallel to Lincoln's assertion of war powers in the denial or limitation of civil rights can be discovered. In certain cases where the Supreme Court invalidated laws on the ground of unconstitutionality dissenting opinion stigmatized the majority decision as unsound and in one instance declared that it rested on a tortured interpretation of the fundamental law. Congress was within its constitutional rights in making broad delegations of power to administrative agencies, although the desirability of such sweeping grants could be, and was, questioned. The tension of the time led many voters to make their first careful study of the Constitution, a useful by-product which can be credited to both sides of the debate.

The demonstration that a powerful President will go farther and do more than a mediocre or average incumbent was merely an addition to previous lessons on this subject. The word "politician" was frequently applied as a term of reproach, disregarding the fact that the powerful presidents of the past, with the possible exception of Jackson, have had more than an average share of political acumen. The man who lacks it is headed for trouble, whatever his administrative capacity. The headlong creation of administrative bodies, often overlapping or conflicting in the earlier years, swelled the government payroll and gave reason for the fear of setting up an unwieldy bureaucracy. The excuse and partial justification was the urgency of the need.

After all the debates are ended there remains the axiomatic fact that strong Presidents in time of crisis will take strong steps. The case cannot be stated more clearly and succinctly than by George Fort Milton in the concluding paragraph of his excellent study, *The Use of Presidential Power:*

> Irrespective of the individuals who occupy the White House in the kaleidoscopic years to come, it can be confidently predicted that the President of the United States will employ old powers in new ways, or discover new sources of power, if he even begins to cope with the crises which will continue to arise. It is of the essence that a President in a time of crisis find and employ power adequate to the emergency. Weak men in the high office will fumble as Buchanan. Strong men in time of crisis will continue to make great Presidents.[4]

One of the criticisms sometimes leveled at the New Deal is that its measures were experimental in form. This involves a queer misunderstanding of our own past, which can truthfully be described as a series of experiments. The expedients and changes in the application of our public-land policy furnish excellent illustration of this fact. In one of his dissenting opinions Justice Holmes said of the Constitution: "It is an experiment, as all life is an experiment." [5]

It is of the nature of an emergency that it does not follow a prescribed path and cannot be met with orthodox and familiar means. One of the advantages of a democracy such as ours is that it permits the process of trial and error.

How much of a revolution was the New Deal then? So far as constitutional changes or new interpretations were concerned, none at all. So far as purpose can be derived from act, there is strong ground for the conclusion that the administration sought to preserve and strengthen the existing social

---

[4] George Fort Milton, *The Use of Presidential Power, 1789–1943* (Little, Brown & Co.), p. 322.
[5] *Abrams* v. *United States*, 250 U.S. 616.

and economic system rather than to destroy it. The charge of socialism is easier to make than to prove. In form and purpose the New Deal was a return to the pattern of thought and action that stretched from Populist days through the Progressivism of Theodore Roosevelt and the New Freedom of Woodrow Wilson. If this is a just verdict then the decade of the twenties is a regrettable hiatus, a suspension of activity and not a positive program. The speed and range of the acceptance of social responsibility had been a shock to those who hoped and believed that the Coolidge and Hoover administrations heralded a return to what they regarded as older and safer ways.

The label of socialism may not apply, but the desire for a greater socialization of our economy was clearly present. Did the New Deal, with its bewildering array of alphabetical agencies—P.W.A., W.P.A., A.A.A., T.V.A.—bring the depression to an end? In fairness it must be said that the evil of unemployment was not ended, only mitigated. There had been signs of recovery in 1936, but in the fall of 1937 clouds gathered again and the reviving stock market sank back, not to the old depression levels, but far enough to be disturbing. Perhaps it was only a relapse, but patients have been known to die in such circumstances. When a rally began to make itself felt, was it a result of New Deal remedies, or, as many critics have pointed out, a response to the stimulant of approaching war? From 1938 on we have lived in an atmosphere of war, near or remote, and we have not found the sure cure for unemployment.

CHAPTER XVII

The Old and the New Supreme Court
(D. R.)

As we have seen, the so-called Roosevelt Revolution did not follow the lines of historic revolutions. There was no popular uprising and seizure of power. No forceful overthrow of a government. No abrupt transfer of governing power from one ruling class to another. The Constitution of the United States remained visibly unaltered from the day President Roosevelt took office to the end of his four terms, with the one exception of the ratification of the Twenty-first Amendment (repealing the prohibition amendment); and that amendment had been proposed before he was inaugurated.

But, in the period from 1933 to 1945, the Roosevelt influence wrought such changes in the operations, the methods of administration, and the authority exercised by the federal government, as to constitute a political revolution of first magnitude. A large majority of the electorate was persuaded to approve, or at least acquiesce in, two major developments of governing power: first, the assumption by the federal government of an authority and responsibility to evolve and to regulate a national economic system which would protect and promote the general welfare; second, the enlargement of the powers of the Congress and the President so that they might be able to fulfill this new responsibility.

This enlargement of congressional power required a corresponding diminution of power in state governments and in the federal judiciary. However, the opposition of state governments never seriously embarrassed the revolutionary forces. The traditional strongholds of states rights were in the South where traditional support of the Democratic party made it easy for a nationalistic administration of Democrats to retain the support of popular majorities. The obvious need for national solutions of national problems made it difficult for conservative Republicans in the North and West to arouse popular opposition in states where Republican leaders for decades had preached nationalism and scorned "reactionary" pleas to preserve the powers of local self-government.

With the enormous power of unlimited income taxation (granted by the Sixteenth Amendment in 1913) the federal government was now able to raise vast sums for unemployment relief, for expenditure in public works, for home owners' relief and aid in home building, for subsidies to agriculture, and for loans to industry, and thus to pour millions upon millions of dollars into every state. No politician could, if he would, persuade his constituents to reject such bounty. Christmas still came only once a year; but the new-found Santa Claus came every day.

The obstruction of the federal judiciary presented for a time the only effective barrier to the spread, with breathtaking speed, of federal controls over the living and working conditions of all Americans. Some blockading was inevitable in the high court where the preservation of constitutional limitations upon federal power had long been regarded as its most solemn duty. This had been sternly fulfilled by the justices, according to their lights, in the era of "judicial supremacy."

The philosophic, economic, and political views of those eventually described as the "old judges" have been reviewed in a previous chapter. The modification, and overruling, of the "older" opinions of the Supreme Court began with the shifting of the majority judgment through which the "court packing" proposal was finally done to death. Then, by the successive retirements of Justices Van Devanter (1937), Sutherland (1938), Cardozo (1938–died), Brandeis (1939), Butler (1939–died) and McReynolds (1941), President Roosevelt was able to appoint Justices Black (1937), Reed (1938), Frankfurter (1939), Douglas (1939), Murphy (1940) and Byrnes (1941). With the retirement of Chief Justice Hughes (1941), the President elevated Justice Stone to Chief Justice and appointed Justice Jackson (1941); and, after the resignation of Justice Byrnes (1942), he named Justice Rutledge (1943).

Thus it is evident that a definitely "new" Supreme Court came into being before the entry of the United States in World War II in December, 1941. Before his death, in 1945, President Roosevelt had appointed eight of the nine justices to the position which each then held. (This included the elevation of Justice Stone.) No one well acquainted with Franklin D. Roosevelt would suspect him of knowingly investing anyone with the power to frustrate him. Who would be likely to do so!

The Roosevelt Revolution established the dominant influence of a strong chief executive, subject only to some restraint by strong leaders of bi-partisan forces in Congress and to little restraint by a partisan Supreme Court. In one view this was no revolution at all because from early times strong Presidents such as Jefferson and Jackson had sought to dominate the Congress, and to insure their programs against obstruction by maintaining or creating a sympathetic Supreme Court. In another view, however, it was a veritable revolution because of the unprecedented expansion of federal authority which had been growing ever since the Civil War and then was rapidly accelerated by the successive national calamities of World War I, the Great Depression, and World War II.

The necessities of this era not only had forced an autocratic leadership upon the President but also had created a popular demand for such a leadership. The people in large numbers wanted the President to solve their common problems and, when his programs met their hopeful approval, they wanted the Congress to write them into law, and they didn't want the Supreme Court to nullify them. When the President tapped the public resources of wealth and credit, and the private taxable resources of those who had made or could make "surplus" money, and this kept a golden flow of assistance moving to the less fortunate, he acquired the support of voting majorities. When he created huge bureaucracies to administer all these popular projects, he not only acquired the support of a vast number of federal employees and federal dependents, but also increased his powers of patronage with which to gain and maintain the support of the national legislators.

In this manner, and largely because of the earlier passage of the income tax amendment, the way was prepared for a strong executive to achieve that "executive supremacy" (as President and as Commander in Chief of the armed forces in two world wars) which had been so feared by the framers of the Constitution. Only the Supreme Court for a brief period blocked the way. When this barrier was overcome the reality of the "revolution" was made plain.

Following the resignation of Justice Roberts in 1945, and the deaths of Chief Justice Stone (1946), Justices Murphy (1949) and Rutledge (1949), and the appointments by President Truman of Justice Burton (1945), Chief Justice Vinson (1946), and Justices Clark (1949) and Minton (1949), the Court remained a "new" Court, in the sense of being fundamentally different in its philosophy from the "old," pre-Roosevelt Court.

There has been no such unanimity of opinion in the "new" Court as would permit anyone to assume in advance what opinion even a majority would agree upon in a particular case. But there have been certain underlying predispositions of at least a majority—and probably a large majority—that have given reasonable assurance that expansions of federal authority by laws enacted by the Congress and by generous exercises of granted or implied powers by the Executive Department, were not likely to be checked by any strict constructions of the Constitution—except possibly where certain civil rights were involved.

Accordingly it is necessary to assume that the federal government is now well fortified for the comprehensive exercise of powers which twenty years ago were held closely restricted by constitutional provisions, intended to protect local self-government and individual liberty. These are: the power to regulate commerce, the power of taxation, and the treaty power.

The only effective restraint upon the sweeping exercises of these powers lies today, apparently, in the self-restraint of a majority of the members of Congress. An understanding of how this devitalization of the Constitution and abnegation of judicial authority has come about is essential to an understanding of the reality of the Roosevelt Revolution and the development of a new governing power in the United States.

In historical retrospect we can see plainly those fears of governmental power that animated the framers of our Constitution. Those fears might or might not animate the same men if they were facing today, in changed economic and political conditions, the similar problem of constructing a government strong enough under these conditions to protect the general welfare but not strong enough to become a political tyranny.

The founding fathers feared the power of government to rule over industry—to control the making of a livelihood.

They feared the power of a centralized government to subordinate local self-government to remote and concentrated controls.

They feared the power of unrestrained lawmaking, in any government, to deprive a people of individual liberty to pursue happiness so far as their individual ambitions would move them and their individual abilities would permit.

These fears were written into the constitutions of the several states in the form of rights of citizens against the government and limitations upon the lawmaking powers of state legislatures.

Most emphatically these fears were written into the Constitution of the United States, by granting only carefully limited and defined powers of lawmaking to the Congress, by reserving to the separate states "or to the people" all powers "not delegated" to the United States (except those prohibited to the states), and by enumerating the rights of the people as individuals *against* the federal government, in the Bill of Rights, and then finally by providing that, "The enumeration in the Constitution of certain rights shall not be construed to deny or disparage others retained by the people."

From 1787 to 1937—one hundred and fifty years—these fears remained as vital influences controlling the interpretation and enforcement of the Constitution by the Supreme Court. At times it seemed that they were brushed aside under pressure of events that demanded the solution of new economic and political problems. But always when the "clear and present danger" became evident that fundamental principles were being ignored and obvious restrictions upon excessive governmental power were being flagrantly violated, there would be warning voices or stern rebukes from a judiciary which was conscientiously endeavoring to support and defend the Constitution as the supreme law of the land.

This comment does not imply that the "new" Supreme Court has been any less conscientious than the "old" Court.

It is only intended as an introduction to a comparison between "new" and "old" opinions so that the profound change in interpretation of constitutional limitations may be made plain. There is just as much conscientious devotion to a public duty in seeking to loosen the binding force of ancient doctrines and restrictions so that government may meet its new responsibilities, as there is in striving to hold fast to restraints upon political power which one believes have everlasting virtue. The important thing for a student of history to understand is what and when and how changes in government are brought about. Then he may not be misled by the use of the same words to mean utterly different activities or concepts, as when, for example, Soviet spokesmen refer to the objectives of communism as "democracy," and describe the imposition of a tyranny as a "liberation."

The most obvious change in the philosophy of the "new" Supreme Court has been revealed in its increasing deference to legislative and executive judgment. This has been extended far byond the time-honored refusal to review the wisdom of the ways and means chosen by a legislature for the exercise of a conceded power. The Court has always been loathe to hold that a law was "unreasonable" or "arbitrary" merely because it might be criticized as undesirable. An opinion of the "new" Court in 1940 [1] reasserted this old and well-established doctrine.

> Those matters, however, relate to questions of policy, to the wisdom of the legislation, and to the appropriateness of the remedy chosen—matters which are not our concern. If we endeavored to appraise them we would be trespassing on the legislative domain.

There was nothing revolutionary in such a doctrine. The contribution of the Court to the success of the Roosevelt

[1] *Anthracite Coal Co. v. Adkins*, 310 U.S. 381.

Revolution became evident, however, in its novel acceptance of the opinion of a majority of Congressmen that they could extend their own lawmaking powers beyond the limits strictly defined in the Constitution. When, for example, the Court unanimously held: "The power of Congress over interstate commerce is not confined to the regulation of commerce among the states," [2] even a Congressman who had read the Constitution might be shocked.

The reason given by the Court had a plausibility that might satisfy or confuse a "man-in-the-street." It was that commerce wholly within one state might "affect" commerce "among the states." But, a puzzled farmer might say: "If I raise grain as food for myself and my livestock, that may 'affect' interstate commerce in such grain, because I won't buy such grain raised in other states; but if the federal government has only a power to regulate what *is* interstate commerce how can it have any power to regulate my raising a crop for my own use? If that is any kind of 'commerce,' it certainly isn't interstate commerce."

However, such a farmer's objection to federal regulation of his local work, his self-support and his individual liberty, has been definitely overruled by the Supreme Court.[3] The new doctrine has been declared repeatedly by the Court that if, in order to exercise a "granted power" (such as regulation of interstate commerce), it is an "appropriate means" for the Congress to exercise a power *not granted* (such as regulation of local production for local use), the Congress can lawfully exercise such an unlawful power.

This is a truly revolutionary doctrine; but one essential to full judicial support of the Roosevelt Revolution. Under it the national lawmakers are now authorized to exercise powers never granted to them, but on the contrary specifically denied to them, whenever they find that such an exercise of

---

[2] *U.S.* v. *Darby*, 312 U.S. 100.
[3] *Wickard* v. *Filburn*, 317 U.S. 111.

an unlawful power will assist them in exercising a lawful power. There was an attempt to establish such a doctrine to aid the national government in the throes of a civil war. It was denounced by the Supreme Court in words which still reverberate in the courts. Military tribunals had been established in areas which were not battlefields; but the Supreme Court denied their authority (although they were obviously "appropriate means" to aid in the exercise of a conceded war power). The court held: [4]

> The Constitution of the United States is a law for rulers and people, equally in war and in peace, and covers with the shield of its protection all classes of men, at all times, and under all circumstances. No doctrine, involving more pernicious consequences, was ever invented by the wit of man than that any of its provisions can be suspended during any of the great exigencies of government.

The revolutionary character of the new Supreme Court doctrine lies in its disregard for the plain meaning of plain words written in the Constitution which the Court is sworn to support. The jurisdiction of the Congress, although *geographically* extending into the areas of all the states, was expressly limited by the Constitution to the *subject matter* of "commerce among the several states"; which would confine federal laws to regulating activities or movements of persons or things in interstate commerce, or which interfered with or controlled such interstate commerce. This meaning of the plain words in the Constitution is so plain that the Supreme Court was compelled to say that the power of Congress is not confined within the limits defined by these words, but that it can assume a power to regulate anything which "affects" commerce. This doctrine destroys practically all the visible limits on federal power, because almost every activity in a state might "affect" interstate commerce. Crime, local cus-

[4] *Ex parte Milligan,* 4 Wall, 2.

toms or habits, social relations and health conditions, all "affect" interstate commerce. But it had been the settled law of the Constitution from the time of its adoption that these matters of "internal concern" were left to state regulation under the state police power. No such police power was granted to the Congress and it was uniformly held by the Supreme Court, until very recently, that the limited grant of a jurisdiction to the Congress to regulate interstate commerce did not and could not authorize the exercise of any federal power over such subjects of the reserved powers of the states as purely local production and trade.

The age-old rule of law is that no government official can exercise any authority outside the limits of his jurisdiction, which are prescribed by the statute or constitution from which he derives his authority. This may be a geographical limit or a subject-matter limit. For example, no state court can summon a witness and compel his attendance when he is in another state, no matter how helpful this might be to the administration of justice. No state police officer can himself arrest and bring back a criminal from another state. A state legislature cannot enact a law to regulate persons and properties and activities in another state.

All this is elementary law. But, the fact that there are no *geographical limits* (within the United States) to the exercise of the powers of the national government seems to have blinded many lawyers to the important fact that *subject-matter limits* are equally rigid limits of any legislative jurisdiction and power. From this it would logically follow that although the Congress was granted jurisdiction to regulate persons and things moving in interstate commerce, and activities interfering with, or obstructing, or designed to regulate such commerce, it was granted and has no jurisdiction whatsoever over the production, purchase and sale of goods wholly within a state, or over other local activities of persons not engaged in interstate commerce nor seeking to regulate interstate commerce, even though such activities may have an incidental effect upon what is interstate commerce.

It was the overriding of this constitutional limit upon federal jurisdiction, by the Congress with the sanction of the Supreme Court, that accomplished a revolutionary change in the government of the United States in the short space of less than fifteen years. This investing of the federal government with supreme and unlimited power to regulate the economic, and incidentally the social, life of the nation may have been desirable or undesirable; but it was not brought about as the result of additional grants of power by a constitutional amendment. It was accomplished by the assumption and exercise of an unconstitutional power by the Congress and the sanction of such power by the Supreme Court.

Those who think that this extension of federal power is undesirable may find some comfort in noting that a power extended by this method may be abandoned or nullified without the difficult, protracted procedure of amending the Constitution in order to repeal a misguided amendment, which was necessary to repair the grievous error of the prohibition amendment.

The purpose of the foregoing account of the essential part played by the "new" Supreme Court in the expansion of the federal commerce power has not been to express any futile dissent, but simply to make it clear that revolutionary changes in our form and methods of government can be accomplished by congressional assumptions and exercises of powers never granted to Congress (or even expressly denied) so long as the Executive Branch will administer and the Judicial Branch will sanction such unauthorized lawmaking. The fundamental theory of popular government is that all governmental authority is created and granted by the people and that no public official can exercise any power which is not granted, or any power beyond the limits of the jurisdiction granted. In the course of the New Deal, however, exercises of power not granted by the people were proposed by executive officials, were written into laws by legislators, were sanctioned and enforced by the judiciary, and finally were administered by the executives who proposed them. Thus a new method was revealed for making revolutionary changes in the government of the United States without bloodshed or popular approval by means of a constitutional amendment.

It has been argued that in this new method popular government has been preserved because the collaboration of all branches of government is necessary, which would be impossible if these public officials did not genuinely represent the will of the people. But, it is of the essence of popular government that the people themselves must deliberately grant and limit all power to be exercised over them. A people who were induced to invest their representatives with unlimited power to make and enforce laws would not establish a popular government but a political tyranny.

By the same token people, induced to sit idly by while their representatives vote to exercise powers of government not granted, but in fact denied to them, are not enjoying "popular government." They are merely tolerating the destruction of popular government. They do not enjoy the opportunity of deliberately granting to their representatives large powers which may be used for evil as well as good ends. They simply consent to, or even applaud, an exercise of power that for the moment promises to benefit them. They do not knowingly grant a new or extended power that may eventually be used to injure them. Thus is developed government of the people, perhaps for the people, but not by the people.

After this intensive review of the revolutionary extension of the federal commerce power a more summary explanation may be attempted of the absence of a restraining influence from the Supreme Court upon recent or imminent expansions of two other federal powers: the power of taxation and the treaty power.

It was inevitable, after the passage of the Sixteenth Amendment, that the power of income taxation would give to the federal government ability to raise and spend enormous sums of money, which would increase vastly the powers of the central government.

In retrospect it appears that the opposition of those who opposed the amendment on the ground of its "socialistic" possibilities might have sought more wisely and successfully to place some limitation on the percentage of income subject to federal expropriation rather than to have opposed absolutely a power of taxation which the national government sorely needed to meet modern demands of national defense. In this manner the disparity which developed between federal and state powers to protect and promote the general welfare might have been avoided, with the result of less dependence of the people of the several states on the federal return of moneys collected from them.

There are now practically no visible limits to the imposition and spending of federal taxes, except the toleration and capacity of the people to bear them. There was an historic dispute [5] as to whether the federal taxing power was limited by the Constitution to taxes for the purpose of carrying out the enumerated powers of the federal government. The Constitution authorized taxes "to pay the Debts and provide for the common Defence and general Welfare of the United States." The argument was plausible that, since the federal government was one of limited enumerated powers, the only "general welfare" confided to the federal government lay within the field of its specifically granted powers. On the other hand the argument was: Why was a taxing power specifically granted which must be implied anyhow for the execution of the enumerated powers?

The Supreme Court finally decided this dispute in 1936,[6]

[5] Discussed in Chapter III.
[6] *U.S. v. Butler*, 297 U.S. 1.

but the only reason cited for its approval of the Hamilton-Story construction, that a separate additional power had been granted as against the Madison limiting construction, was not impressive. The Court, in the opinion of Mr. Justice Roberts, stated that it would be mere "tautology" to regard the grant of the taxing power as simply supplemental aid to the execution of other granted powers, because, of course, the taxing power would be implied in the granted powers, as necessary and proper to their execution.

The learned justice thus brushed aside the long debates in the Constitutional Convention as to how the taxing power should be and must be limited. Nevertheless, in his opinion, Justice Roberts pointed out that even Hamilton "never suggested that any power granted by the Constitution could be used for the destruction of local self-government in the States." And his final decision was that the Agricultural Adjustment Act was invalid because it attempted to extend Congressional power to the regulation of agricultural production, which was a power reserved to the states, and thus attempted to use the federal taxing power as a "means to an unconstitutional end."

In this case the dissenting Justices, Stone, Brandeis and Cardozo, would have upheld the tax on the ground that it provided for a voluntary acceptance of payments made to farmers "to promote the general welfare." But, their opinion also held that "The power to tax and spend is not without constitutional restraints. One restriction is that the purpose must be truly national. Another is that it may not be used to coerce state action."

Nevertheless, the entire court set aside the one clear definition of a "national purpose" which was made by the writers of the Constitution when they specifically enumerated all the powers of the national government and expressly wrote that all others were "reserved to the States respectively, or to the people." Thus, again, the door was left wide open for the

Congress to decide what was a national purpose and for the Supreme Court then, with its new humility, to sanction the judgment of Congress. Through this open door came the Social Security Act,[7] and then the expenditure of general taxes to support a new agricultural regulation act, which was enacted in the asserted exercise of the federal commerce power, which was now sufficiently enlarged by a legislative-judicial collaboration to cover even regulation of the local raising and use of grain to feed a farmer's own family and his own livestock.

In a courteous obeisance to the Constitution it is still judicially noted that a "line must be drawn" between "the general welfare" and what is not "general." But the Supreme Court has unanimously agreed that this "is a practical question" and that "it will require a very plain case to warrant the courts in setting aside the conclusion of Congress in that regard." [8]

Justice Roberts, speaking for a majority of the Court, said in 1936 that the Constitution closed the door to any "scheme for purchasing with federal funds submission to federal regulation of a subject reserved to the states" and that Hamilton and Story would have both agreed that the taxing power could not "be used for the destruction of local self-government in the states." Only one year later the door was flung wide open by the Supreme Court. This is not an adverse criticism of the Court. It is the simple recording of a fact. It emphasizes again that "the Constitution is what the judges say it is."

We come now to a brief discussion of the recent expansion of the treaty power. Under the Constitution a treaty with another nation becomes a part of the "supreme law of the land." A treaty can be adopted by the signature of the President and its subsequent approval by a vote of two thirds of

---

[7] *Steward Machine Co.* v. *Davis*, 301 U.S. 548.
[8] *Cincinnati Soap Co.* v. *U.S.*, 301 U.S. 308.

the Senators "present," that is, by two thirds of a quorum. There is the possibility of a later nullification of a treaty by a conflicting law enacted by the entire Congress, or by a refusal of the Congress to pass laws necessary for the execution of the treaty, or by a refusal to appropriate money necessary to carry it into effect. However, a treaty may be partially or entirely self-executing, as, for example, a treaty giving aliens a right to own land. Then state laws denying such a right are immediately nullified and alien ownership of land will be upheld by the courts.

Until recently treaties were normally only an agreement between the United States and one other nation and would establish rights and impose duties governing reciprocally the relations and intercourse between the two nations and between their respective citizens. A treaty would only incidentally establish rights and duties governing the internal relations and activities of the citizens of a nation with one another. In a word, a treaty would only supersede state laws of local self-government in minor and comparatively unimportant cases.

When, however, the United States made a treaty with many other nations, in approving the Charter of the United Nations, an unprecedented extension of federal power, over an indefinite number of matters of hitherto only domestic or local concern, became imminent. Some of the provisions of the charter have already been held by the courts to be self-executing, and therefore to have nullified conflicting state laws, as for example those forbidding alien ownership of land. The Senate is now being asked to ratify "Conventions" adopted by delegates to the United Nations—on the ground that we are morally if not legally obligated to put these subsidiary treaties in effect.

If the Human Rights Covenant and the Genocide Convention were approved by the Senate they would, according to their sponsors, empower the Congress to exercise a far-reaching control over commercial and social relations of inhabitants of the United States with one another. One example would be a new federal power to prevent discriminations because of race, color, or religion. Another example, offered by the Genocide Convention, would be the creation of a new set of crimes, punishable not only by the federal government but also through international tribunals. Thus, by exercise of the treaty power, an indefinite federal jurisdiction to supersede the jurisdiction of the states over local crimes may be established, if the arguments of the proponents of this enlarged federal power, and of the advocates of an international super-government prevail.

It would be impractical and unwise, in this historical review of the growth of government in the United States, to enter upon any discussion of the merits or probabilities of such a revolutionary change in the form and processes of our government. The numerous questions involved are being hotly debated. What may be done or what can be done without submission of amendments to the Constitution presents issues of great complexity and uncertainty. It seems only pertinent and practical here to point out that the methods of eliminating constitutional restraints upon the exercise of federal power, which have been used recently in expanding the commerce power and the taxing power will surely be employed. Indeed they are being employed.

The first step is to persuade the Congress that, under a broadly stated grant of power, it can extend that power beyond all previously accepted limits. The next step is to persuade the Supreme Court that it should defer to the judgment of the Congress, not only as to how it should exercise its conceded powers, but also as to the need to exercise powers not granted as "appropriate means" to exercise powers that have been granted.

This second step may not be as difficult as the first because of the deference which the Court has always paid to the exercise of the treaty power. In the leading case of *Missouri* v. *Holland*[9] it was held, on the basis of many precedents, that a treaty may override the power of the states to control "the great body of private relations." It was, however, also observed that the treaty before the Court "does not contravene any prohibitory words to be found in the Constitution." Also it was said: "We do not mean to imply that there are no qualifications to the treaty-making power." But, it is evident that, if there is no flagrant violation of prohibitions or limitations clearly laid down in the Constitution, there is no likelihood of the Supreme Court undertaking to nullify or to refuse to enforce the provisions of a treaty.

It is particularly significant that the "old" Supreme Court, with only one dissent, approved an opinion asserting that the treaty power did not depend upon a grant in the Constitution, but "would have vested in the federal government" as one of the "necessary concomitants of nationality."[10] The historical basis for this conclusion, which was that the states had no "sovereignty" with which to make treaties and hence could not grant any, is historically inaccurate. This unhappy divorcement of the treaty power from the Constitution indicates the strong probability that the Supreme Court will not apply any constitutional limitation to treaty lawmaking if there is any way to avoid it.

In concluding this survey of the expanding powers of the federal lawmakers and the diminishing judicial restraint upon the exercise of these powers, we may summarize by stating that, with the increasing stature of the United States in the family of nations, the federal government has certainly become leviathan in the dual system of government which was inaugurated in 1787. Possessed of a commerce power, a taxing power, and a treaty power with which to override state laws, the preservation of the safeguards of local self-govern-

[9] 252 U.S. 416.
[10] *U.S.* v. *Curtiss-Wright Export Corp.*, 299 U.S. 304.

ment and individual liberty rests at this writing largely in the self-restraint exercised by the Congress in its legislation. That exercise of self-restraint will be strongly influenced by the self-restraint, or the lack of it, exhibited by the President in his party leadership, his uses of his great executive power in both foreign and domestic affairs, and his outstanding influence in educating and guiding public opinion.

In the end, the enlightened intelligence or unthinking emotionalism, the sound or unsound instincts, of the American people will determine whether they have the capacity for self-government under the self-imposed restraints of the Constitution they wrote, and which they can revise, or whether they will choose to submit to the rule of masterful men who are ready and willing to accept the responsibilities and to gather the dubious profits of wielding unlimited power over the lives of their fellow men.

CHAPTER XVIII

Hopes of a Welfare State
(A. B.)

SUCH A STUDY as this would be incomplete without a tentative projection of the past into the future. However diffident he may be, a historian can hardly avoid the role of minor prophet on occasion. That task is made more difficult at this time by the new and heavy problems in world affairs forced upon us by our successful share in the recent war and by the uncertainty and fear that surround our present position in Europe and Asia. At the same time these changes make it imperative for us to look at the future calmly, whether with hope or fear. The word "welfare" in the title of this chapter may be reassuring, but it has little value as evidence or argument for the future. All governments, by virtue of their relation to the people governed, must plead the general welfare often in defense or explanation of acts that have no visible relation to the public interest. Terms such as these are not self-defining or automatic in their operation. This much at least we should have learned from the experience of the totalitarian states. In our own history these terms have had many interpretations and will have others in the years to come.

For the student of our governmental structure and procedure the great change since 1941 has been in the size and appearance of the problems with which we are forced to deal. The steps taken to insure an adequate supply of trained men and the necessary supplies for their use brought no new questions involving constitutionality or political technique. It can be written to the credit of democracies that in our hour of greatest danger we proved that we could move swiftly and with determination and efficiency in our defense. The blow at Pearl Harbor had immobilized several essential units of our navy and greatly impaired effectiveness in the air. The losses were made good, and our fighting force built up with a speed and to a level without parallel in our history. The record of our high command was impressive. The politician-general of malodorous memory was happily absent. And the miracle was accomplished without laying violent hands on the Constitution.

The ending of the war in the summer of 1945 found the government facing a multiplicity of problems. The mammoth defense industry must be turned back to peacetime production as quickly and as painlessly as possible with a minimum of delay and unemployment. This was done to the happy confounding of the gloomy prophets of collapse and depression. Some of the difficulties of a democracy in a long, drawn out emergency were revealed in the widespread and powerful demand for the immediate release of the young men of the country from the armed services. Our responsibilities in Japan and Germany where effective civil government had disappeared were heavy. Here was presented one of the baffling paradoxes of modern, full-scale war, the obligation of the conqueror to rebuild that which he has only recently destroyed. The disavowal of further responsibility in the war areas was not as general as after the first World War, but it was enough to illustrate our immaturity as a world power. This is still one of our handicaps.

It is further revealed in a widespread objection to such actions as the Marshall Plan aid to Europe and the still more disputed appropriations for the rehabilitation of depressed areas in other parts of the world. The argument in substance has been that such high-minded enterprises should not be undertaken until our domestic problems have been solved. To this observer such an argument is the result of a failure to understand the nature of what we call "social and economic problems." These are not susceptible of definite and final working out as are those which confront the engineer or the scientist. It is of the nature of human entanglements that they can be compromised and adjusted, but the nearest approach to a final test is that we are enabled to continue living together in an organized and stable society. To hope for more is to look forward to the day when all marriages will be happy and permanent. The only formula is that of trial and error which has been our political practice throughout our history.

The act which contained greater possibilities of constitutional disagreements and difficulties than any war measure was the forming of the United Nations in San Francisco. The charter announces that this is an agreement among sovereign powers for the purpose of providing an alternative to war among nations. Our dilemma arises from the fact that the document, although recognizing national sovereignty, in effect proposes that member nations relinquish some of the rights and prerogatives pertaining to sovereignty. While the Congress in principle retains its constitutional right to declare war, the provision for dealing with an aggressor state clearly limits the freedom of Congress to choose. Furthermore the provision for United Nations control of a combined force acting to repel aggression creates a combined authority not previously in being. The basic concept of a united world, even though the scope of action is severely limited, implies the surrender or delegation of some sovereign powers formerly held close within national boundaries.

The sending of United States forces into Korea brought into view an obscure question of constitutional implication that is not a new one. Was this a logical use of the President's power as "Commander in Chief of the Army and Navy of the United States"? To call this a police action instead of a war is a mere quibble. The Japanese pretended, at least until the attack at Pearl Harbor, that the war in China was only "the China incident," but no one believed them, the Chinese least of all. Changing names does not conceal the visible reality of war. What we know of the debates in the Constitutional Convention makes it sufficiently clear that the delegates understood that the power of the President over our armed forces was continuously active and was not confined to a time of actual war. Some of the statements make it appear that the President might, if he so chose, take command of forces in the field. Lincoln did not go to this extreme, but some of his instructions to his generals amounted to tactical as well as strategic decisions.

The necessity of a formal declaration of war by Congress before beginning hostilities is equally unclear. When, for example, was the Civil War authorized by Congress? And the Mexican War? The President's speech to Congress on December 8, 1941, was a statement of fact, not a request for authorization. Formal declarations do not start wars and the absence of a declaration does not prevent them. Former Governor Dewey has declared that the presidential right to direct the "deployment" of troops is clear. It is, but when is a deployment not a deployment?

The issue involved in the Marshall Plan and its collaterals is one of policy rather than of constitutionality. There are, of course, important domestic questions connected with such a move, primarily fiscal. How much can we afford to spend and in what ways does such spending serve the national interest? On this point the Constitution sheds no light. Our commitments and entanglements beyond our own borders are not only huge and perplexing, but they are essentially different from any that we have faced before. From the viewpoint of practical politics, which both the Administration and the Congress must take, the pathetic search for a road that is both safe and sure is wishful thinking. Every course is studded with hazards and the outcome is still heavily speculative.

One road at least seems closed, that which leads us securely back within our own borders. The inescapable fact is that we are one of the two great powers of a world that is now, as it has always been, the arena of a struggle for power. As always we are called upon by many of our own people to declare the ends for which we fight. One seems reasonably clear. If there is a sharp difference between ourselves and Russia that reaches down to spiritual bedrock, it is that of individual versus state. Throughout our development as a nation our belief in the integrity and the importance of the individual has been manifest. The state exists to serve the individual. In the totalitarian system which Russia embodies the state is the be all and end all for which the individual exists.

The importance of the individual is not only the sufficient justification for our faith in a democratic society in which the final decision, the ultimate exercise of sovereignty, rests with the people speaking freely through the ballot, but it also offers such guide and guaranty for the future as can be found. The temptation to take refuge in words is almost irresistible, even in this day when such brave words as freedom, order, loyalty, and democracy are being tortured to such base meanings as to call for the formation of a Society for the Prevention of Cruelty to Words. Totalitarian leaders boast of the democracy and freedom which they have called into being and point with pride to overwhelming approval in elections offering a choice between yes and no, with no carrying such sinister implications as to put it out of circulation.

In any attempt to view the future, whether with hope or with alarm, the historian must look to the past for his most reliable evidence. Human progress is a combination of change and continuity. Our first recourse in dealing with the new is to draw on our own past. The Passamaquoddy duck that flew backward because he was more interested in where he had been than where he was going may have been wiser than he seemed. To know where we have been is at least essential to an understanding of our probable course in the future. Specific challenges and our responses are impossible to foresee with any accuracy. Exactly what we shall do under given circumstances remains uncertain, but the manner of our doing can be charted reasonably well. Here an inventory of our own past is useful.

The right to vote is inseparable from citizenship. It was not always so. Manhood suffrage did not become universal until around the end of the first quarter of the last century. Womanhood suffrage came with the Nineteenth Amendment in 1920. Much is made in certain quarters of the difference between a republic and a democracy and the superiority of the former. This resembles the shadowboxing of metaphysicians. The right to vote is severely democratic; the business of government is carried on by representatives of our free choosing. What the framers of the Constitution preferred is water over the dam. The new states, beginning with Vermont, stipulated manhood suffrage, and finally the original thirteen followed suit. The voice of the people as spoken through the ballot is seldom the voice of God, and often not very wise, but it is a determination as of that time until it is altered by the same voting process. Its significance lies in the fact that we have made the choice freely and, if mistakenly, the mistake is of our own making. Only once have any of us refused to accept the decision as binding. That was in 1860.

The picture of the free citizen in the voting booth, "alone

with his conscience and a lead pencil," is appealing and too rare. For how much of the world's population does it exist, except as a faint hope for the future? Perhaps one sixth, possibly not so many. We shall not lightly nor easily surrender this basic right. Whatever our acts in the future, they must meet this acid test directly or indirectly.

There is our Constitution, the oldest fundamental document of government now in existence. We have amended it, construed it, at times stretched it, but we have been scrupulous to stay within its bounds. Foreign observers, chiefly British, have criticized it for its rigidity, but the great judges, beginning with Marshall, have given it flexibility in its application to specific instances. The tenor of decisions on thorny constitutional points, especially presidential rights, implied powers, and the exact meaning of the Fourteenth Amendment, has changed from time to time and later courts have reversed earlier decisions; but on such a clear issue as the civil rights of the individual the Supreme Court has stood fast on the assertion that the Constitution meant what it said. Ironic comment has called attention to occasions when the Court has expressed the will of God by a vote of five to four. But in some such cases a dissenting opinion has in the long run had more influence than the prevailing decision. Those who fear radical changes or executive usurpation have little cause for alarm as long as the Supreme Court is the guardian and the exponent of the Constitution. This observer gives the Constitution and the Court a long life expectancy.

The struggle between the executive and legislative arms of the government is endemic in our system. Washington resented what he regarded as the presumptuous interference of the Congress and after one experience in the Senate declared that he would never enter that bear pit again. Jackson and Lincoln had their troubles and most second-termers have encountered congressional opposition. In general, strong Presidents have had their way more often than weak ones, which is only to be expected. With the growing complexity of political forces and actions the tendency has been for presidential power to increase. This is intensified in times of war or other emergency, but as long as Congress holds the purse strings executive usurpation is a practical impossibility.

At the present time, as on previous occasions, there is a considerable demand that Congress take charge, especially to reduce expenses and to clarify and state our foreign policy. As to the first, Congress has the power at all times to refuse to vote appropriations asked for by the Executive Branch and to substitute other items of their own choosing. But there are certain untouchables in the national budget. First, of course, the debt charges, unchangeable except by refinancing at a lower rate of interest. At present, defense items are on the same sacrosanct list. Federal salaries can be reduced but not without careful consideration of the cost of living and the prevailing rate of pay in private employ. The rude hand of economy is likely to disturb the sacred cow of patronage, of which Congress is not unaware. A pertinent illustration is the River and Harbors Bill, "pork barrel" of long tradition. Here is the golden opportunity for Congressmen to demonstrate their devotion to the interests of their constituents. It is possible that Representatives may voluntarily use the ax on these items, but the odds are not attractive.

The sense of a vested interest in particular parts of the budget handicaps Congress in any serious move for economy, as has been shown in the opposition to proposals for sweeping reorganization of administrative agencies and procedures in the joint interests of efficiency and economy. Officeholders cling tenaciously to their posts, but most Congressmen keep even tighter hold on the powers of patronage. Our governmental experience points to the conclusion that the momentum for substantial economy must come from the Executive Branch. It is a reasonable assumption that the total of government expenditures will increase with the increase of government problems and functions, especially in times of abnormal strain and difficulty, such as the present. As the strain decreases, special expenses will shrink, but it is vain to hope for a return to the old level. In general the trend of the line is upward.

The safest test is the relation of expenditure to national income over a long period. For the short run the rise and fall of the curve will tend to correspond to the formula of Lord Keynes, in spite of theoretical dispute. In times of depression and widespread need, government will tend to offset private retrenchment. The alternative is acute social and political tension and weakness, such as no government can safely contemplate. The two directions in which major reductions can be sought in the long run are those where it is most difficult to bring them about, debt service and the national defense. The debt can be reduced, and the need for large-scale defense can diminish.

The problem of government which is the most difficult to solve is taxation. How much of a tax burden will our economy carry without serious impairment? Has that process of weakening already begun? The answer to the first question is doubtful; probably more than the conservatives fear and less than the extreme Keynesians believe. The danger point exists, but we are only beginning to examine the ways in which its location can be determined. In our more recent experiences unusual relief and defense spending have stimulated the economy rather than the contrary, indicating a negative answer to the second question. As in private enterprise a desirable budgetary change is in the reduction of fixed charges relative to controllable items. Only in that manner can flexibility be obtained. Incidentally there is need of a modern unified budget such as exists in well-run private enterprises. Our present patchwork quilt of estimates and hopes with only vague reference to expected income is hardly to be called a budget at all.

How far can Congress determine or control foreign policy, beyond its present powers? And is such a change desirable? Here the observer is bound to be skeptical. Foreign policy at any given time is the result of a combination of tradition, principle, prejudice, and expediency, requiring the close attention of trained minds. The persistent process of adjustment, compromise, and maneuver by which policy is applied is beyond the powers of a large body of representatives lacking special training and knowledge. Our State Department, which for long periods has been among the lesser objects of attention and interest, is now, and for a long time to come will be, the department of greatest importance. Its direction requires highly competent hands and unity of effort and purpose, conditions hardly to be expected in Congress.

Nevertheless Congress has a function of the first importance in this field, that of open, serious debate of principles and objectives. Education and clarification are needed now more than ever and hearings and discussions of our course should supply some. Another useful service rendered by Congress is through investigations carried on by standing or special committees. In spite of the wild charges made in some committee hearings, Congress has a clear duty to examine and, if justified, to censor or condemn. There is need for reform of the procedure of some of the hearings, but a heavy burden of proof lies on the shoulders of the critics who would dispense with the hearings altogether. As the problems arising in our complicated society increase in form and number the drafting of adequate legislation becomes more professional and Congress will be forced to rely increasingly on administrative agencies for the form and phrasing of laws. This tendency will force Congress to make more use of its investigative powers.

If, as seems likely, we must call in the expert in ways not previously necessary, a double danger will confront us, a top-heavy bureaucracy and an undue centralization of power and function. This is a risk to which all governments are exposed except the very weakest of which little is expected. Even in private enterprise there is a tacit conflict between financial and operational control. The hazards appear to be greater in totalitarian countries where all the functions of government, legislative, executive, and judicial, are in the hands of a small central body with a few powerful individuals holding the reins. Democracies have the power to limit the risks, but hardly to eliminate them.

Our present national debt, somewhere in the neighborhood of $285,000,000,000, is a prodigious fact, for all our wry jests and ill-timed humor. We call solemn attention to the pressing necessity of its reduction, but it continues to grow with each annual budget, and the government personnel shows little sign of shrinking. Incidentally, the hoped-for cuts in income-tax rates fail to materialize. Lord Keynes' formula for the minimizing of government expenditures in time of prosperity is as essential as his prescription for government spending to take up the slack, if and when depression comes. It was an old maxim of diplomacy that commitments should never outrun ability to perform. This is still sound doctrine in government operations as well as private.

In foreign policy our problems are the usual combination of political, economic, and financial, with marked overtones of the emotional. What ends do we seek? And how much are we prepared to pay in order to gain them? Our ability to produce more goods than our home market can consume has been amply demonstrated. To say only this is an oversimplification. If, in gaining more customers, we also create more competitors, have we gained or lost? In the period immediately after the war, Congress sought to draw a line between restoration of the devastated areas of Europe and recovery of their ability to produce goods. Specifically, should Germany be aided in the rebuilding of her heavy-goods industries in the Ruhr? These had been the chief source of the material of war and might be so again. Mr. Henry Morgenthau, Secretary of the Treasury, proposed that the Germany of the future should be restricted to agriculture as a guaranty against the building of the machines of combat. How large a population could such an economy support? And how much could or would such a Germany buy from us? Again shadowboxing and metaphysical, at that! In the end, the Germans decided for themselves. A new German army is in the making, approved by us, preparing to join in the defense of Western Europe, and German automobiles are rolling along our highways. Apparently it is an easy step from enemy to ally. But where did rehabilitation stop and reconstruction begin?

Politics and finance are inextricably interwoven in our efforts to thread a way through to a coherent foreign policy that corresponds to the realities of the time. Consider the thorny problems of the Near East. Here the world of the Arab and the vital interests of the West are grappling in a confused struggle. Egypt strives to lead the Arab world. The countries of the Bagdad Pact—Iran, Irak, Pakistan, and Turkey—lean to the West in opposition to Egypt and the Arabians of the Saud. England and France, both suspect of colonial ambitions, go with the Bagdad nations. Where do we stand and why? It is vain to assure ourselves that we stand for justice and peace. These are to be gained only at a price.

What course does our love of justice prescribe toward Israel? Here the Arabs represented by Nasser in Egypt and Ibn Saud in Arabia are bluntly clear in their statements of policy. The Israelis must go! Saud and Nasser may go, but the antagonism will remain. The position is confused and conflicting. On the record we are friendly to the Jewish hunger for a homeland where they can bring their long wandering to a secure end. But we also have a hunger and a need for the oil that underlies Arabian sand. Can we mix Arabian oil with our friendship for the Israelis without an explosion? The complications are many, and there is always the threat of Soviet intervention. Will Soviet tanks and planes for Egypt be followed by troops? If that happens, what course will we take? Lately we joined in the United Nations warning to England and France to withdraw their forces from the Suez area, and, in so doing, seemed to give aid and comfort to Colonel Nasser and his Russian friends.

Here in the vast area stretching from North Africa to the borders of Afghanistan and north to the Russian border is need for both rehabilitation and reconstruction. In Old Testament times this land supported a large population, much larger than today. Israel and Turkey have made a promising beginning in irrigation works and reforestation, pilot plants that point the way for a better future. Much remains to be done. It is still a hungry land and both justice and peace wait on the food supply, here, as elsewhere in the Asiatic world. Our statements on Near East policy speak in large, vague terms of military and economic aid. Are they necessarily collateral? And how much of each and in what form? Our intentions are unclear. As long as this is the case, our support at home and in the Congress will be hesitant and unwilling. Specifications are lacking and voters grope doubtfully in the darkness. Would it not be the part of wisdom to turn back to the old policy of a high protective tariff and abandon our high hopes of world leadership and reform?

Our towering national debt oppresses us and we view each new budget with alarm that mounts as we approach the income tax deadline. Justice and peace come high, and we are unsure of our willingness to foot the bill. Here is a case where our experience of a hundred and seventy years offers us little guidance, and there is so little room and time for experiment. To that extent our old practice of trial and error seems outmoded. To add to the complexity of the situation, our understanding of the geography of the Near East is uncertain, as it might well be. What and why is Jordan; where does Lebanon begin and end? What are we supposed to do and where? Finally, how much will it all cost? Obviously, we cannot foot the bill for a brave new world all on our own, particularly a world that we are ill-prepared to understand. And that seems to be the case for our dream of world leadership.

It must not be forgotten that the title of this chapter is "Hopes of a Welfare State." What kind of a state is that? A theoretical answer is easy: a state that has for its prime purpose the welfare of its people. That takes in all states that endure longer than overnight or that exist by virtue of the ignorance and credulity of their people. To reach an acceptable definition of the term, attention must be given to the form and powers of the government and its relation to the rest of the world. What has already been said in this chapter applies to one or the other, or both, of these considerations. Whatever we do must be done with what we have in the world as it is. The inner question that must be answered in policy and action is the meaning of welfare. The road to a definition is beset with semantic pitfalls, bristling with such words as socialism, communism, dictatorship, paternalism, and bureaucracy, all of them loaded with unpleasant implications. Nevertheless it is necessary to look for a way through. Our historical record of change by experiment shows a steady expansion of the field of governmental action.

The Constitution is our first large exhibit of the evidence available. That was an experiment by compromise, adjustment, and postponement. The states were jealous of the powers that they had assumed during the Revolution and suspicious of any form of centralized power, which to the delegates to the Convention smacked of royal prerogative. Only Hamilton was openly in favor of strong centralization. A President with power was merely a king or, at the least, a royal governor in disguise. Was the Union an organic entity or a gentlemen's agreement? It took a long and costly war to answer that last question. Jefferson, the chief supporter of a relatively weak central government, bought the Louisiana

Territory by executive act. "I stretched the executive authority until it cracked," he said. Experiment, trial and error! Little importance was attached to the possibility of new states in the future and the constitutional provision for their admission was of the vaguest and most general character, "New States may be admitted by the Congress into this Union." But new states came fast, three before the end of the first decade, and they came on equal terms with the original thirteen. The founding fathers agreed in their dislike of parties and hoped there would be none. By 1832 the party and the party convention had elbowed their way in.

The struggle over slavery and the war that ended it brought changes but made little alteration in the basic pattern except to determine the organic nature of the Union. Presidential authority increased under the pressure of war needs, but Congress had its way in the reconstruction and readmission of the states lately in secession. This too was accomplished outside the Constitution, although the congressional action had some faint resemblance to constitutionality.

The generation following the war was a period of political stalemate and of colossal economic growth. The government continued the policy of tariff protection of American industry and aided in the financing of railroads by land grants and guarantees of railroad bonds. In other respects it played the part of passive and indifferent bystander, with few indications of any sense of responsibility or concern, except for Cleveland's use of his executive power to expel cattlemen, mining companies, and settlers from public lands that they had entered without legal warrant. The economic and social thought of the time was clear—that the good of all was best served through the free-for-all of unrestricted competition. An equitable portion of the benefits gained by the upper strata would filter down automatically to the lower levels. At the best it was a combination of guesswork and wishful thinking, without the historical justification that could be claimed for the free enterprise theories of English Liberalism. Under the surface, opposition and resentment were growing.

In the last decade of the century the ferment of discontent that had been working under the surface broke through. The farmers formulated their demands in the Populist and Democratic platforms of 1896. The language was often violent but the demands and proposals were couched in familiar terms and involved no changes in the form or power of government. What the farmers sought was political power to do the things that they believed needed doing. The changes that they desired were to be accomplished within the traditional pattern of American political procedure. What they desired was the political opportunity to establish and maintain their freedom in ways sanctioned by long use.

The two decades from 1900 to 1920 saw a continuous process of development of governmental activities in the form of controls, directives, and restraints in what hitherto had been the sacred field of free enterprise. The details have been outlined in Chapter XII, The New Nationalism and Social Responsibility. Underlying these changes and extensions was the firm belief that two rival powers were struggling for the upper hand, the one economic and the other political. The implied issue was: Will the people rule or be ruled? Can individuals retain their freedom in a complicated modern society against the encroachments of organized wealth while the government keeps to the role of policeman and umpire?

To say that our future course is not likely to present radical deviation from that which we have followed in the past is too easy, although it does serve to emphasize the important part that habit plays in human behavior. A disastrous war or a severe and long continued depression can drive us out of our accustomed ways, but the predictability of such happenings is too uncertain to permit analysis of the disruptive effects they might produce. So far we have weathered wars and depressions without serious danger of revolution.

There are two immediate dangers in the development of the Welfare State that must have careful and continuing attention. The first is that of an overload of taxation and restriction on our economy. Fears and warnings to the contrary notwithstanding, our basic faith is still in free enterprise. Our ability to maintain the governmental activities that make up the sum total of our welfare experiments to date depends upon our ability to pay the cost. Much of our extension so far can be justified as necessary to keep enterprise free in the widest possible sense. Where we have ventured beyond that we are entering dangerous ground. There will be continuing need for re-examination in the interests of economy and efficiency, if for no other reason. So far our acts have defined welfare as the steps deemed necessary for the protection of the individual and to guard him against forces that would encroach upon his legitimate freedoms.

The other ever-present danger is the shrinkage of individual freedom by its subordination to the interests of a group. How to reconcile a high degree of individual freedom with collective freedom is a large question and a real one, as many labor union members should be able to testify. Labor unions are obvious responses to industrialization in a democratic society, but democracy is in danger within unions themselves. Rank and file rebellion against official or committee domination is a healthy sign not too often in evidence. Here the most potent weapons of democracy are the familiar ones of free speech, regular and frequent elections, a free vote, and a fair count. Democratic rights and the freedom of the individual can be lost in a series of obscure battles in dark corners.

In the minds of most of us, labor union action is associated with strikes, involving work stoppage and the prevention of other men from working. This was the old technique. The older leaders held the strike to be their last and best weapon, even though the cost to labor might be more than any advantage gained. Strikes have grown less reckless and violent, but the threat of them is always present. We attempt to set up a special category of strikes that are contrary to the public interest, but the idea is unreal. Every strike of whatever kind carries with it the possibility of conflict with the common good through their interference with normal activity. There is no place for strikes in a welfare state that really seeks the common good.

The same dictum holds good for monopoly, whether established by labor or industry. Monopoly is a denial of the right of free enterprise to remain free. There are obvious economies in a monopoly, but we must realize that these are secured at the cost of freedom and, in the long run, both small consumer and small producer pay the bill. Complete free enterprise is possible only in a state of complete freedom to buy and sell, to make, and to consume. Anything less is a denial and a limiting of the true welfare state.

These dangers and others associated with them are inherent in our society and will continue to exist. Our freedoms are more likely to be lost through our own blindness and the corrosion of disuse than by frontal attack from open enemy. For the present, the danger of formal organized movements, such as Socialism and Communism, is largely imaginary. The argument that we may become a socialist state without our own knowledge or intent is speculation. It is always open season for guessing.

The title chosen for this book is not an accident. Its accuracy has been proved repeatedly in our history. It took courage to break with England and set our feet on an untried and dangerous road. That has been repeated in diverse ways all the way down to the present. We have had the courage and resourcefulness to meet new challenges, often unwillingly and slowly, but always with an ultimate willingness to do that which seemed to need doing. We have had large advantages of time and space, sometimes to our own deception. Are our hazards and the urgency of our needs greater now than in the past with corresponding limitation of our room for experiment? This is altogether likely, but as an offset we have at our command a large stock of political wisdom which we have won from our experience. We have now not only our own courage but the courage of those who brought us this far.

The temptation to be rhetorical is great, but sometimes it is necessary to speak out in meeting. Nowhere else in human history have so many people worked together for so long a time to build a political structure compounded of a sense of the integrity of the individual and of his right to an equitable share in the common welfare. It will not be destroyed easily.

CHAPTER XIX

Fears of a Welfare State
(D. R.)

ONE OF THE DIFFICULTIES in discussing any political issue is the constant corruption of words and phrases in political debating which thereafter prevents their use to define accurately the subject of one's approval or disapproval. The corruption of the word "democracy" in communist propaganda has made it appear that an advocate of "democracy" must or should believe in equalitarianism enforced by a "dictatorship of the proletariat." If you claim to be a "democrat" you are told that you must believe that all men are created "free and equal"—not only in political rights but in every way. You must believe that by the voting power of an unrestrained majority the government should enact laws to enforce this mythical equality of all persons in all social relations and in the distribution of the fruits of industry, regardless of their individual abilities or their contributions of service to industry or to the welfare of their fellow men.

On the other hand, anyone who advocates "social responsibility" is likely to be promptly classified as an orthodox "socialist." He will be denounced as a socialist if he asserts that an individual possessed of large economic or political powers should be compelled to accept a social responsibility to use such powers in such ways that society will be benefited and not harmed by the freedom of action that it permits and protects him to exercise. Yet there is a fundamental difference between the advocate of free enterprise who concedes that the government should prevent him from using his freedom to injure the general welfare, and the socialist who thinks that the government should compel all men to work as servants of the political rulers of the state.

It should be recognized that all advocates of a welfare state are not orthodox socialists. In the United States the strongest support of a welfare state comes from those who are sincerely opposed to the inevitable tyranny of a government of orthodox socialists, even if they would be gentle tyrants and would not resort to the cruelty and terror and ruthless use of force employed by communist socializers.

Fears of the development of a welfare state in America do not generally arise from opposition to any acceptance by the government of a responsibility to prevent abuses of private power by those who manage private industries. These fears arise because of the temptation to which reformers are so inclined to yield, to substitute political management for private management as the quickest and easiest way to enforce a social responsibility.

Why waste time trying to persuade big business managers to accept obligations of public service? Why waste energy in trying to prevent them from making excessive profits out of underpaid labor and overcharged consumers? Why not simply have the government take over the powers of private management and operate industries for the benefit of both workers and consumers? That is the way the argument runs for more and more government controls.

The best way to answer it is not to rely on appeals to fears of "socialism" and "communism" but to marshal the evidence to convince well-meaning humanitarians that more and more government controls must inevitably lead to a government that will eventually fail miserably to fulfill its promises, or will be forced to adopt the tyrannies of national socialism to conceal or to postpone the revelation that its promises can never be fulfilled. As one who is now convinced that this is the menace of what is being advocated as a welfare state by many who are not apostles of national socialism, I offer a summary statement of the evidence on which I base my convictions.

The so-called welfare state is not an assured force for good merely because it proposes to organize a nation for universal service to the general welfare. These were the proposals of Hitler, Mussolini, and Lenin. These are the proposals of all orthodox socialists and of all dictators in the modern world. On the other hand modern free-enterprisers do not propose to organize a nation merely for the profit and glory of a favored few. That concept of a "free economy" and the "survival of the fittest" is as dead as the dodo.

We will make more progress in our efforts to develop government in the service of the common good if we assume that this is the aim of both the socializers and the free-enterprisers, and if we then debate the real issue which is: What extent or limitation of government regulation of industry will be most effective to advance the general welfare? In this debate we can assume that the accepted aim of our society, and our reason for supporting a government, is to advance the general welfare.

What is called the welfare state may be defined as a government which assumes the direct and unlimited responsibility of assuring to all citizens a decent livelihood and financial security against the hardships that may result from unemployment, ill-health, disability or old age. However, such a responsibility cannot be met without giving to the government power to plan and control the operation of all productive enterprises and the distribution of all income and products in conformity with government requirements. In such a welfare state the function of all private associations which are engaged in, or affect, production or distribution must be to act as instruments or agencies of the government in meeting its assumed responsibility.

Even those who oppose the development of such a welfare state ought to concede that it *is* the responsibility of our government to establish an adequate legal structure for a society of men and women, who are living and working together for mutual protection and correlative gains. This legal structure should be an authentic house of voluntary cooperation in which citizens can organize and operate voluntary associations through which the opportunity to earn a decent livelihood and to gain financial security against hardship will be assured. The opponents of the compulsory welfare state believe that when political force is used to *compel* men to associate, and to operate their associations, in conformity with political programs, then the inherent vigor of a free people and of a free economy is destroyed. They believe that our material progress will be retarded by this loss of vigor far more than it can be advanced by the disciplinary efficiency of compulsory cooperation. They are sure that our spiritual progress will become a spiritual retreat.

A good example of the two opposing concepts of government is found in the choice between government *protection* and government *control* of labor organizations. It has been our governmental policy for many years to protect labor unions from destruction by, or subservience to, the economic power of large employers. In order to promote an equality of bargaining power, labor unions have been aided by law to organize wage earners in such numbers that they could confront employers with a choice between paying good wages or being unable to operate their properties.

The economic powers of employers and of organized employees have been abused by both; but, so long as neither could dominate the other, the principle of voluntary cooperation has been maintained. The government has always had, and should exercise, a police power to correct these abuses—and even to require both parties to break deadlocks when their inability to agree becomes seriously harmful to the national welfare. But the use of police power to restrain and to punish wrongdoers is utterly different from the use of police power to conscript and to reward right doers.

If, however, the government should assume an unlimited and direct responsibility for the wage earner's livelihood and security, government wage fixing would become a continuing and imperative duty. Then the fixing of a wage for any important group of workers would require the equalization of wages for all other groups, and, inevitably, the determination of reasonable prices for consumers and of reasonable compensation for the owners of properties which are used to provide employment or shelter or services for the workers.

We cannot forget that an underlying factor in the cost of living is the cost of products of the soil, the food, the fuel and the raw materials of industry that are the products of agriculture, forestry and mining. The largest factor in all costs is labor cost. How could a government assure a decent livelihood and employment to industrial wage earners without controlling all the other labor upon which the welfare of industrial workers depends? It should be evident to industrial labor that a welfare state cannot meet its responsibilities to all the people without subjecting all the people to detailed regulation of the working and living conditions of all.

Indeed, the inevitable march of political control is now clearly forecast in the recent official proposal of our nascent welfare state to guarantee an income to farmers. But, what value would a guaranteed income have for farmers if there were no accompanying guarantee of the purchasing power of that income? How can a farmer's buying power be guaranteed unless there is a control of the prices which a farmer must pay for what he buys? How can industrial prices be controlled without a control of industrial labor?

The difficulty of persuading labor unions to support a welfare state, which would enslave them, was met by the socialist leaders of the Labor Party in Great Britain by promising a miracle. Sir Stafford Cripps (Chancellor of the Exchequer) said in February, 1946: "No country in the world, as far as I know, has yet succeeded in carrying through a planned economy without the direction of labor. Our objective is to carry through a planned economy without the direction of labor. . . ." Three years later, despite all its good intentions, the Labor Government had to announce the issuance of directions compelling men to remain in mining and in agriculture.

Of course there is no fair comparison between the cruelly enslaved labor of Russia and gently "directed" labor of Britain. It would be silly to prophesy that an American welfare state would promptly enslave the industrial workers and the farmers who voted it into power. That would be as silly as calling the Taft-Hartley Act a "slave law." It is even more silly to contend that a welfare state can fulfill its promises, and guarantee a decent livelihood and financial security against hardship to all able-bodied citizens, without exercising a supreme authority to plan and direct the operation of all major industries and to determine the proper compensation and working conditions for all essential workers.

Advocates of the welfare state insist that political programs backed by the coercive power of government force are necessary to advance the general welfare. Then why are they so anxious to pretend that there will be no use of force to regiment the workers into the service of a police state? Why do they not admit the truism that the promise of economic security through a politically planned and directed economy is a promise to use force to compel obedience to government directions? Why do they not offer their bribe to wage earners and farmers in plain terms which would be: "Give us your votes and, as the political representatives of your organizations, we will run the welfare state so that your members will be left free from compulsory service and yet have economic security provided by taxing and coercing the rest of the people"?

The reason that there is no such candor, no such fundamental honesty, in the welfare state program is that, when clearly explained, it becomes evident that the nascent welfare state must become eventually a state of national socialism, or else engulf us in the most calamitous depression of our history. It is no defense of national socialism to assert that a complete socialization of our political economy might at least make it financially possible to maintain an orderly society under rigid control of a national police. But, the attempt of a government to eliminate the incentives and profits of private enterprise, while relying on the taxes and capital produced by private enterprise to sustain its operations, is foredoomed to failure.

To make it plain why a welfare state must become totalitarian or become insolvent, it is only necessary to reveal exactly how our government has been able to carry the enormous load of its present expenditures. The man in the street is unwilling or unable to analyze this fiscal problem. But no student or teacher of political science can shun the tiresome task.

For the later scrutiny of political scientists I would be glad to present a comprehensive analysis of this fiscal problem. But, to shorten the present chapter I will now offer only a few conclusions from such an analysis:

1. We have devalued the dollar, borrowed over 200 billion dollars and in various other ways inflated our national income in *dollars* to 2½ times what it was twenty years ago.

2. We have increased the federal receipts and expenditures from around 3 billion dollars in 1929 to over 70 billion dollars in 1953.

3. In addition to payments for national defense and interest on debt, the national government is expending about 25 billion dollars per year for the general welfare of ourselves and other people. There will be a serious question of our ability to finance the illimitable costs of another great war, if we continue thus to exhaust our financial resources.

4. The *introductory* program for a welfare state which the President brought forward in 1950 will add another 25 billion dollars to annual national expenditures. This calculation was made by the staff of the Senate Committee on Expenditures in the Executive Departments; it was reported to the Senate by the committee chairman, Senator McClellan. He estimated that the *increase* in the tax burden to pay for this initial program would be $166 annually for every man, woman and child in the United States; and that *total* federal taxes would then amount to 30 per cent of present national income.

5. If we add state and local taxes to the federal, this would "make the annual tax obligation of the American people more than 40 cents out of every dollar they earn."

6. The major part of all taxes are, and must be, paid by persons of small or moderate incomes.

7. As the voters become too much exhausted or exasperated by increased direct taxation of incomes, political spenders resort more and more to indirect taxes, concerning which millions of people are either ignorant or strangely indifferent. The indirect taxes paid today by the average family have been carefully computed to exceed $700 per year. When direct taxes on small incomes are added, it becomes a proven fact that the average wage earner's family is already paying over $1000 a year for the support of an infant welfare state that has only just begun to bite!

Any competent student of the fiscal and operating problems of the infant welfare state must see that, with the development of its vast public projects, taxation will become so confiscatory, the regulation of management and labor so detailed, private property rights so reduced, and private enterprise so smothered by political controls, that the emergence of the mature welfare state as a state of national socialism is inevitable.

Apparently the concealed justification for taxing people so that the government may spend their individual earnings to advance their individual welfare is that the masses of the people are morons who should not be trusted to spend their own money. It is assumed that they should be glad to have their money spent for them by professional politicians trained and experienced in the art of spending other people's money. Of course this argument isn't made openly because even humble people resent being treated like children. So they are told that they are made more secure by investing their money with politicians than with business men. Business men are pictured as cold, greedy, fat exploiters, while politicians are those genial backslappers who call you by your first name and work day and night to find ways to buy things for you with your money which you wouldn't buy for yourself.

There are many things of common use which may wisely be paid for through government, such as roads and parks and common-school facilities. But the welfare state proposes to take more and more of a man's earnings to buy things for his *individual* use which he ought to be free to buy less or more of according to his individual need or desire. It proposes to substitute a common standard of living and a common, compulsory pursuit of happiness for the individual rewards and the individual pursuit of happiness which have inspired the American people to raise themselves through voluntary cooperative enterprises to the highest standard of living, coupled with the greatest individual liberty, ever enjoyed by 170 million human beings.

Why shouldn't you buy your own health insurance, or any other insurance against misfortune, from your own selected insurance organization? Millions upon millions of people have done it. Why shouldn't you organize voluntary cooperatives to buy and sell things for you? Millions of people all over the world have done it. Why shouldn't you use your own labor organizations to provide unemployment insurance either alone or in cooperation with employers? Labor unions can pay strike benefits when men refuse to work; why should they not pay unemployment benefits when men are unable to find work?

The point which I am trying to make briefly is that the major offerings of a welfare state are simply offerings to do for you what you can do better, more cheaply, and with greater satisfaction, for yourself. In so doing you can save yourself from dependency on political favor, political integrity, and political wisdom, those three weak reeds upon which no man who has common sense and a knowledge of history will ever wish to become dependent. Three weak reeds upon which no man who has a backbone of self-reliance will be willing to lean.

If, on the other hand, we were resolved to preserve the proven vigor and productiveness of a system of private enterprise, we have ample evidence that we could meet our social responsibilities without accepting a compulsory socialism. We could go forward patiently to expand the cooperative powers of our present private, voluntary associations. The government would lend its aid in legalizing such collective projects as the organization of corporations, cooperatives, trade unions and trade associations; and the government would impose such restraints as are necessary to prevent private monopolistic controls of commerce and to preserve competition and a free purchasing power as the natural and impartial regulators of prices and production.

Furthermore, it should be accepted that, in the emergencies of war, national disaster, or serious economic disorder, the government should take such action as is temporarily necessary to develop and make effective the maximum power of our nationally organized resources to meet the emergency demands upon them. It should be our established doctrine that such political controls of our lives and work are fundamentally evil, like fighting fire with fire and bullets with bullets. We should make it an everlasting rule to end political tyranny and denials of individual liberty just as soon as the emergent calamity that enslaves us has been overcome.

Time will not permit any adequate exposition of how all the social responsibilities that are supposed to demand the creation of a compulsory welfare state can be fulfilled through voluntary associations of a free people. But I would like to refer to the stimulating and comprehensive exposition of our capacity and willingness to meet these responsibilities, which is presented by a representative group of industrial leaders in a book entitled *The New Outlook in Business,* published by Harper & Brothers in 1940. When I list among the twenty-two authors, Charles R. Hook, Richard R. Deupree, Robert E. Wood, Walter D. Fuller and Wallace Brett Donham, it may be understood why I think that a reading of this book [1] would be more enlightening than any further argument by me. Also, I believe that the plans and programs of these practicing economists offer more trustworthy guidance than those of the theorizing economists who are befuddling the American people today with roseate visions of a make-believe welfare state.

There are two major excuses for substituting political support for self-support, and political discipline for self-discipline, which merit brief discussion.

One is the excuse that because some men make too much money out of others, they should be compelled by taxation to share their gains with those whom they exploit; or, because some localities are more prosperous, their gains should be shared with poorer localities. Let us disregard the counter-argument that the forced service of the more competent to

[1] Now out of print, but available in many libraries.

the less competent, and the levelling down of humanity to a common standard of living, is not a democratic but a communistic doctrine. Nevertheless, we may well agree that the exceptional profits of fortunate individuals or favored communities should be taxed away to maintain the common defense and to promote the general welfare. It is a proven fact that if every dollar of income in excess of a fair compensation for personal services, or for the use of private properties, were siphoned into the United States Treasury, this would provide only part of the federal revenue needed to pay for national defense, national administration of justice, and national expenditures for public works of general value. A major part of all essential public revenues must be obtained by a direct or indirect tax deduction from the earnings of the great mass of workers of small or moderate incomes. So the revenues of the expanding welfare state will necessarily come from increased deductions from the earnings of those who are the proclaimed beneficiaries of this additional government spending.

The second excuse for a paternal collection and spending of a worker's earnings is that voluntary cooperation will fail to advance the welfare of the cooperators as far as compulsory cooperation would. It is argued that the thriftless or unfortunate, who most need protection, will not or cannot insure themselves. It is also argued that in any industry a chiseling minority will break down the best devised programs for preserving an ideal balance between producing and consuming power. As one of the administrators of the notable NRA experiment, I am familiar with these arguments and believe that I can appraise their merits with the aid of an unusual amount of experience and with, perhaps, an unusual impartiality of judgment. I still believe in the voluntary self-government of industry, which was the announced objective of the NRA. I never believed in the compulsory political government of industry which NRA dabbled in, while floundering down the road to Limbo.

There will always be chiselers and black marketers to sabotage and subvert every cooperative program of private associations or political governments. But business and social ostracism is more effective than criminal prosecution to discipline recalcitrants. There is always some sympathy for the rebel against government who asserts his right as a free man to live and work as he pleases. There should not be the same sympathy for the cheat or sharper who will not abide by the rules of fair play adopted by his neighbors and co-workers. To gain an undeserved support, the business cheater always poses as a little David fighting the Goliath of monopoly.

The American people are rightfully afraid of monopolies, but they have been educated to recognize only a business management monopoly. They tolerate labor monopolies that curtail production, create scarcities and raise prices with a ruthlessness that no business management monopoly ever dared to exhibit. They are being seduced into approval of the oppressive monopolies of a welfare state, although for centuries the common people of every nation on earth have been fighting to free themselves from compulsory service to government monopolies operated by political tyrants.

Once upon a time it was the supreme law of our land that there was no "due process of law" by which our national government could deprive a man of the liberty to support and protect himself and his dependents by his free labor and his free use of his own earnings. The government could only tax him to support the strictly limited powers of the government to provide for the common defense and the *general* welfare. It could not tax him to enable the government to take care of his *individual* welfare or the *individual* welfare of his neighbors. It could not deprive him of his "unalienable right" to take care of himself, or to make a fool of himself.

Today, following the socialist dogma that the individual

citizen should be made the bond servant of the general welfare, the courts have invented a new "due process of law" with which the national government can deprive a farmer of the right to raise grain on his own land for his own consumption, unless he obeys government orders limiting the amount of grain he can raise and fixing the prices at which he can sell it. Today, the national government, by using this new "due process of law," can deprive a worker of the right to spend, to save and invest his own earnings as he wishes, for the economic support and protection of himself and his family. He can now be compelled to pay taxes which transfer a substantial part of his earnings to the government so that it can then provide such economic protection for him and for others as the government decides to be in the interest of the general welfare.

If ten to twenty per cent of a man's subsistence earnings can be taken from him today there is no legal barrier against taking from him thirty to forty per cent tomorrow, which, according to British precedents, will be required to support a young welfare state. In such a political economy, of what use will be private, voluntary associations, except to serve as pressure groups to try to elect and control public officials so that, in the political distribution of a worker's earnings, he may get back as much as possible after paying a few million political employees for spending his money for him?

For such lowly and limited functions private associations may survive in the welfare state. They may also serve to maintain the illusion that we are a free people, free to organize, to debate, and to petition the government for the redress of grievances, subject, of course to laws restricting and controlling lobbying and propaganda so that a dominant political party will not be unduly hampered by a too vigorous opposition.

It would not be accurate to define associations as "private" or "voluntary" which are, and will be, organized and maintained with political aid in order to make effective government regulations. Such dependent associations might well be compared to "company unions," which national trade unions have always denounced as mockeries of voluntary organization.

The conclusion of this short survey is obvious: Private, voluntary associations and enterprises, as an influential factor in our political economy, will not and cannot survive in a compulsory welfare state. Their powerful influence in the expansion and enrichment of our American way of life will disappear in the politically planned and directed economy of national socialism.

The evils of even a benevolent national socialism have been too often portrayed to make it necessary here to detail all the fears aroused by such a prospect. But two might be briefly emphasized. The first arises from the historical knowledge that incentive of private profit (which means not merely money but any personal satisfaction) has driven millions upon millions of human beings for many thousands of years to work hard to better their own lives and, as a result, to make possible a better life for all other human beings. The evidence of this experience is overwhelming in its proof that no other incentive has ever been so effective a motive power for industrial and social progress.

The attempt to substitute a voluntary desire or an enforced obligation to work hard for others, for the incentive of private profit has been tried a thousand thousand times and has never been successful except when altruism rises out of a profound faith in Deity and an urgent desire for divine approval or an urgent fear of divine wrath. The materialism of the orthodox socialist does not invoke but, on the contrary, destroys the faith which has made it possible for a great human spirit now and then to drive a human body to accomplishments utterly beyond the ability of ordinary men and women. It cannot be seriously contended that ordinary human beings have ever worked hard, or ever will work hard, except under the incentive of fear, or of faith, or of private profit. It must be conceded that without hard work no society can prosper and progress.

The second fear of the advance of national socialism applies also to any variety of a welfare state which seeks miraculously to free men from want and fear and yet make them work hard. Political experiments throughout the world in the last forty years have proved repeatedly that the mental powers of public officials are soon corrupted and overwhelmed by the enormously complicated problems which a paternal, centralized government must attempt to solve for a modern industrial society. When people are left free to solve their individual and local problems by experiments in voluntary cooperation, they may suffer the ills and losses resulting from foolish family management, or weak corporate management, or poor political management of local affairs. But these will not afflict entire nations with the suffering and disasters that have been caused by the misguidance of a Hitler or a Mussolini or any other of the power maniacs, many of whom unfortunately are still alive.

The possibility that ordinary men will find a way to manage fairly well a small, simple, and local business is obviously much greater than that a few extraordinary men will be able to train and direct a few million ordinary bureaucrats to manage wisely and efficiently the family, local, national, and international business of a nation of 170 million people.

The entire American experiment is based on faith that men have a capacity for self-government. This means that they must be left free to manage their own local affairs and not be subjected to the intimate control of their lives by a select class of supermen who are given or assume the power to save them from their own incompetence to govern themselves. Experimenting with the covert tyrannies of a welfare state may cost the American people a large part of the inheritance of natural and accumulated wealth, and the heritage of liberty, with which they entered the twentieth century. If they waste only their wealth and sacrifice their liberties trying to help one another, the great American experiment may go on. Brave men may still be able to keep themselves free.

The gravest danger threatening the life of our great experiment in self-government arises from the gradual but already evident transformation of our national welfare state into an international welfare state. We begin by accepting our "responsibility" as a great nation to look after the welfare of all other nations. We end by accepting the "responsibility" of all other nations to look after our welfare. Our mental corruption and our material deterioration have proceeded in the darkness of self-deception. Those who love to play God and regulate the lives of others and make them over in the image of their noble preceptors have assumed a national leadership.

It might seem as though the project of reforming ourselves and improving the fleshly enjoyment as well as the spiritual virtue of our lives would be sufficiently large to absorb all our reforming energies for a few more decades. But the desire to play God is insatiable and cannot be confined. So our moral leaders guide us hurriedly away from the unsolved problems of poverty and crime in the United States and exhort us to load up our airplanes and fly to the aid of the poor, underprivileged Polynesians.

When moral exhortations fail they appeal to selfishness and fear. If you do not willingly accept your duty to uplift the Polynesians, you are told you cannot sell tractors and moving pictures unless you educate and enrich those people so they will want and be able to buy tractors and moving pictures. Also you are warned that discontented, unelevated Polynesians will be taken over by Communists and organized into armies to conquer the United States. Therefore, as a matter of both good business and self-preservation, you must take over this new "white man's burden" and "wait on sullen peoples" all over the world.

But of course no one nation should arrogate to itself the authority of world reformation. All nations should unite to establish and enforce righteousness not only in international relations but in the relations of men to one another everywhere, which the United Nations are now trying to accomplish through the Human Rights Covenant and the Genocide Convention. All local customs, habits, and laws should yield to international law enforced by international government.

Thus arises the danger that, not only local self-government within the United States, but even a national power of self-government will gradually be surrendered to an international authority so little responsive to individual needs and desires that it will not be and cannot be self-government. That would mean the end of the great American experiment. That prospect arouses the deepest fear of encouraging the development of a welfare state in the United States of America.

CHAPTER XX

That Manifest Destiny
(A. B. and D. R.)

A. B. says:

The belief in a special purpose or destiny is not the peculiar property of any nation or people. Evidence of it is at least as old as the recorded history of the Jews. It was the element which saved Alexander's conquering sweep through Asia from being only a piratical raid. The German version of manifest destiny was explicit long before Hitler. It was an important feature of Hegel's philosophy of history, and it was urged as an important reason for the establishment of German colonies in western America in the eighteen thirties.

In our own case the assumption of a special divine plan for the new nation made itself felt early in the nineteenth century, as two facts became evident, a wide expanse of territory, especially after the purchase of Louisiana, and the rapid growth of population, 30 to 35 per cent every ten years. Surely God had chosen this continent and these people as the stage for and the performers in a new drama, a greater civilization at a higher level than any previously seen. The combination of cheap land and rapid increase of population strength made such a concept seem logically tenable. The early assumptions of semi-aristocratic control by property owners held at the time of the framing of the Constitution lost their significance as the ownership of land became widely possible and the equalitarian forces of manhood suffrage and free public education gave a democratic coloration to the whole social system.

The Civil War put an end to Calhoun's dream of aristocratic agrarianism, and the growth of manufacturing wealth in the North threatened the development of a new industrial aristocracy, arrogant and irresponsible. This power clashed with the equalitarian agrarianism of the West and South in a struggle of growing bitterness that reached its climax in the free-silver campaign of 1896. By this time the pattern of domestic change had been clearly set. The overseas thrust that was part of the result of the Spanish-American War precipitated a noisy argument over something called imperialism, but this soon passed and attention turned again to domestic concerns. That was the age of Theodore Roosevelt and his Progressive movement, soon to merge into the new freedom of Woodrow Wilson.

The kaleidoscope of war, normalcy, depression, the New Deal, and war again moved too swiftly and in such confusion and darkness after 1917 that even speculation as to the total meaning of this period of more than thirty years is idle. If there is to be a large sweeping interpretation of our history it must rest for the present on the period that ended in 1914. That was the end of an intelligible world, and the beginning of another that is still lacking clear form and meaning.

Is there a manifest destiny visible or clearly implied in that older world? In the judgment of this observer there is. It lies primarily in the desires and accomplishments connected with this movement of people across a continent, making their own trails and building their society and their government as they go. The process that began at Plymouth and Massachusetts Bay and to a lesser degree at Jamestown continued all the way. Its elements were such simple forces as the desire for land and an opportunity. To those ends they cleared the land, organized villages, cities, and commonwealths. The land was theirs and the government as well, to make or to spoil, and we have done both. It was self-government because most of the time no other kind was possible, and for the most part we wanted no other kind. It is still ours if enough of us want it or must have it.

The particles composing these elements have changed in form and texture from raw wilderness, through the agrarian and rural, to the industrial and urban. If the will to organize and to carry on in voluntary and unofficial ways, as well as more formal and legal ways, that was, and is still, so marked in the smaller towns and the rural districts, is still strong in our more complex and crowded areas the process is still valid. For the present the conclusion is evident that at least in the earlier period the destiny that shaped and guided us was in ourselves, compounded of our desire for a place to stand and a determination to assert and maintain our individual rights and integrity together with our recognition of the equal rights of our neighbors. In the degree that we have kept these simple principles clearly in view we have been true to our destiny.

* * *

D. R. says:

The ultimate goal of the United States of America cannot be defined or planned with any more precision than the ultimate goal of human life. We only make, or fail to make, progress toward the visions of our faith—whatever that may be.

The political faith that has seemed to be the continuing inspiration of Americans from colonial days to the present time has been a faith in the capacity of human beings for self-government. Just what is self-government and how it can be established and maintained are propositions subject to endless debate. What is truth, or righteousness, or justice? Individually we learn by trial and error not only how to seek to satisfy our desires but also what our desires are. For most of us few desires remain constant from the cradle to the grave.

The destiny of the American people may not be to perpetuate what is loosely called the American way of life, or the American form of government. But, for over three hundred years they have persistently sought to develop and to perpetuate a society in which the political government is organized to serve the individual citizen, but is denied the power to dominate him. To this unfinished task we are still dedicated. In the short range of human vision this much of our destiny seems manifest.

By all the standards available to our finite intelligence, great progress has been made in the rapid centuries of our great experiment. An ever-increasing population has freed itself from many ills and hardships that had afflicted humanity for previous uncounted centuries. These people have played a great part in a world-wide development of natural resources in the service of human life. These people have enjoyed a freedom from human oppression, and from compulsory service to human masters, such as no comparable society ever before enjoyed for so long a time. They have every reason to persist in their faith that they have been moving on the right road, in the right direction, toward a better life for more and more people.

It may be that in some not far off day the people and the government of the United States may be absorbed into a larger society and government, but presumably with the hope or even expectation that their experiment of self-government will go on. That would be a more reasonable prospect than that so fruitful an experiment would simply come to an irrational end.

A Thomas Edison, having produced an electric lamp,

would not be expected to destroy his laboratory and to advise the world to go back to oil lamps and candles. A Henry Ford, having developed a mass production of automobiles, would not be expected to abandon his efforts and to try to lead the world back to the horse and buggy days.

It should not be expected that a society, successful beyond all previous societies in making life more comfortable and satisfying and hopeful for millions of people, would abandon all further efforts at self-improvement and lead the way back to the political and economic servitude of ancient days.

During these recent centuries brave men throughout the world have been waging and winning lonesome battles and great wars to gain the power of self-government. If there be any manifest destiny for their descendants it would seem to be at least to preserve their heritage, not of expendable wealth but of self-respect, of faith in their capacity to govern themselves, of courage to meet new difficulties with new experiments and to pay the cost of their mistakes gladly in order to retain their freedom to gain the rewards of their own work and sacrifice. To preserve this heritage is such manifest wisdom that, for at least a few more generations of Americans, it can be called their manifest destiny.

With justified immodesty the American people have felt that they were moving in the vanguard of this political advance, experimenting with every new process or doctrine developed in their own land or anywhere else on earth. They have made costly mistakes and paid for them. They have made happy discoveries and profited by them. They have cherished their freedom of self-expression and self-advancement more than any other heritage and have been willing to sacrifice their wealth and comfort and even their lives to maintain these freedoms against menaces which, to a people of less vision, might have seemed—and might have been—remote to at least the present generation.

It is hardly conceivable that, as such menaces become more

imminent, these people will lose the will and the courage to persist in maintaining their faith in the virtues of self-government and in the wisdom arising out of continual experimentation as superior to any fixed design of social, economic, or political organization. In an era when self-confident, would-be masters of the future have been rising to establish governments that "for a thousand years" should rule their subject peoples and relieve them from all the pain and insecurity of self-support and self-government, there still remains in North America the hard core of a faith in the capacity of free men and women to govern themselves. For a time, at least, the limited vision of the human mind can see in the preservation of that faith and the courage to live by it the manifest destiny of the American people.

Index

Adair-Coppage Cases, 220
   rejected, 335 U.S., 221
Adams, President John
   preserves peace; Alien and Seditions Acts, 66
Adams, Samuel, and Boston Town Meetings, 31
Agricultural Adjustment Administration, 273
Amendment, Fourteenth, 160
Amendment, Twelfth, 78
Anthracite coal strike, 203

Bank holiday ordered by President, 270
Bank of U.S. gov't deposits withdrawn, 121
Bryan, Wm. J., 194
Bull Moose campaign, 215
Burr, Aaron, tried for treason, 81

Calhoun, John C., leader of new south, 134
Carolina, the Unalterable Constitution, 15
Chase, Justice
   impeachment, 80
Child Labor Case
   Hammer v. *Dagenhart* overruled in Darby Case, 224

Civil Rights cases, 162
Commerce & Labor, Dept. of, 205
Commerce Power
   convention debate, 53
   extension by Supreme Court, 297
Commission government in cities, 209
Conservation of natural resources, 205
Constitutional Convention, Call for, 45
Constitutional Convention, supreme problem, solutions, 48
Continental Congress, First, 34
   Weaknesses of, 42
Cotton gin, Eli Whitney builds first, 131
Currency, Colonial experiments in, 17

"Democracy," corruption of the word, 328
"Do Something," depression demand, 228
Dred Scott case, 147
"Due process of law"
   profound transformation of, 223, 340

Executive Agreements, like treaties, 260

Farmers' Alliance, 184

Food and Drugs Act, 204
Founding Fathers, Fears of, 294
Fundamental Orders of Connecticut, 12

Garrison, Wm. Lloyd, abolition leader, 141
General Welfare
  convention debate, 55
  Supreme Court construction, 58, 302
Genet, Citizen Edmond
  Minister from France, recalled, 65
Gold standard, U.S. goes off, 271
Granger legislation Munn v. Ills, 181

Hamilton, Alexander
  First Report on the Public Credit, 62
Hepburn Act, 204
Homestead Act, 174

Internationalism, major issue, 263
Interstate Commerce Commission, 183

Jackson, Andrew, President, 128
Jacksonian democracy in White House, 116
Jefferson, Thomas
  campaign developed "party spirit," 67
  election support by Hamilton, 68
  presidency, 70 *et seq.*
  Louisiana Purchase, 74
  attacking Supreme Court, 83
Johnson, President
  tried to carry out Lincoln policies, 157
  Civil Rights Act passed on veto, 159
  Reconstruction Act on veto, 159

Labor unions, 98
Land Ordinance, Northwest, 87
League of Nations Covenant, 246
Lincoln-Douglas Debates, 151
Lochner Case (*L.* v. *New York*), 219
Locke, John, on the origin of gov't, 20
Louisiana Purchase, 74
Lusitania sunk, 240

Manorial lords in New York, 15
Marshall, Chief Justice John
  Marbury v. *Madison*, 71
  conflict with Jefferson, 79
  federal decisions, 82
Mayflower Compact, 4
Mercantilism in the colonies, 16
Migratory Birds treaty, 255
  Missouri v. *Holland*, 256, 307
Missouri Compromise, 133
Monopolies—fear of, but toleration of labor or state, 340
Mormonism, 104
Muller v. *Oregon*, followed by *Bunting* v. *Oregon*, 223

National Labor Relations Act, 282
National Recovery Administration, 273
New England, Cambridge Agreement for, 8
  Town Meetings in, 10
Northern Securities Co., 203
Northwest Ordinance, 88
Nullification Ordinance, 135

Party convention, First, 118
Patrons of Husbandry formed, 180
Pennsylvania, Frame of Government for, 14
Plan of Union, Franklin's, 22
Populist party organized, 192
Proclamation of 1763, 25
Prohibition amendment, 249
Proprietary colonies, 13
Public Utility Holding Company Act, 280
Puerto Rico, Status of, 198

Quebec Act, 25

Republican party born, 142
Revolutionary Doctrine, extension of commerce power, 297
Roosevelt, Theodore, First Message of, 201

Securities Exchange Commission, 280
Sherman Anti-trust Act, 183

INDEX

355

Slaughter House cases, 162
Socialism
  welfare state advocates not orthodox socialists, 329
  evils of national socialism, 342
Social Security Act, 285
Spanish-American War, 197
Specie circular, 122
"Spoils system," 118
Stamp Act opposed, 27
  Congress, 29
Supreme Court conservatism
  stimulates progressive movement, 164
  nullifies minimum wage law, 227
  nullifies New Deal laws, 231
Supreme Court Justices
  rapid changes, 1937-1943, 292
  further changes, 1945-1949, 293
Supreme Court remaking
  demanded, 231
  achieved, 233
  "new" philosophy, 296
  extension commerce power, tax power, treaty power, 301

Taft-Hartley Act, 283
Taney, Chief Justice Roger B., 144
  attitude toward slavery, 145
  liberal opinions, 146
Tennessee Valley Authority, 277
"Tippecanoe and Tyler Too," 124
Townshend, Chas., tax measures and writs of assistance, 30
Treaty Power—extra constitutional, 257

expansion by Supreme Court, 304
historically inaccurate, 307
Trust agreements appear, 176

Union Pacific railway built, 172
United Nations Charter, Declaration of Human Rights, 257
  Extension of federal power, 305
Utrecht, Treaty of, and slavery in colonies, 20

Van Buren, Martin in Cabinet, 117
Virginia Bill of Rights, 39
Virginia, Charter of, 6
  Tobacco in, 7

Wabash Pacif. & St. Louis R.R. v. Ills., 182
Welfare State definition, 330,
  promoted by English socialists, 333
  may become totalitarian fiscal problem, 334
  substitutes common for individual standards, 336
  major excuses for, 338
  national leads to international, 344
Whig party appears, 120
Williams, Roger, Founds Rhode Island, 12
Woman Suffrage, Seneca Falls Declaration, 103
  Amendment, 249
Works Progress Administration, 275
World War I, America enters, 242

APR 24 1956